Wellington's Peninsular War Generals and Their Battles

When I reflect upon the characters and attainments of some of the general officers in this army, and consider that these are the persons on whom I am to rely to lead columns against the French, I tremble and, as Lord Chesterfield said of the generals of his day, "I only hope that when the enemy reads the list of their names, he trembles as I do."

Lieutenant General Viscount Wellington, commander of the forces in Spain and Portugal, to Colonel Henry Torrens, Military Secretary to the Commander-in-Chief of the British Army, 19 August 1810.

Wellington's Peninsular War Generals and Their Battles

A Biographical and Historical Dictionary

T A Heathcote

With a foreword by Gordon Corrigan

Pen & Sword
MILITARY

First published in Great Britain in 2010 by
Pen & Sword Military
an imprint of
Pen & Sword Books Ltd
47 Church Street
Barnsley
South Yorkshire
S70 2AS

Copyright © T A Heathcote, 2010

ISBN 978-1-84884-061-4

The right of T A Heathcote to be identified as Author of this Work has
been asserted by him in accordance with the Copyright, Designs and
Patents Act 1988.

A CIP catalogue record for this book is available from the British Library.

Typeset in 11pt Ehrhardt by
Mac Style, Beverley, E. Yorkshire

Printed and bound in the UK by MPG Books Group

Pen & Sword Books Ltd incorporates the imprints of Pen & Sword
Aviation, Pen & Sword Maritime, Pen & Sword Military, Wharncliffe Local
History, Pen and Sword Select, Pen and Sword Military Classics and Leo
Cooper.

For a complete list of Pen & Sword titles please contact
PEN & SWORD BOOKS LIMITED
47 Church Street, Barnsley, South Yorkshire, S70 2AS, England
E-mail: enquiries@pen-and-sword.co.uk
Website: www.pen-and-sword.co.uk

Contents

Foreword

The soubriquet 'polymath' is greatly overused – often inaccurately – but if it applies to anyone it surely does to Dr Tony Heathcote: scholar, linguist, author, historian, reserve soldier, amateur sailor and hugely knowledgeable and amusing companion. I first met Dr Heathcote when we were both at the Royal Military Academy Sandhurst over thirty years ago, I as the commander of a company of my battalion lent to Sandhurst and then as the commander of Burma Company, and he as the Curator of the Sandhurst Collection. Rather in the way that the assistant cultural attaché at an embassy is more often the chief resident spy, the curatorship of the Sandhurst Collection entailed far more than responsibility for paintings and the mess silver (extensive though that was), but extended a tentacle or two into virtually every aspect of Academy life. A huge potential source of blackmail (although never used as such) was his guardianship of the personal files of everyone who had ever passed through Sandhurst – I well remember Dr Heathcote allowing me to look at my own file and my amazement at discovering that what I had thought to be my clever concealment of all sorts of unpleasant character traits as an officer cadet was well known to the authorities and accurately recorded by them. Tony Heathcote's first love was Asia; his doctoral thesis was on British policy in Baluchistan and he has published extensively on the British Indian Army, the 1857 Mutiny and the Afghan Wars, but he has also produced three reference books which, if they are not already on the shelves of every military historian, certainly should be: *The British Field Marshals*, *The Admirals of the Fleet* and most recently *Nelson's Trafalgar Captains*: succinct, accurate, informative and immensely readable biographies of everyone who ever held those ranks or appointments. Now he has turned his attention to Arthur Wellesley, first Duke of Wellington and, in my opinion at least, England's greatest general.

Well before the appearance of Wellington, the British had decided that they would pursue military policy on land with a professional, rather than a conscript, Army. Professionals cost more than levies and so that Army would be small. British campaigns on land of necessity would usually be fought as part of a coalition and often in difficult or undeveloped terrain. To be a successful British general meant being able to co-operate with allies and having an understanding of logistics – that unsexy, undramatic, often boring and absolutely vital aspect of military management without which you can do nothing. Leading an attack on an enemy position is easy: organising the feeding, transportation, accommodation, supply and medical care of an army in an inhospitable country a long way from home is not. Arthur Wellesley joined the Army because there was no other avenue for advancement open to the younger son of impoverished Anglo–Irish gentry, and it was an Army that due to the years of peace since the Seven Years War and a reluctance to spend money was going through one of its periods of incompetence, inward looking and poor leadership. The French Revolutionary and Napoleonic Wars gave Wellesley his opportunity, and it is for his command of the Anglo–Portuguese army in the Iberian Peninsula that he is remembered, but he learned his trade – particularly about operating in a coalition and how to manage logistics in the Third World – in India, whither he went as a battalion commander laden with debt and returned as a reasonably comfortably-off major general. Wellesley was probably no better a tactician than John Moore, but unlike Moore he understood the political imperatives of what he was doing, and could operate with difficult allies and with the Royal Navy. Much has been written about Wellesley/Wellington, and biographies of some of his subordinates are on the shelves – Picton, the irascible Welshman; Stapleton Cotton, the man Wellington considered to be one of the few cavalry officers capable of commanding more than a squadron; 'Daddy' Hill, who was only ever heard to swear twice; Craufurd of the Light Division and Paget/Uxbridge/Anglesey, who lost his leg at Waterloo, are probably the best known, and a biography of Thomas Graham is in preparation, but many of Wellington's subordinate commanders and staff officers are just names to most. In this much-needed addition to the literature of the period Dr Heathcote shines a scholarly light on another of the characteristics that made Wellington a great general – his ability to use the strengths of his subordinates and compensate for their weaknesses. Wellington had very little say as to who would command his formations and, in an age when commissions were purchased, it was very difficult to sack anyone, but he generally managed to place his juniors where they could operate to the best advantage to the army or where they could do least damage to it. This book describes not only the better known divisional commanders but also men like William Erskine, who was probably mad; John Sherbrooke who, as the second lieutenant colonel in the 33rd Foot, taught the young Arthur Wesley much of the minutiae of regimental soldiering and who to this day has a Canadian regiment named after him; Karl Alten, the German officer who took over the Light Division after the death of Craufurd, and William Carr Beresford, illegitimate son of the Marquis of Waterford who, while no great field commander, performed near miracles in reconstituting the Portuguese army until its soldiers were every bit as good as their British comrades. The staff is not neglected and George Murray, the quartermaster-general (chief of staff in modern parlance), James McGrigor, the chief medical officer, Richard Fletcher, the Royal Engineer, and Alexander Dickson of the Royal Artillery are all included. The last three were not generals but owing to the system of promotion by seniority were effectively doing the job of generals, as those generals who did exist in their respective arms were mostly too old, too fat or too confused to carry out the duties of the appointment. Heathcote also looks at the battles and, while the well known ones are covered, he does not neglect the lesser-known but equally interesting clashes.

Wellington was not necessarily a warm or approachable man – but then nice chaps don't win wars – but by his understanding of the political restrictions on waging war; by his intellect that allowed him to plan ahead and yet remain flexible; by his ability to keep his army in the field, well fed and supplied, far from home and with allies who in many cases were of dubious value, and by his knack of reading men's characters and placing subordinates where they could operate to the limit of their varying abilities Arthur Wellesley was a great general and a great man by the standards not just of his age but of any age – and there are many parallels with British military operations today. This admirable book will serve not only as a work of reference for the cognoscenti, but also as a fascinating record of fascinating men in a fascinating time for the general reader with an interest in the history of this nation and of warfare everywhere.

Gordon Corrigan

List of Illustrations

Portraits
1. Sir William Beresford, Viscount Beresford [2]
2. Sir Galbraith Lowry Cole [9]
3. Sir Stapleton Cotton, Viscount Combermere [11]
4. Robert Craufurd [12]
5. Sir Thomas Graham, Lord Lynedoch [19]
6. Sir Rowland Hill, Viscount Hill [21]
7. Sir John Hope, Earl of Hopetoun [23]
8. Sir George Murray [28]
9. Sir Edward Paget [30]
10. Sir Thomas Picton [33]
11. Sir John Sherbrooke [36]
12. Sir Charles Stewart Vane, Marquess of Londonderry [40]

Statues
1. Sir Stapleton Cotton, Viscount Combermere [11] (Chester)
2. Sir John Hope, Earl of Hopetoun [23] (Edinburgh)
3. Sir James McGrigor [27] (Camberley)
4. Sir Charles Stewart Vane, Marquess of Londonderry [39] (Durham)

Maps
1. The Iberian Peninsula, North-Western theatre. 1808–14
2. Battle of Talavera, 27–28 July 1809
3. The Campaign in Walcheren, August–September 1809
4. Battle of Busaco, 27 September 1810
5. Battle of Fuentes D'Onoro, 2nd day 5 May 1811
6. Battle of Albuera, 16 May 1811
7. Badajoz and its defences, March–April 1812
8. Battle of Salamanca, (Los Arapiles), 22 July 1812
9. Battle of Vitoria, 23 June 1813
10. San Sebastian and its defences, June–September 1813
11. Passage of the Nivelle, 10 November 1813
12. France, South-Western theatre, 1814
13. Battle of Waterloo, 18 June 1815

Introduction

At a time when the British Army's campaigns generally involve coalition warfare, undertaken with limited resources, in harsh terrain, alongside the unreliable forces of failing states, the Peninsular War (now halfway through its bicentenary) remains well worthy of study. Revisionist historians have claimed the war for the Spaniards, stressing the part played by Spanish regular troops as well as the partisans from whose activities the word 'guerrilla' passed into the English language. The results of their scholarship cannot be denied, but there is still a lingering view among post-revisionists that Spain was no more liberated by the Spanish in the Peninsular War than France was by the French in the Second World War. For all the gallantry of Spanish officers and soldiers when given a fair chance, the traditional British view is that their Army consisted of Don Quixotes in the saddle and Sancho Panzas in the ranks. Wellington declared that he never met any Spanish officer who could be made to understand the nature of a military operation, and accepted the post of C-in-C of the Spanish armies at the end of 1812 only when he was certain that their troops would be fed, paid and disciplined. His supreme command in the Peninsula included an army of British and Neapolitan troops from Sicily that operated in eastern Spain from 1812 onwards, but the army under his direct orders was a multi-national force of British, Portuguese and Spanish formations. It is the British generals of its Anglo-Portuguese element who are the subjects of this book.

Wellington's Peninsular War generals are widely regarded as being better subordinates than independent commanders, a perception that owes much to their great Chief himself. Although even the best must suffer from comparison with a Wellington, this book shows that, while some of his generals failed when trusted with independent commands, others succeeded and deserve more credit than they are often given. Generally treated as mere extras in the story of Wellington's campaigns, many of them had achieved much before they joined him, and went on to have distinguished careers in their own right. They spanned a period of history full of excitement and drama and their adventures and personal lives stand comparison with those of fictional heroes such as Harry Flashman, Matthew Hervey and Richard Sharpe.

Strictly speaking, the only British general in Wellington's Peninsular War army was Wellington himself, who was promoted to that rank (and, even then, only local to Portugal and Spain) on 31 July 1812. Before that, the army had been commanded by lieutenant generals, first by Wellington, as Sir Arthur Wellesley, then briefly by Sir Harry Burrard and Sir Hew Dalrymple, next by Sir John Moore, and finally again by Wellesley (after September 1809, Wellington). There was at this time no firm link between the rank of a general officer and the level of the formation under his command and, as the following pages demonstrate, a lieutenant general might command a division, a corps (in Wellington's army, an ad hoc grouping of two or more divisions) or an army. Major generals commanded either divisions or brigades. Brigades might also be commanded by brigadiers, a title that appears in the Army Lists of the day only in the section for officers holding local rank, or in the 'remarks' column of that for substantive colonels. Brigade commanders below the rank of major general were called brigadier generals, in the same way that officers commanding warships were then called captains, regardless of their actual rank in the Navy List. Craufurd commanded the Light Division as a brigadier general, and though eventually promoted to local major general, was still a substantive colonel when killed in action at Ciudad Rodrigo. Despite the Army Lists showing colonels commanding brigades as brigadiers rather than brigadier generals, for practical purposes they counted as generals.

Wellington's Anglo–Portuguese army, at its largest, consisted of two cavalry and eight infantry divisions, each of two or more brigades, together with a number of independent brigades. The numerous changes among their generals during the five years of the war produced too many for all to be covered in detail in a book of this nature, which accordingly includes only the best-known of the divisional commanders, together with a selection of the principal staff officers and heads of supporting arms and logistic services, who, though not generals in Wellington's army, would have ranked as such in modern armies.

Until the reforms of the 1970s, introduced to bring the British Army into line with its NATO (meaning United States) allies, British staff officers included adjutant-generals and quartermaster-generals, each with their deputies, assistants and deputy assistants. Allies were frequently puzzled to find that a deputy assistant adjutant and quartermaster-general was neither an adjutant nor a quartermaster, still less a general, but a major of the personnel (later G1) and logistics (later G4) branches. In Wellington's time, the staff of the quartermaster-general's and adjutant-general's branches also performed duties that were allotted to the general (later G3) staff when this was formed in the British Army in the early twentieth century.

The importance attached by Wellington to his logistics, deriving as much from his first campaign, in the Low Countries, as from his later ones in India, is well known. He was the first British commander to mention medical and commissariat officers in despatches and these two services are represented in this book by McGrigor and Bisset respectively. Wellington's gunners are represented by Dickson and Robe, and his engineers by Elphinstone and Fletcher. Controlled by the Board of Ordnance, not by the Commander-in-Chief of the British Army at the Horse Guards, the two Ordnance Corps (the Royal Artillery and the Royal Engineers) always felt that Wellington gave them less than their due.

This selection produces a total of forty-one officers, giving a cross-section of the senior British military officers of their day, whose lives illustrate the social as well as the operational history of the Army. Nineteen were born in Scotland, a tribute to that country's martial traditions and also (as they include the Medical, Commissariat and at least two of the four Ordnance officers, who were trained in scientific subjects) its educational system. Nine came from English families. Only six belonged, like Wellington, to the Anglo-Irish Protestant Ascendancy that later produced a much higher percentage of the Army's officers. Three were Welsh, or at least had estates in Wales. Two were Germans, subjects of the Elector of Hanover and serving him in the King's German Legion. One was a West Indian, having been born on his family's plantation in St Kitt's. Their social origins faithfully reflect those of most senior officers at that time. Eighteen were the sons (in some cases, the heirs) of peers or baronets or were otherwise connected to noble families. Eleven were the sons of other landed proprietors. Those from middle-class backgrounds (the Medical, Commissariat and Ordnance officers among them) included five sons of naval or military officers not included among the above and seven from other groups, clergymen, merchants, etc. Their marriages show the way in which great families maintained the matrimonial alliances that strengthened their dominant position in Georgian society, a constant theme in the novels of their contemporary, Jane Austen (whose nephew married the widow of one of Wellington's Peninsular War generals). The early death of so many of their wives illustrates the hazards of married life for women of all classes, who at this period had at least as great a risk of mortality, and a greater certainty of pain, in child-bed, as did their husbands on the battlefield.

Wealth and family influence is an advantage in any profession at any time. In the Georgian Army, the purchase system allowed officers to gain early promotion by investing large sums to obtain advancement within their regiment, or transfer from one regiment to another. Despite its name, the purchase system was not one in which individuals bought and sold their commissions solely in accord with market forces, regardless of military rank. In order to obtain his commission, a potential officer had first to be recommended to the Commander-in-Chief by a patron of recognised social status. Friends or families of an MP or peer who supported the government of the day had a great advantage in this respect, as corruption was rife even by the standards of the early twenty-first century. The sons of businessmen or industrialists, no matter how wealthy, were rarely accepted.

Appointment and subsequent promotion depended on the existence of a vacancy in the appropriate rank and regiment and, at least in peace-time, possession of the necessary funds. In addition to the regulation sum, rising with each step, that an officer was required to lodge with the authorities, there were also over-regulation payments, varying according to circumstances, made to the officer whose departure created the vacancy. To prevent favouritism, a vacancy at any level had first to be offered to the senior qualified officer of the rank below it in the same regiment. An officer whose promotion in his regiment was blocked by the operation of this rule could transfer to another one, generally by paying compensation to the officer whose place he took. Although in theory this worsened his prospects, as he immediately became the junior of his rank in the new regiment (though retaining his existing seniority in the Army as a whole), in practice he would select a regiment in which large numbers of vacancies were expected, so that he would rise rapidly to the top of his list and gain promotion to the next rank soon afterwards. Such transfers were normally arranged through firms of specialist brokers (who also acted as officers' bankers) known as army agents and could involve officers passing through the rolls of several regiments in succession without actually doing duty in any of them. In times of expansion, when new regiments were being raised, commissions and promotions were granted without purchase, often in return for a specified number of recruits (whom rich landed families could find among their tenants). Promotion to fill vacancies left by officers who died on active service was by regimental seniority, without purchase, hence the common toast to 'a bloody war or a sickly season'. Such promotion was more likely to occur in regiments serving in unhealthy stations and those seeking advancement were more willing to go with, or transfer to, regiments ordered to the West Indies or India than those who chose to stay at home.

Several examples of these practices may be found in the early careers of Wellington's generals. His brother-in-law, the Honourable Edward Pakenham, son of the Earl of Longford, became a major within five months of joining the Army, while still aged only 16, and a lieutenant colonel commanding a battalion on operations in less than five years. The Honourable Charles Stewart, son of the Marquess of Londonderry, rose from ensign to captain in thirty days, to major in ten months and to lieutenant colonel in just over two years. His namesake, the Honourable William Stewart, son of the Earl of Galloway, became an ensign aged 12 and a lieutenant colonel aged 21. James Willoughby Gordon became an ensign aged 10 and Colville an ensign in the 28th Foot (recruited from his family's Ulster stronghold) aged 11. Lowry Cole became a cornet of dragoons at the age of 15. Paget reached the rank of lieutenant colonel at the age of 18 and Wellington at the age of 24. Fifteen of the forty-one officers chose to serve in the unhealthy West Indies at an early stage in their careers, as did ten, along with Wellington, in India.

The purchase system applied only in the cavalry and infantry. Officers of the Ordnance corps were trained as gentlemen cadets at the Royal Military Academy, Woolwich. Purchase was not allowed in these corps, and promotion by seniority meant they might still be regimental lieutenants when in their 40s. Medical and commissariat officers in effect purchased their appointments by buying out their predecessors, as was normal for public offices at the time, and still is, in the private sector, for professional partnerships and the like.

Regimental promotion carried promotion to the same rank in the Army as a whole, but went only as far as lieutenant colonel. A parallel system, not requiring purchase and known as brevet promotion from the six-monthly brevets or official documents in which it was normally published, allowed otherwise-qualified officers to be promoted in the Army to ranks for which there was no vacancy in their regiments. Although an officer remained at the lower rank in his regiment, he held the higher, brevet, rank in the Army and, when employed on extra-regimental duty, was paid at the higher rate. Lieutenants and captains in the Household Cavalry or Foot Guards held brevet commissions in the Army as captains and lieutenant colonels respectively. Most colonels held their rank in the Army, by brevet, rather than in their regiments, where the establishment normally provided for only one colonel at a time. Colonels in the Army were promoted to major general by brevet as vacancies on the establishment occurred, in order of seniority, and thereafter rose through the ranks of general officers in the same way. Those promoted by the same brevet took seniority among themselves according to the dates of their previous commissions. Colonels of regiments were appointed, without purchase, regardless of existing regimental seniority and commonly had no previous connection with their regiments at all.

Brevet promotion did not guarantee employment in the rank it conferred, as there were always more colonels and generals than commands for them to hold. Appointment was by nomination, so that it was important for an ambitious officer to maintain a network of connections by appearing regularly at Court or at the Horse Guards, one reason why many of Wellington's generals went home from the Peninsula on leave. The only way that a general could be promoted over his seniors on the active list was by local promotion which, specific to a given theatre, kept the individual in the same place in the Army List. Nevertheless, it brought him employment, pay and status, often to the chagrin of those superseded in this way. Wellington's first promotion to general was local, and fourteen of his senior officers in the Peninsula first became lieutenant generals by local promotion.

Most of Wellington's generals were also regimental colonels, appointed by the Crown as a reward for previous good service. Their pay as such, plus the officially-sanctioned 'off-reckonings' from contracts for equipping and maintaining their regiments, provided a permanent income that continued when they ceased to be employed as general officers. Whenever the Army was reduced in size, regiments were disbanded in numerical order, the juniors first, without any of the special pleading that accompanies such decisions in modern times. It was therefore safer to be the colonel of a senior regiment than of a junior one, and most of the generals in this book can be seen 'trading-up', as colonels, from one regiment to another. As additional rewards for good service, general officers could be given governorships or captaincies of establishments in the United Kingdom, which brought both an income and an official residence. Such posts could be held in succession in the same way as colonelcies, as demonstrated by Sir Edward Paget who was captain of Cowes Castle, governor of the Royal Military College, Sandhurst, and finally governor of the Royal Hospital, Chelsea.

Wellington's attitude towards his generals has been described by one of his recent biographers as that of a 'control freak'. Certainly, the motto on his armorial bearings, *Virtutis Fortuna Comes* ('Fortune is the companion of valour') might equally well have been 'Why do I have to do everything myself round here?' His view of his generals in 1810 appears at the front of this book. Early in 1811, when almost all his general officers returned home either on medical grounds or to deal with important private affairs, he complained that no sooner had he trained generals who knew their business than they went away, leaving him to start again with a new set. Even after reaching the Pyrenees, he wrote home that, despite all his victories, his generals had no confidence in themselves and, though heroes in his presence, they were as children in his absence. His highest praise was for those who obeyed his orders as they were given. His greatest blame was heaped on those who departed from them. This is only to be expected of any great military leader and Napoleon himself declared that the first duty of a soldier is obedience. Wellington may have carried this principle to extremes, but having lived through the 1789 Revolution in France and the 1798 Rising in Ireland, and witnessed the Duke of York's disastrous campaign in the Low Countries, he was always conscious that only discipline stands between an army and an armed mob.

In fact, most of Wellington's generals arrived with combat experience to their credit, and many had previously served together in the same way as had Nelson's 'band of brothers' in the Mediterranean. Sixteen had been in the Low Countries in 1793–95 and eleven at the Helder in 1799. Fourteen were in the Egyptian campaign of 1801. During 1807, six were in the River Plate expedition and eight were with Wellington at Copenhagen. Their other operational theatres had included the Mediterranean, Mysore (where two of them had fought alongside Wellington), South Africa and the West Indies. Three had seen active service in the American War of Independence.

As fighting soldiers, they undertook all the risks of their profession. Four of them were killed in action; one was drowned at sea and two were involved in other shipwrecks; twenty-six were wounded, many of them several times and some very seriously; seven became prisoners of war. Several contracted malaria or other fevers, in one case fatally. After leaving Wellington, three became Commanders-in-Chief, India, where Cotton took the previously impregnable stronghold of Bharatpur. In the American War of 1812, Sherbrooke conducted a successful campaign in Maine, and Pakenham a disastrous one at New Orleans.

Many of Wellington's generals played an important part in civil life. Thirteen were elected Members of Parliament and seven sat in the House of Lords. Murray, quartermaster-general in the Peninsula, sat in Wellington's Cabinet as Secretary of State for War and the Colonies and in Peel's first Cabinet as Master-General of the Ordnance. Ten served as colonial governors, covering between them Barbados, British North America (Canada), Cape Colony, Ceylon (Sri Lanka), Grenada, the Ionian Islands, the Leeward Islands, Mauritius, Nova Scotia and Trinidad. As for their regiments, Wellington claimed that, after the Napoleonic wars, he saved the Army by hiding it in the colonies.

In a work of this nature, which is intended to be consulted as a reference book rather than read as a continuous narrative, there is unavoidably some repetition. To reduce this to a minimum, whenever an officer is first mentioned in an entry other than his own, his name is followed by the sequential number in which he is listed in the Contents pages, in **bold** and within square brackets [...]. In the same way, battles, campaigns and expeditions in which at least five of the generals took part are indicated, with their dates, in **bold** and summarised, in chronological order, in the second section of the book.

I take this opportunity to acknowledge all those whose advice, encouragement and assistance contributed to this book, and especially Dr Peter Thwaites, my successor as curator of the Royal Military Academy Sandhurst Collection; his successor, Dr Anthony Morton; Andrew Orgill, Librarian of the Royal Military Academy Sandhurst, and his deputy, John Pearce; the ever-helpful staff of the National Portrait Gallery, London; my old NATO comrade-in-arms, Lieutenant Colonel Dianne Smith, United States Army (Retd); and most of all my wife, Mary, who sacrificed her Bridge while she performed the customary tasks of an academic spouse by proof-reading the MSS and undertaking the picture research. All errors are the sole responsibility of the author.

T A Heathcote
Camberley, October 2009

The Biographies

ALTEN, Major General Sir CHARLES (KARL), Count von Alten, KCB (1764–1840) [1]

Charles (Karl) von Alten, the youngest son of August, Freiherr von Alten, was born on 12 October 1764 at Burgwebel, Hanover. In 1786 he was appointed a page of honour to George III as Elector of Hanover and later became an ensign in the Hanoverian Foot Guards. Following the outbreak of the French Revolutionary War in February 1793, he served as a captain in the Hanoverian contingent in the **Low Countries (March 1793–April 1795)** where, during 1794, he commanded an outpost line along the River Lys. In May 1803 the French occupied Hanover and disbanded its Army. Alten was among those who reached England to carry on the fight under British colours. With a reputation as a capable officer of light infantry, he joined the newly-raised King's German Regiment, a light infantry corps that in December 1803 became the nucleus of the all-arms King's German Legion. Alten was granted a commission in the British Army as colonel commandant of the 1st Light Battalion of the King's German Legion with effect from 18 August 1803 and commanded the Legion's two light battalions in **Hanover (8 November 1805–15 February 1806)**, at **Copenhagen (16 August–7 September 1807)** and in the **Baltic (May–June 1808)**.

Alten and his two battalions joined the Peninsular War in August 1808. They served with Sir John Moore's army in his advance from Portugal into Spain, and formed part of the rearguard during the first part of the subsequent **retreat to Corunna (25 December 1808–11 January 1809)**. Evacuated through Vigo, they returned to England and afterwards served at **Walcheren (August–December 1809)**.

Alten was promoted to major general on 25 July 1810 and returned to the Peninsula on 21 March 1811, where he was given command of a newly-formed brigade in the 7th Division, consisting of the two light infantry battalions of the King's German Legion and another German light infantry corps, the Brunswick-Oels Jagers, and led this at **Albuera (16 May 1811)**. On 2 May 1812 Alten was given command of the Light Division, which he led at **Salamanca (22 July 1812); Vitoria (21 June 1813);** the battles of the **Pyrenees (25 July–1 August 1813);** the **passage of the Nive (10–13 December 1813); Orthez (27 February 1814)** and **Toulouse (10 April 1814)**. With the war ended by Napoleon's abdication, he was awarded the KCB early in 1815, when the Prince Regent re-organised the Order of the Bath. During the Hundred Days, following Napoleon's escape from Elba, Sir Charles Alten commanded the 3rd British Division at Quatre Bras (16 June 1815) and **Waterloo (18 June 1815)**, where he was badly wounded. In the victory honours he was made a Hanoverian count and was awarded the Russian Order of St Anne.

As part of the post-war settlement of Europe, Hanover was raised to the status of a kingdom. The KGL was disbanded, with its officers being placed on the foreign half-pay list of the British Army on 24 February 1816. Some officers and men found employment in the new Royal Hanoverian Army and served under Count von Alten in the Allied Army of Occupation in France. Alten returned to Hanover in 1818, where he subsequently became minister for war and foreign affairs, inspector-general of the Army and a field marshal. He retained these posts, remaining a British major general on the foreign half-pay list, until his death at Botzen, Tyrol, on 20 April 1840. He was buried at his family residence in Wilkenburg, Hanover.

BARNARD, General Sir ANDREW FRANCIS, GCB, GCH (1773–1855) [2]

Andrew Barnard, son of the Reverend Henry Barnard of Bovagh, County Londonderry, was born at Fahan, County Donegal, in 1773. He entered the Army during the French Revolutionary War on 26 August 1794 as an ensign in the recently-raised 90th Foot (Perthshire Volunteers) and became a lieutenant in the 81st Foot a month later, just before the regiment embarked for the West Indies. He was promoted to captain-lieutenant and captain on 13 November 1794. Between April and August 1795 he was stationed in French San Domingo (Haiti), at that time under British occupation. Barnard transferred to the 55th Foot, whose flank companies were then serving in the West Indies, on 2 December 1795 and joined the rest of the regiment early in 1796, when it arrived from England with large-scale reinforcements under Sir Ralph Abercromby. He served in Abercromby's recapture of St Lucia (26 April–25 May 1796) and was subsequently engaged in counter-insurgency operations in the densely-wooded mountains of the interior. Severely reduced by tropical fevers, the 55th returned home in 1798 and then served at **the Helder (August–October 1799)**.

On 19 December 1799 Barnard transferred to the 1st Foot Guards as a lieutenant in the regiment and captain in the Army. He was promoted to major in the Army on 1 January 1805. During 1806 and 1807 he served as second-in-command of a company in the 3rd Battalion, 1st Foot Guards, in the British garrison of Sicily, where King Ferdinand of Naples and Sicily had taken refuge after a French invasion drove him from his mainland kingdom. Barnard became a major in the 7th West India Regiment on 6 January 1808 and was promoted to lieutenant colonel on 28 January 1808. He was appointed inspecting officer of militia in Canada in July 1808 and, after transferring to the 1st Foot on 18 December 1808, returned home in August 1809. He exchanged to the 95th Foot (Rifles) on 29 March 1810 and became the commanding officer of its newly-raised 3rd Battalion, with which on 29 July 1810 he joined Graham [19] at Cadiz. Barnard commanded this battalion at Barossa (5 March 1811), where he was twice wounded. After joining Wellington in Portugal during August 1811, he was given command of a brigade in the Light Division, with which he subsequently served at **Ciudad Rodrigo (7–19 January 1812)**. He succeeded to the command of the Light Division when Craufurd [12] was killed and the senior brigadier, Major General John Vandeleur, was wounded in the storming of the city, and was noted for his efforts to restore discipline in the subsequent pillage.

Barnard remained in acting command of the Light Division at **Badajoz (17 March–6 April 1812)** and returned to regimental duty in May 1812 as commanding officer of the 1st Battalion, 95th Rifles, with which he served at **Salamanca (22 July 1812)**. He was promoted to colonel on 4 June 1813 and was at **Vitoria (21 June 1813)**, **San Sebastian (29 June–8 September 1813)**, the **passage of the Nivelle (10 November 1813)**, where he was shot through the lung, **Orthez (27 February 1814)** and **Toulouse (10 April 1814)**. He was awarded the Army Gold Cross with four clasps and, with the war ended by Napoleon's abdication, became a KCB in the victory honours of January 1815.

Sir Andrew Barnard returned to active service for the Hundred Days, when Napoleon returned from Elba, and led the 1st Battalion, 95th Rifles, at Quatre Bras (16 June 1815) and **Waterloo (18 June 1815)**, where he was slightly wounded. He commanded a division in the Army of Occupation and was awarded the Russian Order of St George and the Austrian Order of Maria Theresa. He was promoted to major general on 12 August 1819 and awarded the KH in the same year.

In 1821 Barnard became groom of the bedchamber to George IV and on 25 August 1822 was appointed a colonel in the Rifle Brigade, the former 95th Rifles. He continued his career as a courtier, becoming an equerry to George IV in 1828, clerk-marshal and chief equerry to William IV on the latter's accession in 1830 and, after the King's death in 1837, to Queen Adelaide until her death in 1849. He became a GCH in 1833, lieutenant general on 10 January 1837 and a GCB in 1840. Barnard was appointed governor of the Royal Hospital, Chelsea, on 26 November 1849, and was promoted to general on 11 November 1851. He died in office at the Royal Hospital on 17 January 1855, and was buried in the cemetery there. Prior to the funeral, in-pensioners who had served under him in the Peninsula asked permission to file past him. They secretly each brought in a laurel leaf and after they left, his coffin was found covered with these tributes from his old veterans.

BERESFORD, General Sir WILLIAM CARR, GCB, GCH, Viscount Beresford (1768–1854) [3]

William Beresford was born on 2 October 1768, the natural son of an Irish peer, the 2nd Earl of Tyrone, created Marquess of Waterford in 1787. He was educated in Yorkshire before attending a French military academy at Strasbourg during 1785. On 27 August 1785 he became an ensign in the 6th Foot and in 1786 went with it from Ireland to Nova Scotia, where a hunting accident left him blind in his left eye and facially scarred. He was promoted to lieutenant in the 16th Foot on 25 June 1789 and became a captain on the unattached list on 24 January 1791, from which he joined the 69th Foot in Ireland on 31 May 1791. Following the outbreak of the French Revolutionary War in February 1793, the 69th embarked as marines for the Mediterranean Fleet and served at **Toulon (August–December 1793)**.

In February 1794 Beresford landed in San Fiorenzo Bay, Corsica, with a British force supporting local patriots and led a storming party against a solidly-built tower at Mortella Point. The strength of this medieval fortification, which had defied a naval bombardment and had to be taken from the landward side, so impressed British officers that large numbers of 'Martello Towers' were then built to protect English shores from a threatened French invasion. Beresford was promoted to major on 1st March 1794 and became a lieutenant colonel on 11 August 1794, commanding the 124th Foot, a regiment then being raised from his father's estates in Waterford. When this was disbanded in the following year, he transferred to command the 88th Foot, the Connaught Rangers, on 16 September 1795.

In November 1796 the 88th sailed for the West Indies, but the convoy was dispersed by violent storms in the Channel so that only three companies and the surgeon, McGrigor [27], arrived there. The regiment spent most of the next three years in Jersey, prior to being ordered to India, and Beresford was promoted to colonel on 1 January 1800. From Bombay (Mumbai) they served in **Egypt (March–October 1801)** where hostilities ended in October 1801 as part of a general armistice, leading to the restoration of peace by the treaty of Amiens (25 March 1802). War with France was renewed in May 1803 and Beresford became a brigadier on 11 February 1804.

The Dutch settlement at the Cape of Good Hope, restored by the British to the French-dominated Batavian Republic under the terms of the treaty of Amiens, was recaptured in January 1806, with Beresford leading a detachment that landed 16 miles north of Cape Town. From the Cape, he commanded a descent on Buenos Aires in the first phase of the campaign on the **River Plate (June 1806–July 1807)**. Recovering from their surprise, the Spanish recaptured the city on 12 August 1806 and Beresford surrendered to the Spanish regulars, on terms allowing his troops to return to England. The British aim of encouraging the colonial population to rise against the Spanish authorities had, however, succeeded only too well, and the Argentinians, whose militia had suffered heavy casualties, repudiated the agreement. The British were marched several hundred miles inland but Beresford and his fellow prisoner, Lieutenant Colonel Dennis Pack, escaped to a British force (originally intended to reinforce Buenos Aires) at Montevideo. He returned to England where he had been appointed colonel of the Connaught Rangers on 9 February 1807.

At the end of December 1807, after the French occupation of Portugal, the British occupied Madeira with 4,000 men under Beresford, who governed in the name of the Portuguese Prince Regent. Promoted to major general on 25 April 1808, Beresford became familiar with the Portuguese and in July 1808 asked to join the British army in the Peninsula. After the Convention of Cintra (Sintra), by which the French agreed to evacuate Portugal in return for being taken home, with all their possessions, in British troopships, Beresford was appointed commandant of the British troops in Lisbon. This involved him in carrying out the terms of the Convention despite protests from the Portuguese that the French were leaving with stolen property. He insisted, however, on the French evacuating the Portuguese border fortress of Elvas and leaving its artillery behind. Beresford commanded a brigade in Sir John Moore's advance into Spain in November 1808, the **retreat to Corunna (25 December 1808 –11 January 1809)** and the battle of **Corunna (16 January 1809)**.

While Sir Arthur Wellesley was despatched with reinforcements for the British troops left in Lisbon, a new alliance was concluded with the Portuguese by which the British provided a commander-in-chief and a cadre of officers and sergeants to train and lead the reconstituted Portuguese Army. Those who volunteered for this role were promoted by one rank in the Portuguese service, and Beresford himself, selected after several others declined the post, was made a Portuguese marshal with promotion to local lieutenant general in the British Army on 16 February 1809. Within months, 25,000 Portuguese soldiers of the new army, armed, equipped, rationed and paid from British sources, and brigaded alongside British formations, were ready to take the field. From then on, Wellesley (after September 1809, Wellington) commanded an army that was an allied, rather than an entirely British, force.

In May 1809, as Marshal Soult retreated from Portugal, Beresford led his troops cautiously into action in support of the main British force, with a caveat from Wellington 'Remember that you are a commander-in-chief and must not be beaten.' After crossing the Douro from Lamego, he unexpectedly drove back a French division and took Amarante on the only major road left into Spain, thus forcing Soult to abandon his guns and wagons and struggle across the mountains to Galicia. When Wellington advanced into Spain, Beresford was left to guard the Portuguese frontier, but his troops had gained Wellington's approval and British financial aid was increased. When the French again invaded Portugal, Beresford's men fought well at **Busaco (27 September 1810)**. On 16 October 1810 Beresford was awarded the KB, followed on 19 October by a Portuguese peerage as Count of Trancoso, with the Portuguese Order of the Tower and Sword. On 1 January 1811, in the absence of Hill **[21]** on sick leave in England, Wellington appointed Sir William Beresford commander of the Allied troops in southern Portugal. Following the unexpected surrender of the Spanish fortress of Badajoz (11 March 1811), Beresford was ordered to recapture it before its defences could be repaired. He succeeded in recovering Campo Mayor (25 March 1811), but failed to prevent the French garrison from retreating to Badajoz with all its heavy guns. He laid siege to Badajoz from 5 to 13 May 1811 before abandoning his works in order to meet a relieving army under Soult.

In the subsequent battle of **Albuera (16 May 1811)**, French cavalry inflicted severe casualties on the 2nd Division and reached the rear of the British line, where Beresford himself, caught up in the *mêlée*, seized an enemy lancer by the throat. Although Soult was prevented from reaching Badajoz, Beresford's first report dwelt upon his heavy losses to such an extent that

Wellington ordered him to redraft it in more positive terms. Most observers, Wellington foremost among them, blamed Beresford for a faulty deployment and failing to manoeuvre his troops effectively. Aware that the day had been saved by the stubbornness of his men rather than his own leadership, Beresford took his army back to Badajoz where, on 27 May 1811, he was succeeded in command by Hill [21], on the latter's return from England. He then resumed his administrative functions in Lisbon, possibly suffering from a post-traumatic stress disorder. In 1811 he was appointed governor of Cork, a post he retained *in absentia* until 1820. From June 1811 to May 1814 he was Tory MP for County Waterford, a seat owned by his brother, the 2nd Marquess of Waterford.

Beresford was promoted to substantive lieutenant general on 4 June 1811 and, after rejoining Wellington in the field in March 1812, commanded a corps comprising the 3rd, 4th and Light Divisions at **Badajoz (17 March–6 April 1812)**. Despite reservations about his ability in a separate command, Wellington continued to hold Beresford in high regard and kept him on his staff in the subsequent advance to **Salamanca (22 July 1812)**, where Beresford was wounded in the chest by a musket-ball. After several operations, surgeons in Portugal removed a piece of his coat from the wound in April 1813. He returned to Lisbon in October 1813 to deal with Portuguese demands for a separate field army, arising from a national feeling that the achievements of their men had received insufficient credit. Wellington refused, declaring that, despite their merits, the Portuguese would only disgrace themselves unless supported by British troops and logistics. Beresford rejoined him and served in the invasion of France, where he commanded major formations at the **passage of the Nivelle (10 November 1813)**, the **passage of the Nive (10–13 December 1813)** and **Orthez (27 February 1814)**. He was then detached with 12,000 men to Bordeaux, where the mayor declared his city's defection to the Bourbon cause, though Beresford declined to offer more than the protection of its inhabitants pending the outcome of international negotiations. At **Toulouse (10 April 1814)**, he commanded Wellington's left flank and captured the ridge dominating the city. In the victory honours he was created Baron Beresford of Albuera and Waterford on 17 May 1814 and became a GCB on 2 January 1815. He was also created Duke of Elvas in the Spanish nobility and a knight of the Portuguese Order of San Fernando.

Contrary to Wellington's advice, Lord Beresford continued as C-in-C of the Portuguese Army and, with Portuguese politicians failing to agree on forming an administration, was for a time virtually head of the government. The decline of trade, poverty caused by the ravages of war and heavy taxation (much of which was resented as going to the exiled Court in Brazil), and the continued employment of British officers in the Army aroused much discontent. In 1817 an attempted *coup*, aimed at replacing the British, was severely repressed. Beresford went to Brazil to urge the former Prince Regent (who had succeeded to the throne as John VI in 1816) to return to Lisbon, but had to suppress another *coup* there. Beresford became colonel of the 69th Foot in March 1819. In July 1821, following rebellions in Lisbon and Oporto, John VI returned from Brazil and promised to grant a constitution. Foreign officers were dismissed and Beresford himself, who had gone to Brazil on a second mission to the king, was not allowed back. In the series of civil wars between constitutionalists and absolutists that affected Portugal for the next ten years, Beresford twice declined command of the Army.

In March 1823 he was created Viscount Beresford and purchased the estate of Beresford, Staffordshire. He became colonel of the 16th Foot on 15 March 1823, was promoted to general on 27 May 1825 and in the same year became governor of Jersey, a post he retained until his death. Under Wellington as prime minister (January 1828 to November 1830), he held office as Master-General of the Ordnance. He married his cousin, Louisa Hope (*nee* Beresford), one of the richest widows in England, on 29 November 1832, and purchased the estate of Bedgebury Park in the Weald of Kent, where he died on 8 January 1854. He was buried nearby in Christ Church, Kilndown, a church built and endowed by him in 1841.

BISSET, Commissary General Sir JOHN, KCB, KCH (1777–1854) [4]

John Bisset was born in Perth in 1777. He joined the Commissariat Department (a civil branch whose officers wore uniform with the cocked hat and sword of a staff officer but had no direct powers of command over the military) in 1795 and, with intervals on the half-pay list, served in the United Kingdom as a commissary general of hospital stores and provisions. After serving at the **River Plate (June 1806–July 1807)** and **Walcheren (August–December 1809)**, he was appointed commissary-general of Wellington's army in the Peninsula on 31 July 1811, in succession to the capable Robert Hugh Kennedy, whose wife had insisted on his returning to the United Kingdom.

Wellington's ability to keep his army concentrated, a vital element in his operational plans, depended on the commissariat supplying food and forage for thousands of men and animals. Although the fullest use was made of local purchase, the commissaries were frequently hard pressed to obtain provisions from the infertile tracts through which the army had to pass. Local dealers were reluctant to accept unfamiliar British bank-notes, and the British Treasury, struggling to fund a world war, had little gold to spare for the Peninsula. Supplies came mostly from overseas, brought under the protection of the Royal Navy to coastal bases and then taken forward to chains of depots and magazines (thirty-seven in Portugal alone), established along the army's lines of communication. With limited inland navigation and few good roads, the commissariat depended on a force of 10,000 pack mules, locally hired along with their professional muleteers, men accustomed to long-distance journeys. These were supplemented by local ox-carts, but the primitive vehicles normally used in Portugal proved so cumbersome that Wellington forbade their use and ordered Bisset to design a new pattern. The prototypes, using materials captured from the French, were constructed in Portugal during the winter of 1811–12, and orders were placed for another 800, to be made in England. Each cart was allotted six draught bullocks (two yoked and four as reliefs) owned by the commissariat, and driven by locally-engaged civilians. Every few days, convoys of mules and ox-carts left the bases carrying food-stuffs, rum, boots, clothing, ammunition, firewood, hay-bales and all the other combat supplies on which the army depended.

The commissariat was organised in the same way as other branches of the staff, with a hierarchy of deputies, assistants, deputy assistants, and clerks. Most of those in the Peninsula were stationed at the base depots, from where a deputy assistant commissary or clerk took charge of each convoy. In areas close to the enemy, military escorts were provided, but if these did not have their own officer, there were often brawls between soldiers and civilians, or sometimes collaboration between them to steal attractive items from the loads. A further problem for the commissary was to ensure that the drivers (whose pay was usually months in arrears) covered the maximum distance on each daily stage. Moving at two miles in the hour, the trains could maintain regular re-supply to static installations, but had difficulty in keeping up with the army on the move.

There were the usual difficulties between the fighting arms and the logistic services on which they depended. One German commissary complained that British soldiers were as helpless as nestling birds and knew only how to open their mouths to be fed. Commissaries with the divisional and brigade staffs were often exposed to danger from brigands and enemy patrols as they went about their work of buying and bringing in animals from local farmers to provide the soldiers with fresh meat. In the regiments, however, men commonly regarded the commissariat as a set of selfish bureaucrats, full of embezzlers and as ready to steal the soldiers' supplies as they were reluctant to share their hardships. Commissaries complained that while regimental officers took the best billets and could relax after the day's march, they themselves had to work on their accounts and ledgers until late into the night. Wellington was well aware of the importance of logistics and, after **Salamanca (22 July 1812)**, mentioned Bisset in despatches, the first time in British military history that the commissariat was so recognised.

Wellington's move from Madrid to **Burgos (16 September–21 October 1812)** left his magazines still located along the route from Lisbon to Madrid. In the subsequent **retreat from Burgos (21 October–19 November 1812)**, Bisset and Kennedy (who returned as commissary general just before the retreat) moved their stores back along a route furthest away from the enemy, in accordance with orders from the quartermaster-general, Gordon [18]. As this route was also furthest away from the army, the troops almost starved before reaching the magazines of Ciudad Rodrigo. Bisset survived the war, though without the decorations awarded to officers of the fighting arms. In William IV's 1830 coronation honours, however, he was made a knight bachelor and awarded the KCH. In 1840 he published *Memoranda regarding the Duties of the Commissariat on Field Service abroad*, a valuable manual drawing together the lessons learned on his campaign experiences. He was awarded the KCB in 1850 and died in his native Perth on 3 April 1854.

BOCK, Major General EBERHARDT OTTO GEORG, Baron von Bock (1755–1814) [5]

Eberhardt von Bock was born in 1755 on his family estate at Elze, a few miles west of Hildesheim, Lower Saxony, in the then Electorate of Hanover. Following family custom, he joined the Hanoverian Army in 1774 and served as a junior officer in the 5th and 13th Infantry Regiments until 1779, when he transferred to the Hanoverian Life Guards, in which he was promoted to rittmeister (captain of Horse) in 1784, major in 1788 and lieutenant colonel in 1799. When the French occupied Hanover and disbanded its Army in July 1803, some of the disbanded troops took service as mercenaries in the French Hanoverian Legion but a larger number, including Bock and Alten [1], escaped to England and formed the King's German Legion, a force of all arms raised in December 1803. Bock assembled four troops of cavalry that in April 1804 became the nucleus of the 1st Dragoon Regiment of the King's German Legion, with Bock himself granted a commission in the British Army as its colonel commandant. He served in **Hanover (8 November 1805–15 February 1806)**, where recruits were found for a newly-raised 2nd

Dragoon Regiment, and in 1806 was permitted to assume the title of Baron von Bock.

After returning from Hanover, the King's German Legion was stationed in Ireland, where von Bock was promoted to major general on 25 July 1810 and given command of a heavy cavalry brigade, composed of his two dragoon regiments, in 1811. This formation joined Wellington in Portugal on 23 March 1812 and served in his advance into Spain. After **Salamanca (22 July 1812)**, riding at the head of his leading squadron, von Bock routed two French squadrons at Garcia Hernandez (23 July 1812), though it was reported that due to his short sight he had to ask one of his officers to point out the direction of the enemy. On the night of 22–23 July, the British cavalry commander, Sir Stapleton Cotton [11], was badly wounded and, with its three senior generals having become casualties, command of the 1st Cavalry Division passed to von Bock.

After Cotton's return in October 1812, von Bock's brigade took part in the **retreat from Burgos (21 October–19 November 1812)**. Reduced to 300 men, it made a desperate charge at Villodrigo (23 October 1812) and was driven back by superior numbers. When Cotton was evacuated home for further medical treatment in December 1812, von Bock again assumed command of the division. Wellington amalgamated his two cavalry divisions into a single formation on 21 April 1813, but Cotton did not return until 25 June, so that von Bock led the cavalry during the first phase of Wellington's final advance into Spain and at **Vitoria (21 June 1813)**. He then reverted to command of his brigade, and reached the Pyrenees with it in November 1813. Early in 1814 von Bock sailed for England in the transport *Bellona* but was caught in a Channel storm and drowned when the ship struck the Tulbest Rocks, off the north coast of Brittany, on 21 January 1814. His body was washed ashore at the nearby village of Pleubian, where he was buried on 24 January 1814. His son and aide-de-camp, Captain Ludwig (Lewis) von Bock, perished in the same shipwreck.

BURNE, Lieutenant General ROBERT (1755–1825) [6]

Robert Burne entered the Army as an ensign in the 36th Foot on 28 September 1773, on its return from Jamaica. During the American War of Independence, he served in Ireland and was promoted to lieutenant on 13 January 1777. In 1783 he went with his regiment to India, where he was promoted to captain on 7 May 1784 and served in the Third Mysore War (1789–1792), commanding the grenadier company of the 36th Foot and taking part on 13 September 1790 in the occupation of Sattimungulam (Sathymangalam), Tamil Nadu. When a counter-offensive by Tipu Sultan, the ruler of Mysore, forced the British to retreat, Burne's grenadiers led the vanguard and withstood a charge by Tipu's cavalry at Showera (Cheyur) on 14 September 1790. During the subsequent British advance to Tipu's capital at Seringapatam (Srirangapattana), Burne was at the storming of Bangalore (21 March 1791), Nandidroog (Nandagiri), Karnataka (19 August 1791), and Seringapatam (5–23 February 1792), where the campaign ended when Tipu accepted British terms. Following the outbreak of the French Revolutionary War in February 1793, Burne served in the ten-day siege of Pondicherry, the last remaining French position in India, taken on 23 August 1793. He became a major in the Army on 1 March 1794 and in his regiment on 15 April 1796, and was promoted to lieutenant colonel in the Army on 1 January 1798.

Burne sailed for home on 15 October 1798, but did not reach England until 26 July 1799, as the fleet of East Indiamen had to wait for three months at St Helena for a naval escort. He became a lieutenant colonel in the 36th Foot on 15 November 1799 and served with it in the British garrison of Minorca until the war ended and the island was restored to Spain by the treaty of Amiens (25 March 1802). Burne then commanded his regiment in Ireland from August 1802, in **Hanover (8 November 1805–15 February 1806)** and on the **River Plate (June 1806–July 1807)**, after which his officers gave him a presentation sword and a purse of 120 guineas as a mark of their admiration for his leadership during the fighting in urban areas of Buenos Aires. He was promoted to colonel in the Army on 25 April 1808 and, with his regiment, joined a force assembling under Sir Arthur Wellesley for another expedition to South America.

The troops were sent instead to support the patriot risings in the Peninsula and landed in Portugal at the beginning of August 1808. Burne commanded the 36th at **Rolica (17 August 1808)** and **Vimiero (21 August 1808)**, for which he was mentioned in despatches. Wellesley asked Lord Castlereagh, the Secretary of State for War and the Colonies, for some further recognition of 'this old and meritorious soldier', adding 'The 36th are an example to this army.' Burne was accordingly rewarded with the governorship of Carlisle Castle, though he remained with his regiment in the Peninsula and served in Sir John Moore's advance into Spain, **retreat to Corunna (25 December 1808–11 January 1809)** and battle of **Corunna (16 January 1809)**.

Burne's next campaign was in **Walcheren (August–December 1809)**, where he led the 36th in the siege and capture of Flushing (Vlissingen) and became a colonel on the staff. He joined Wellington in the Peninsula in March 1811 as commander of a brigade formed by the 1st and 2nd battalions of the 36th and allotted to the 6th Division. After serving in the battle of **Fuentes d'Onoro (3–5 May 1811)** and the subsequent pursuit of the French garrison of Almeida, Burne was promoted to major general on 4 June 1811 and led the 6th Division from November 1811 to February 1812.

Burne then went home on medical grounds and commanded the troops at Lichfield in 1812–13 and Nottingham in 1813–14. Never having led a major formation in battle, and lacking influential connections, he was not mentioned in the victory honours of 1814, though he retained the governorship of Carlisle, with its daily pay of nine shillings and sixpence. He was promoted to lieutenant general on 19 July 1821, and died at Stanmore, Middlesex, on 16 June 1825.

CAMPBELL, Lieutenant General Sir ALEXANDER, baronet, KCB (1760–1824) [7]

Alexander Campbell, fourth son of John Campbell of Baleed, Perthshire, was born on 20 August 1760. He entered the Army on 1 November 1776, at the beginning of the American War of Independence, as an ensign in the 1st Foot, in which he was promoted to lieutenant on 25 December 1778. He became a captain in the 97th Foot, (raised on 13 April 1780 as a regiment of marines) and served at sea in the first relief of Gibraltar (May 1781) and in the battle of Dogger Bank (5 August 1781). With the 97th, he was then in the garrison of Gibraltar from March 1782 until the great siege ended in July 1783. When the treaty of Paris (3 September 1783) brought the war to an end, Campbell went on half-pay on 23 September 1783, prior to his regiment being disbanded in the usual post-war reductions. In 1784 he married Olympia Elizabeth Morshead, the eldest daughter of a Cornish squire.

In 1787 the Board of Control for the Affairs of India, the government ministry set up to oversee the East India Company, decided that four new regiments of the British Army should be raised for service in India. The Company's Court of Directors protested and at first refused them passage on its ships. It was eventually overruled by a special Act of Parliament, but with the concession that the regiments' officers would be drawn equally from the Company's own unemployed officers and from British Army officers on the half-pay list. On 25 December 1787 Campbell became a captain in the senior of these regiments, the 74th (Highland) Regiment of Foot, which reached India in June 1789. Campbell joined them in 1793 and was appointed brigade major of the British Army's element of the East India Company's Madras Army in 1794. During 1795 he was commandant of Pondicherry, the last remaining French territory in India, captured by the British following the outbreak of the French Revolutionary War in February 1793. In December 1794 Olympia Campbell died, leaving him with a young family of three daughters and two sons, both of whom later followed him into his regiment.

Campbell was promoted to major in the 74th on 1 September 1795 and to lieutenant colonel in the Army on 4 December 1795. During 1797, with Colonels Arthur Wesley (the future Duke of Wellington) and Sherbrooke [36], he joined an expedition against the Spanish Philippines but it only reached Penang before being recalled to Calcutta. Campbell commanded the 74th in southern India during the Fourth Mysore War (1798–1799), where he was commended for his regiment's performance at Mallavelly (Mallaveli) on 27 March 1798 and mentioned in despatches at the storming of Seringapatam (Srirangapattana), where Tipu Sultan, ruler of Mysore, died fighting on 4 May 1799. In the post-war settlement, Mysore came under British control, with Wesley (by this time Wellesley) appointed as garrison commander and commissioner. Under Wellesley, Campbell took part in various minor operations against local chieftains who, in the aftermath of Tipu's fall, took up arms against the new British Raj. In 1800 he was appointed commandant of Bangalore, Tamil Nadu, and then, for the second time, of Pondicherry.

In Europe, late in 1800, Denmark and other Baltic states revived the League of Armed Neutrality, aimed at breaking the British naval blockade of France. Nelson's attack on the Danish fleet at Copenhagen (2 April 1801) forced the Danes to withdraw from the League, but the news did not reach India before Campbell captured the Danish trading factory of Tranquebar (Tharangambadi) on the Coromandel coast, Tamil Nadu. During the 2nd Maratha War (1803–05) Campbell, given command of the Madras Army's northern division in 1802, planned to move northwards against Cuttack, Orissa, held by the Maratha Bhonsla Raja of Nagpore. Ill health forced him to quit the field at the end of the first march, but the campaign proved a British success and gained Cuttack for the East India Company. He commanded the coast defences at Vizagapatam (Visakhapatnamu), Andhra Pradesh, when a convoy of East Indiamen in port there was attacked on 15 September 1804 by a French squadron from Mauritius, only to be driven away by the 4th-rate *Centurion* and Campbell's shore batteries.

Campbell was promoted to colonel on 25 September 1805, two days after his elder son, Lieutenant John Morshead Campbell of the 74th Foot, was killed serving under Wellesley at Assaye, Maharashtra (23 September 1805). Three of Campbell's nephews also died on active service with the 74th in India, two in 1801 and the third at Assaye. When Wellesley left India for

Europe in March 1805, Campbell was appointed to Mysore in his place. He remained in India as commandant of Trichinopoly (Tiruchirappalli) and head of the southern division of the Madras Army until returning home in 1808.

Campbell then served on the staff in Ireland until January 1809, when he was given command of a brigade in the Peninsula. When Wellington organised his army into divisions in June 1809, this brigade became part of the new 4th Division, with Campbell commanding both formations. At **Talavera (27–28 July 1809)** he held Wellington's right flank where, after driving back a French attack, he kept his men well in hand and did not allow the pursuit to go too far. Wounded in the thigh, he was mentioned in despatches for his courage and judgement and went home to convalesce. On 27 December 1809 he was appointed colonel of the York Light Infantry Volunteers, a corps of English and German sharpshooters. Campbell resumed command of his old brigade in the Peninsula during January 1810, was promoted to major general on 25 July and became the first commander of the new 6th Division when this was formed, with his old brigade as its nucleus, on 6 October. He commanded this division at **Fuentes d'Onoro (3–5 May 1811)** and in the blockade of Almeida, where he was among those wrongly blamed for failing to prevent the escape of the French garrison. He returned home on medical grounds in November 1811, and was awarded the KB early in 1812.

On 9 March 1812 Sir Alexander Campbell became C-in-C and local lieutenant general in the Ile de France (Mauritius) and Ile de Bourbon (Reunion), the French Indian Ocean colonies captured by the British in 1810. His younger son, Major Allan William Campbell of the 74th Foot, was wounded at Sorauren (28–30 July 1813) in the battles of the **Pyrenees (25 July–1 August 1813)** and died of his wounds at Pamplona in November 1813. Campbell became a substantive lieutenant general on 4 June 1814, and a KCB in January 1815. He was created a baronet on 6 May 1815, followed by appointment as colonel of the 80th Foot (Staffordshire Volunteers) on 26 December 1815. Campbell left the Indian Ocean in August 1816, when Reunion was handed back to the restored French monarchy as part of the general post-war settlement of Europe, though Mauritius was retained by the British to prevent it ever again becoming a base for French privateers.

Campbell was appointed C-in-C of the East India Company's Madras Army on 6 December 1820 and married Elizabeth Anne Pemberton, the daughter of a clergyman, with whom he had two more children, a daughter and a son who died soon after birth. On 3 July 1821 he was granted a special remainder to his baronetcy, allowing the succession, failing direct male heirs, to pass to his grandsons in the female line. He died in office at Madras (Chenai) on 11 December 1824 and was buried there. His baronetcy was inherited by his eldest daughter's son, Alexander Cockburn, who added the name Campbell to his own, and later became a prominent settler and magistrate in Western Australia.

CLINTON, Lieutenant General Sir HENRY, GCB (1771–1829) [8]

Henry Clinton, younger son of the future General Sir Henry Clinton, British C-in-C in North America during the American War of Independence, was born at Weybridge, Surrey, on 9 March 1771. Brought up by an aunt after the death in 1772 of his 26-year-old mother, Clinton attended Eton College from 1782 to 1785 with his elder brother, the future General Sir William Clinton. He became an ensign in the 11th Foot on 10 October 1787, before touring France, Germany, and the Austrian Netherlands (Belgium) during 1788. The centralising reforms of the Austrian Emperor Joseph II led to insurrections in his non-German dominions, including the Austrian Netherlands, where there was a rebellion to preserve the long-established local constitution. At the same time, Joseph II concluded an alliance with Russia, aimed at Prussia, but involving him in a war against the Ottoman Empire. With much of his army committed to operations along the Danube, Joseph was forced to seek Russian help against the Belgian revolt. This aid included a contingent hired from the Duke of Brunswick, who had previously supplied Hessian troops to the British during the American War of Independence. Lieutenant General Freiherr Riedesel, commanding this contingent, had served under Sir Henry Clinton in the war in America and repaid his comradeship by finding the young Clinton a place as a volunteer with the Brunswickers. Concessions by Joseph II's successor, Leopold II, ended the revolt and Clinton became an ensign in the 1st Foot Guards on 12 March 1789 and a lieutenant in the Army. He obtained promotion to captain on 6 April 1791, on transfer to the 15th Foot, and returned to the 1st Foot Guards on 30 November 1792 as lieutenant in the regiment and captain in the Army.

Clinton was appointed aide-de-camp to the Duke of York in January 1793 and, after the outbreak of the French Revolutionary War a month later, served under him in the **Low Countries (March 1793–April 1795)**. He was promoted to major in the Army on 22 April 1794, and was wounded at Camphin, near Willems (10 May 1794). After becoming a lieutenant colonel in the 66th Foot on 30 September 1795, Clinton joined it in the West Indies, where he served in counter-insurgency operations in the British Windward Islands and at the recapture of St Lucia (26 April–25 May 1796). He became captain in the 1st Foot Guards on 20 October 1796, retaining his seniority as lieutenant colonel in the Army, but was captured by a French ship while on passage back from the West Indies and was not exchanged until 1797.

In a gracious gesture, General Lord Cornwallis (whose relations with Sir Henry Clinton had been strained since Cornwallis's surrender at Yorktown led to the British defeat in the American War of Independence) selected the young Clinton as one of his aides-de-camp when appointed Lord-Lieutenant of Ireland in June 1798. They arrived during the **Irish Rising (May–September 1798)** and Clinton was present at the surrender of the French General Humbert at Ballinamuck, County Longford (8 September 1798). In 1799 he served on the staff of Lord William Bentinck, British commissioner with the Russian army under Suvarov operating alongside the Austrians in northern Italy, and was present at Suvarov's hard-won victories over the French on the Trebbia (19 June 1799) and Novi (14 August 1799) and the advance through the St Gothard Pass. A subsequent attempt to drive the French out of Switzerland ended in a series of disasters for the Allies and Clinton returned home, where, on 23 December 1799, he married the Honourable Susan Charteris, a daughter of the Earl of Elcho. In 1800 the British Cabinet sent the politician and spymaster William Wickham to Switzerland in a diplomatic mission to ensure that British subsidies were keeping Austria and Russia in the war. When Clinton was appointed military assistant in the mission, his new bride insisted on following the drum and going with him. Later that year, Clinton served with the British mission to the Austrian army in south-western Germany before becoming assistant adjutant-general, Eastern District, in June 1801.

Clinton was appointed adjutant-general of the East India Company's Bengal Army in January 1802, with promotion to colonel on 25 September 1802. During the 2nd Maratha War, he served in the decisive British victory over the Maharaja Sindia of Gwalior's French-trained army at Laswari (1 November 1803). Clinton left India in March 1805 and reached Europe just as Austria, alarmed at Napoleon's ambitions and heartened by promises of British subsidies and Russian military aid, re-entered the war against France. Clinton was appointed British military commissioner with the Russian army under Kutuzov and was present when the Austrians and Russians were defeated at Austerlitz (2 December 1805). The outcome of this battle freed the French armies in Italy to invade Naples, where King Ferdinand of Naples and Sicily had been joined by British and Russian troops. French successes forced Ferdinand and his British allies to Sicily, while the Russians sailed to Corfu.

Clinton arrived in Sicily in command of a composite battalion of flank companies of the Foot Guards late in 1806 and spent most of 1807 as garrison commander at Syracuse under Sir John Moore. Clinton returned to Scotland at the end of 1807, where he unsuccessfully stood for election as MP for Haddington, East Lothian, a seat owned by his father-in-law. Given command of a brigade in January 1808, he served in the **Baltic (May–June 1808)** and returned to politics later that year, when he was elected Tory MP for Boroughbridge, North Yorkshire, a seat owned by another of his noble relations, the Duke of Newcastle.

Following the Cabinet's decision to support the patriot risings in the Peninsula, Clinton landed in Portugal on 21 August 1808 as adjutant-general under his fellow-Guardsman, Lieutenant General Sir Harry Burrard, who had superseded Sir Arthur Wellesley in command of the British army there. Following Wellesley's victories at **Rolica (17 August 1808)** and **Vimiero (21 August 1808)**, Burrard decided to accept French proposals for an armistice and was strongly supported by both Clinton and Murray [28], the quartermaster-general. Another Guardsman, Lieutenant General Sir Hew Dalrymple, governor of Gibraltar, arrived to take over from Burrard on 22 August 1808 and maintained this decision, leading to the Convention of Cintra (Sintra). The French agreed to evacuate Portugal (the declared aim of the British expedition) in return for being taken home, with all their public and private possessions, in British troopships. Popular indignation at these terms, which allowed the French to retain all the plunder they had taken in Portugal and placed no restrictions on their subsequent return to the Peninsula, resulted in Dalrymple (whom Clinton later described as unfit to command) being recalled early in October 1808. Burrard was superseded by Sir John Moore, under whom Clinton remained as adjutant-general during the subsequent advance into Spain and **retreat to Corunna (25 December 1808–11 January 1809)**. Clinton organised the army's embarkation but was absent from the final battle, suffering from dysentery. As adjutant-general he was responsible for discipline, but the high standards he sought to enforce led to complaints about his abusive language and unreasonable behaviour. During 1809 he served as adjutant-general in Ireland, followed by promotion to major general on 25 July 1810.

Clinton returned to the Peninsula in October 1811 and was given command of the 6th Division on 9 February 1812. During Wellington's advance into Spain in the summer of 1812, this division invested the French forts covering the bridge over the Tormes at Salamanca and carried them by storm on 27 June 1812. At **Salamanca (22 July 1812)** Clinton led his men forward to recover ground lost by the 4th Division and then advanced under intense fire, with both sides suffering heavy losses, until the French line opposed to him gave way. While Wellington marched on to Madrid, Clinton was left to hold Cuellar with his own division, a brigade of cavalry and five newly-arrived infantry battalions. From there he took part in the siege of **Burgos (16 September–21 October 1812)** and the **retreat from Burgos (21 October–19 November 1812)**.

During the retreat, together with William Stewart [39] and Lord Dalhousie [34], commanding the 1st and 7th Divisions respectively, he incurred Wellington's anger by departing from the route they had been ordered to take to Ciudad Rodrigo. On 26 January 1813 he went home on sick leave. Clinton was promoted to local lieutenant general (Spain and Portugal) on the staff on 8 April 1813 and was appointed colonel of the 1st Battalion, 60th Foot (Royal American Regiment), on 20 May 1813. He briefly resumed command of the 6th Division on 25 June 1813 and was awarded the KB on 29 July 1813 but again went home on sick leave. After returning to the 6th Division in October 1813, Sir Henry Clinton led it at the **passage of the Nivelle (10 November 1813)**; the **passage of the Nive (10–13 December 1813)**; **Orthez (27 February 1814)** and **Toulouse (10 April 1814)**. At the end of the war, following Napoleon's abdication, he was awarded the Army Gold Cross with one clasp and the Portuguese Order of the Tower and Sword.

Clinton was then appointed Inspector-General of infantry with promotion to substantive lieutenant general on 4 June 1814 and his KB was converted to GCB when the Order of the Bath was reconstituted in January 1815. At the beginning of the Hundred Days, after Napoleon's escape from Elba, Clinton was given command of the 2nd British Division, which he led at **Waterloo (18 June 1815)**. In the subsequent inter-allied exchange of awards to senior officers he received the Austrian Order of Maria Theresa, the Russian Order of St George and the Netherlands Order of William of Orange. He commanded a British division in France in the Army of Occupation but, following the death of his wife in August 1816, his health declined. He went to Lyons as an invalid in 1817 and resigned his seat in Parliament in 1818. Clinton retired to his country estate at Ashley Clinton, near Lymington in the New Forest, Hampshire, where he died on 21 December 1829. He was buried beside his wife in his family's ancient parish church of St Mary Magdalene, Barkway, near Royston, north Hertfordshire, where a memorial to him was put up. He was an efficient staff officer and a competent commander, but his insistence on observing the details of military formality and protocol was thought to be excessive even in a Guards officer.

COLE, General the Honourable Sir GALBRAITH LOWRY, GCB (1772–1842) **[9]**

Galbraith Lowry Cole, born in Dublin on 2 May 1772, was the second son of an Irish peer, Lord Mountflorence, who was created a viscount in July 1776 and Earl of Enniskillen in August 1789. The Honourable Lowry Cole, as he became on his father's advancement, studied at the University of Stuttgart, Wurtemberg, and entered the Army as a cornet in the 12th Light Dragoons, on the Irish establishment, on 31 May 1787. He transferred to the 5th Dragoon Guards with promotion to lieutenant on 31 May 1791 and to captain in the 70th Foot on 30 November 1792. Following the outbreak of the French Revolutionary War in February 1793, the 70th sailed from Ireland in September 1793 for a campaign against the French West Indian colonies, where Cole took part in the capture of Martinique (February–March 1794), Guadeloupe and **St Lucia (April 1794)**. On 31 October 1793 he was promoted to major in the 102nd Foot, a regiment raised in Ireland earlier that month for service in India, though it was later disbanded without going overseas. Cole became lieutenant colonel of the recently-raised Downshire (County Down) Regiment of Foot on 26 November 1794. This was disbanded in 1796 but Cole remained on the full-pay list and between October 1796 and November 1797 served on the staff of the C-in-C in Ireland, Lieutenant General the Earl of Carhampton, an officer whose extreme sectarian policies led to Sir Ralph Abercromby being appointed in his stead.

From 1797 to 1800 Cole sat in the Irish Parliament as MP for Enniskillen, County Fermanagh, a seat owned by his family, but retired before this body was abolished by the Act of Union in 1801. In 1803 he was elected as MP for County Fermanagh in one of the new Irish seats in the Westminster Parliament, where he remained until 1823. On 12 April 1799 Cole was appointed lieutenant colonel of Villette's Regiment of Foot, a newly-raised corps of Albanian mercenaries intended for service in the Mediterranean theatre. This was disbanded the following year, but Cole remained on the full-pay list and was promoted to colonel in the Army on 1 January 1801. In **Egypt (March–October 1801)** he was military secretary to Lieutenant General Sir John Hely-Hutchinson, who succeeded to the command after Abercromby was mortally wounded at Alexandria (21 March 1801).

Cole returned to the United Kingdom when peace was restored by the treaty of Amiens (25 March 1802). After hostilities with France were resumed in February 1803, he joined the Scots Guards as a captain in the regiment (retaining his Army rank as lieutenant colonel) on 25 May 1803. On

4 August 1804 he became lieutenant colonel commanding the 1st Battalion, 27th Foot (the Inniskilling Regiment). Cole then became engaged to the 32–year-old Honourable Catherine 'Kitty' Pakenham, daughter of an Irish peer, the 2nd Earl of Longford. Ten years earlier the then Major Arthur Wesley had sought her hand, only for his suit to be dismissed by her brother, the young 3rd Earl. She never forgot him, however, and early in 1805, when, as Major General Sir Arthur Wellesley, he returned from India and said he still hoped to marry her, she rejected Cole and married Wellesley in April 1806.

Cole, heartbroken by her decision, went with his regiment to Malta. From there, in November 1805, he landed at Naples in a combined Russian and British force supporting King Ferdinand of Naples and Sicily. Napoleon's victory at Austerlitz (2 December 1805) left Italy open to the French, who invaded Naples and forced Ferdinand and the British to withdraw to Sicily in January 1806, while their Russian allies sailed for Corfu. During June 1806 Neapolitan patriots in Calabria, the 'toe' of Italy, rose against French occupation. Major General Sir John Stuart, commanding the British troops in Sicily, went to their aid with 8,000 men and crossed the strait of Messina to disembark on the mainland at St Euphemia Bay. With Cole as his second-in-command, he defeated a hasty French attack at Maida (4 July 1806), but the arrival of French reinforcements soon forced the British back to their ships. Cole was among those awarded the Army Gold Medal, and became a major general on 25 April 1808. Increasingly frustrated by Stuart's reluctance to undertake further operations on the Italian mainland, he sailed home from Sicily in the summer of 1809.

Cole was given command of the 4th Division in the Peninsula in October 1809 and led it at **Busaco (27 September 1810)**. After the French withdrew from Portugal early in 1811, his division was among the troops assigned to Beresford [3] for the recovery of Badajoz. He was present at Campo Mayor (25 March 1811) and was detached to capture the small French-held fortress of Olivenza, achieved on 15 April 1811 after the arrival of heavy guns from Elvas. He rejoined Beresford at the first siege of **Badajoz (5–13 May 1811)** and, when this was abandoned in order to meet the approach of Marshal Soult with a relieving force, was left behind to destroy the immobile stores. Delayed by the premature removal of a pontoon bridge over the Guadiana, Cole only caught up with Beresford during the night before **Albuera (16 May 1811)**. Initially deployed behind the Allied centre, on seeing the 2nd Division under William Stewart [39] in difficulties, he sent to Beresford for permission to move to its aid. The message never arrived and Cole, left without orders, finally decided to throw his fusilier brigade into the fight.

This turned the battle in the Allied favour, though only after heavy casualties, with Cole himself among the wounded and left unfit for duty until the following July. He was promoted to local lieutenant general on 6 September 1811. In December 1811 he went home and was appointed colonel of the 103rd Foot on 13 January 1812.

After resuming command of the 4th Division in June 1812, Cole served at **Salamanca (22 July 1812)**, where he was again wounded, but rejoined his division at Madrid and served with it in the **retreat from Burgos (21 October–19 November 1812)**. During the winter of 1812–13 he became noted for the hospitality offered at his headquarters, with Wellington saying that Cole gave the best dinners of all his generals, Hill **[21]** the next best, his own being nothing special and those of Beresford and Picton **[33]** very bad indeed. After being awarded the KB in March 1813, Sir Lowry Cole became a substantive lieutenant general on 4 June 1813. He commanded the 4th Division at **Vitoria (21 June 1813)**; Roncesvalles (25 July 1813) and Sorauren (28–30 July 1813) during the battles of the **Pyrenees (25 July–1 August 1813)**; the **passage of the Nivelle (10 November 1813)**; the **passage of the Nive (10–13 December 1813)**; **Orthez (27 February 1814)** and **Toulouse (10 April 1814)**. He was appointed colonel of the 70th Foot on 12 January 1814, became a GCB when the Prince Regent re-organised the Order of the Bath, and was awarded the Portuguese Order of the Tower and Sword.

With the war ended by Napoleon's abdication, Cole became engaged to Lady Frances Harris, the daughter of the 1st Earl of Malmesbury, an eminent diplomat. They were married on 15 June 1815 and Cole did not join Wellington in the Hundred Days campaign until 15 August, after the end of hostilities. He was appointed colonel of the 34th Foot on 21 May 1816 and commanded a division in the Army of Occupation until this was withdrawn in November 1818. He was then appointed governor of Tilbury and Gravesend, London's seaward defences, and retained this post until his death.

In 1823 Cole became governor of Mauritius (Ile de France), in the Indian Ocean, from which French privateers had long preyed on British shipping and which was, on that account, retained by the British in the post-war settlement. Despite opposition from the French planters who had previously dominated the island, he introduced a number of reforms in the colony's educational and administrative systems, though the French *Code Napoleon* remained in force in domestic matters and he could do little for the slave population. He ruled with the aid of a council but, although intended to give the impression of representative government, in fact it merely reinforced his authority. On 16 December 1826, he became colonel of the 27th Foot, with its long-standing connection with his family as the leaders of society in Enniskillen.

In September 1828 Cole became governor of Cape Colony. Some settlers pressed for representative government, but the British Cabinet was reluctant to create an elected assembly when similar bodies in other slave-holding colonies were strongly opposing the growing pressure for emancipation (which would be decreed throughout the British Empire five years later). On his frontier, Boer farmers complained that lost or straying cattle had been stolen by Xhosa herdsmen, and the local authorities responded with punitive raids, irrespective of who the thieves actually were. Xhosas and settlers alike objected to the establishment of agricultural settlements for Khoikhoi (Hottentot) and Coloured people, intended by Cole to give them 'some small portion of the soil of their native country'. Lady Cole supported the education of children of the Coloured community, though in one school, when the girls petitioned to be taught Greek, the idea was opposed by the boys on the grounds that girls already surpassed them in every subject.

The town of Malmesbury, in the Western Cape, was named for Lady Cole's father, and Colesberg, in the same colony, was named for Cole himself. He also gave his name to Sir Lowry's Pass, at the foot of Gantuow Mountain, where a new road was constructed under his direction to improve communications between Cape Town and the interior. Cole was promoted to general on 22 July 1830. He generally supported local military commanders, though forbidding needless bloodshed in police actions against the Xhosas. Missionary and humanitarian influences were suspected of stirring up the Xhosas against the British but, when Cole banned Xhosas from the colony, white settlers objected to losing their cheap labour. In August 1833 Cole handed over to Sir Benjamin D'Urban, another Peninsular veteran, and returned to England, where he lived at Highfield Park, near Hook, in north-east Hampshire. Sir Lowry Cole died there suddenly on 4 October 1842, leaving a family of three sons and four daughters. He was buried in his ancestral vault at Enniskillen, where a tall pillar was put up in his memory on Fort Hill, overlooking the city.

COLVILLE, General the Honourable Sir CHARLES, GCB, GCH (1770–1843) [10]

The Honourable Charles Colville, second son of a Scottish peer, the 8th Baron Colville of Culross, was born on 7 August 1770. He became an ensign in the 28th Foot on 6 December 1781, during the American War of

Independence, at the age of 11, though he did not commence duty until promoted to lieutenant on 30 September 1787. He became a captain on 24 January 1791 and transferred on 18 May 1791 to the 13th Foot, stationed in the West Indies. Following the outbreak of the French Revolutionary War in February 1793, it took part in the capture of French San Domingo (Haiti) in 1794, where Colville was wounded at the storming of Cap Tiburon (2–3 February 1794). He was promoted to major on 1 September 1795 and to lieutenant colonel on 26 August 1796 and returned home in 1797. During the **Irish Rising (May–September 1798)** elements of the 13th were at Vinegar Hill, Enniscorthy, County Wexford (21 June 1798), but it does not appear that either Colville or the regiment as a whole saw active service until August 1800, when they formed part of an abortive British raid on Spanish naval installations at Ferrol.

The troops were then sent on to the Mediterranean, where Colville and the 13th Foot served in **Egypt (March–October 1801)**. During the brief period of peace secured by the treaty of Amiens (25 March 1802), Colville moved with the 13th first to Malta and then to Gibraltar, where they remained as part of the garrison after hostilities with France were resumed in May 1803. He was promoted to colonel in the Army on 1 January 1805 and returned to the United Kingdom with his regiment in December 1805. They were sent to the West Indies in February 1808, where Colville commanded a brigade at the recapture of Martinique (30 January–24 February 1809).

Colville was promoted to major general on 25 July 1810 and in October 1810 was given command of a brigade in the Peninsula, with which he served in the 3rd Division at **Fuentes d'Onoro (3–5 May 1811)**, **Badajoz (19 May–10 June 1811)**, and El Bodon (25 September 1811). On 22 December 1811 he became commander of the 4th Division, which he led at **Ciudad Rodrigo (7–19 January 1812)** and **Badajoz (17 March– 6 April 1812)**, where he was wounded by a musket ball through the thigh and lost a finger of his right hand. After medical treatment in the United Kingdom, Colville returned to the Peninsula in October 1812 and commanded the 3rd Division in the absence of Picton [33] until May 1813. He then returned to his original brigade and served with this at **Vitoria (21 June 1813)**, where he was slightly wounded.

From August to early October 1813 Colville commanded the 6th Division in the absence of Clinton [8] and led it at the **passage of the Bidasoa (7 October 1813)**. He again commanded the 3rd Division in Picton's absence from October and December 1813 and led the division at the **passage of the Nivelle (10 November 1813)**. In December 1813 Colville was given command of the 5th Division, which he led at the siege of

Bayonne (27 February–27 April 1814). At the end of the war, following Napoleon's abdication, he led his men back into Spain and was in charge of the final embarkation of the British infantry at Passages (Pasajes). He was awarded the Army Gold Cross with one clasp, and in January 1815 became a KCB, with advancement to GCB in March 1815 and appointment as colonel of the 94th Foot on 29 April 1815.

During the Hundred Days, after Napoleon's escape from Elba, Sir Charles Colville joined Wellington with promotion to local lieutenant general, and commanded the 4th British Division in the Second Corps under Hill [21]. At **Waterloo (18 June 1815)**, Wellington stationed this corps about 10 miles west of his main position, to guard against a possible French threat to his right flank. This threat did not materialise, so Colville did not take part in the battle, but his division joined Wellington's advance the following day, from which they were detached to take Cambrai, one of the French fortresses still holding out for Napoleon. This was stormed with minimal casualties on 23rd June 1815, and handed over to Louis XIII when he returned to France from his refuge in Ghent.

On 16 February 1818 Colville married Jane Mure, the elder daughter of an Ayrshire landholder, and later had with her a family of two sons and three daughters. He became a substantive lieutenant general on 12 August 1819 and served as C-in-C of the East India Company's Bombay Army from 1819 to 1825, with the award of the GCH. Between 1828 and 1835, in succession to Cole [9], he was governor of Mauritius, captured by the British in December 1810 and retained after the Napoleonic Wars to prevent it ever again becoming a base for French privateers in the Indian Ocean. The terms of the British annexation allowed the French population to retain the *Code Napoleon* and continue with their ownership of slaves and denial of equal rights to freemen of African or mixed descent. Suspicion that a British government would renege on these terms caused discontent and in 1830 Colville was obliged to report to Murray [28], Secretary of State for War and the Colonies, that there was widespread hostility to British rule and that the collection of taxes had virtually ceased. In 1832 the appointment of a noted abolitionist, the Guernsey-born barrister John Jeremie, as advocate general of Mauritius, was followed by rioting in the colony. When the local judges refused to swear him in, Colville sent him home to England. Murray immediately sent Jeremie back to Mauritius, but he again became involved in disputes with the judges, whom he accused of sympathising with slavery (about to be abolished throughout the British Empire). Unsupported by Colville, he resigned in 1833, but later went on to a distinguished career in other colonial appointments. Colville was appointed colonel of the 5th Foot on 25 March 1835 and returned home the same year. He was promoted to general on 10 January 1837 and died at his home, Rosslyn House, Hampstead, Middlesex (later in the London Borough of Camden) on 27 March 1843.

COMBERMERE, VISCOUNT, *see* **COTTON,** Sir STAPLETON [11]

COTTON, Field Marshal Sir STAPLETON, baronet, 1st Viscount Combermere, GCB, GCH, KCSI (1773–1865) [11]

Stapleton Cotton, the second surviving son of Sir Robert Salusbury Cotton, 5th baronet, and his wife Frances, daughter of Colonel James Stapleton of Bodrhyddan Hall, Flintshire, was born on 14 November 1773 at Llewenny Hall (Plas Lleweni), Denbighshire, Clwyd. This mansion, then one of the largest in north Wales, was for generations the seat of the Salusbury family until 1684, when for lack of male heirs it was inherited by Hester Salusbury, wife of Sir Robert Cotton, 1st baronet, of Combermere Abbey, on the borders of Cheshire and Shropshire, and became their main family residence. Stapleton Cotton attended Westminster School and a private military academy in Bayswater before being granted a commission, without purchase, as a second lieutenant in the 23rd Foot, Royal Welsh Fusiliers, on 26 February 1790, possibly in recognition of his father's reputation for lavish hospitality and influence as a long-serving Member of Parliament for Cheshire. Cotton was promoted to lieutenant in the 23rd Foot on 16 March 1791 and became a captain in the 6th Dragoon Guards on 26 February 1793, a few weeks after the outbreak of the French Revolutionary War. He served with this regiment in the **Low Countries (March 1793–April 1795)** in the retreat from Dunkirk during 1793 and at Premont (17 April 1794), Beaumont (Le Cateau, 26 April 1794) and Willems (Tournai, 10 May 1794). On 28 April 1794 he became a major in the 59th Foot, giving him the necessary rank for his promotion on 9 May 1794 to lieutenant colonel in the 25th Light Dragoons, newly-raised for service in India.

After embarking for the East Indies, the regiment landed in July 1796 at the Cape of Good Hope (taken by the British from the Dutch East India Company the previous year) to counter a threatened rising by the Boer settlers. Security was quickly restored and the troops sailed on to Madras where Cotton took part in the Fourth Mysore War (1798–99) and served with the then Colonel Arthur Wellesley at Seringapatam (Srirangapattana), where

Tipu Sultan, ruler of Mysore, was killed fighting on 4 May 1799. At this time, through the death of his thirty-year-old elder brother, Cotton became heir to the family estates and baronetcy, and decided to return home. He was promoted to colonel in the Army on 1 January 1800 and exchanged to the 16th Light Dragoons on 14 February 1800. He married the nineteen-year-old Lady Anna Maria Pelham-Clinton, elder daughter of the 3rd Duke of Newcastle, at Worksop, Nottinghamshire, on 1 January 1801, and joined his regiment at Brighton later in the year. During the brief period of peace with France between March 1802 and May 1803, he commanded the regiment in Ireland and in June 1803 was employed in counter-insurgency operations against an abortive nationalist rising led by Robert Emmett.

Cotton was promoted to major general on 30 October 1805 and given command of a brigade at Weymouth. In the same year he was elected Member of Parliament for Newark-on-Trent, and continued to represent that borough until he entered the House of Lords nine years later. Lady Anna Cotton died of 'pulmonary consumption' (tuberculosis) on 31 May 1807, leaving him with a young son. In April 1809 Cotton was given command of a brigade of light dragoons in the Peninsula. He led the British cavalry in Wellington's advance to Oporto and in support of the **passage of the Douro (12 May 1809)** after which his brigade became part of the Cavalry Division formed on 8 June 1809 under Payne [32]. At **Talavera (27–28 July 1809)**, having last ridden over the French as a young captain at Willems (Tournai) fifteen years previously, he led an unexpected charge by the 14th Light Dragoons and halted a French battalion at a critical moment in the battle.

With the death of his father on 24 August 1809, Cotton inherited not only a baronetcy but also vast debts, incurred by years of high living, generous entertainment and devotion to field sports. He went home to settle his affairs, knowing that the Llewenny estate had already been sold, something that later in life, when his own finances improved, he much regretted. Sir Stapleton Cotton was promoted to local lieutenant general (Spain and Portugal) on 31 August 1809 and returned to the Peninsula as second-in-command of the Cavalry Division in November 1809. On 3 June 1810, when Payne went home, Cotton succeeded him as commander of the Cavalry Division, having gained the soubriquet of *Lion D'Or* from his dashing conduct in battle and the splendour of his uniforms. He served at **Busaco (27 September 1810)** and then covered Wellington's withdrawal to the Lines of Torres Vedras. After spending the winter in the United Kingdom, he rejoined Wellington on 22 April 1811 and led the cavalry at **Fuentes d'Onoro (3–5 May 1811)**.

Cotton became a substantive lieutenant general on 1 January 1812. He remained in command of the cavalry during Wellington's advance towards

Madrid and conducted a brilliant action against the rearguard of the retreating French at Villagarcia, near Llerana, (11 April 1812). At **Salamanca (22 July 1812)**, a successful charge by the British heavy cavalry moved Wellington to exclaim 'By God, Cotton, I never saw anything so beautiful in my life; the day is *yours*.' The same night, returning to the Allied lines, Cotton failed to answer the challenge of a Portuguese sentry and was shot in the arm. He was kept in hospital at Salamanca until late October, when he resumed command of his division and covered the **retreat from Burgos (21 October–19 November 1812)** after which he went home for further medical treatment.

Cotton was appointed colonel of the 20th Light Dragoons on 27 January 1813 and returned to the Peninsula in the following June. He commanded the cavalry during the closing stages of the war, where he served during the battles of the **Pyrenees (25 July–1 August 1813)** despite the unsuitability of the terrain for mounted troops, at **Orthez (27 February 1814)**, and **Toulouse (10 April 1814)**. Cotton was raised to the peerage as Baron Combermere on 17 May 1814 and was decorated with the Portuguese Order of the Tower and Sword and the Spanish Orders of St Ferdinand and Charles III. Wellington's opinion of him was that he commanded the cavalry very well, and better than some who were said to be his intellectual superiors. The British cavalry was always weaker in numbers than its French opponents, and Cotton's great achievement was to husband his resources in men and horses. His outstanding merit, in Wellington's eyes, was that he could be relied on to comply with the orders given him, and carry them out with discretion and zeal rather than using his own initiative to try to improve on them. On 18 June 1814 he married the 20-year-old Caroline Fulke Greville, the daughter of a captain in the Royal Navy and later had with her a son and two daughters. Combermere was awarded the GCB in January 1815.

At the beginning of the Hundred Days, after Napoleon's escape from Elba, most Peninsular veterans expected Combermere to be given command of the cavalry in the Allied army being formed under Wellington in Belgium. Instead, the Duke of York, C-in-C of the British Army, nominated the 3rd Earl of Uxbridge, who, as Lord Paget, had commanded Moore's cavalry in the **retreat to Corunna (25 December 1808–11 January 1809)**. Having run away with the married Lady Charlotte Wellesley, Lord Paget had been judged an unsuitable choice to serve under her brother-in-law (Wellington) in the Peninsula. By this time, however, with his first wife having divorced him and married another general (her long-term admirer, the 6th Duke of Argyll), and Lady Charlotte, divorced by her first husband, having become his countess, Lord Uxbridge was rehabilitated in the eyes of Society and, moreover, was nearly four years senior to Combermere as a lieutenant general. When Uxbridge (later Marquess of Anglesey) was badly wounded at Waterloo, Combermere was appointed in his place and remained in France with the Army of Occupation until 1816.

Combermere was appointed governor of Barbados and C-in-C, Leeward Islands, in 1817 with the award of the KCH and became colonel of the 3rd King's Own Hussars on 25 January 1821. During 1821 his eldest son died, leaving the 3-year-old son of his second marriage to become his heir and eventual successor. Combermere served as commander of the forces in Ireland from 1822 to 1825, and was then, on Wellington's recommendation, appointed C-in-C, India. It was said that when members of the Cabinet questioned Combermere's nomination, on the grounds that Wellington thought him a fool, Wellington answered 'So he is, and a damned fool, but he can take Rangoon', in allusion to the slow progress being made in the war against Burma (Myanmar). Combermere was promoted to general on 27 May 1825, and in the following year led the East India Company's Bengal Army in a campaign against the Jat kingdom of Bhurtpoor (Bharatpur), Rajasthan. The massive fortifications of its capital city, which had previously defied attacks by Mughals, Marathas and British in turn, were carried by storm and a pro-British prince was restored to the throne. Combermere was created a viscount on 8 February 1827 and changed his surname to Stapleton-Cotton in November 1827. He was appointed colonel of the 1st Life Guards on 16 September 1829, shortly before his return from India.

Personally, his homecoming was an unhappy one, as his viscountess, who had not accompanied him to India, then left him after fifteen years of marriage. She died in January 1837, leaving Combermere free to marry in October 1838 the 40-year-old Mary Woolley Gibbings, the only daughter of an Irish landowner. They lived comfortably together, mostly at Combermere Abbey, which Combermere had greatly restored and enlarged, though he also maintained a presence in London as a colonel in the Household Cavalry, member of the Privy Council and, in succession to Wellington after the latter's death in 1852, Constable of the Tower of London and Lieutenant of the County (later a London Borough) of Tower Hamlets. He became a field marshal on 2 October 1855, as one of the three senior ranking generals in the Army promoted at that time, and was awarded the KCSI in 1861. Combermere died at Clifton on 21 February 1865. An equestrian statue of him by Carlo Marochetti was erected at Chester Castle in 1865 and a sandstone obelisk was placed in the grounds of Combermere Abbey following the death of his second viscountess in August 1889. Another memorial to him was installed in St Margaret's parish church, Wrenbury, Shropshire, where he was buried.

CRAUFURD, Major General ROBERT (1764–1812) **[12]**

Robert 'Black Bob' Craufurd, the third son of a Scottish baronet, was born at Newark Castle, Ayrshire, on 5 May 1764. He was commissioned as an ensign in the 25th Foot in 1779, during the American War of Independence, and in the same year became a pupil at Harrow School. In 1781 he was promoted to lieutenant and on 14 August 1783 became a captain in the 13th Foot. After attending the George Augustus University at Gottingen, Hanover, Craufurd became a major in the 75th Foot on 1 November 1787 and went to India with the regiment in 1788. He commanded the 75th in southern India during the Third Mysore War (1789–1792) and was noted as a harsh disciplinarian. With the outbreak of the French Revolutionary War in February 1793, he joined the campaign in the **Low Countries (March 1793–April 1795)** and served on the staff of his elder brother, the future General Sir Charles Craufurd, in the British military mission with the Austrian army. Robert Craufurd remained on the Continent until his promotion to lieutenant colonel in the 60th Foot (Royal American Regiment) on 30 December 1797. During 1798 he served as deputy quartermaster-general of the army in Ireland, where its recently-appointed C-in-C, Sir Ralph Abercromby, described it as a force demoralised by constant internal security operations and formidable to everyone but the enemy. This gave such offence to the Irish government that Abercromby was replaced by Lieutenant General Gerard Lake, who was in office when the long-expected **Irish Rising (May–September 1798)** began. Craufurd was mentioned in despatches for his services in this campaign, especially in the 150–mile pursuit of General Humbert's French contingent to Ballinamuck, County Longford, where it surrendered. During September 1799 Craufurd was with the British military mission to the Russian army under Suvarov in northern Italy and Switzerland (renamed the Helvetic Republic in March 1798). The Russians retreated into Austrian territory at the end of September and Craufurd moved to **the Helder (August–October 1799)**.

On 6 February 1800 Craufurd married Mary, daughter of the architect Henry Holland, and with her later had three sons and a daughter. In 1802, through the influence of his brother Charles, who had married Anna Maria, dowager Duchess of Newcastle, he was elected Member of Parliament for East Retford, Nottinghamshire, a seat owned by his sister-in-law's family. In the Commons, he used his formidable talents as a speaker to attack the Tory Ministers' anti-invasion measures, disparaging the Volunteers (patriotic citizens who formed part-time local units for the defence of their hearths and homes) and urging their replacement by full-time conscripts. He was promoted to colonel on the half-pay list of the 60th on 30 October 1805. When the Whig Ministry of All the Talents came into power on 27 January 1806, the new Secretary of State for War and the Colonies was his personal friend and political ally, William Wickham. Craufurd gave up his parliamentary seat in 1806 in the hope of obtaining a field command, which Wickham secured for him at the end of the year.

Craufurd was given 4,000 men and ordered to round Cape Horn, occupy the Spanish colonial city of Valparaiso, Chile, and establish contact with the British army on the **River Plate (June 1806–July 1807)**. There, the Argentinians had already driven the British out of Buenos Aires, so that after sailing, Craufurd was ordered to join the troops on their way to recapture that city. He commanded a brigade of light infantry in the attack on Buenos Aires (7 July 1807) where he was taken prisoner when the British were defeated fighting in the city's urban areas, though Craufurd's own reputation was enhanced by his performance as a light infantry commander.

When the British Cabinet decided to support the Spanish patriots in their rising against French occupation, Craufurd was given command of a light infantry brigade in a force ordered to Corunna under Sir David Baird. At the end of September 1808 it was decided that Baird's contingent, and 20,000 of the 30,000 British troops already in Portugal, should be commanded by Sir John Moore. Baird landed on 14 October 1808 and after a difficult march joined Moore at Mayorga, Leon, on 20 December 1808. Craufurd served with the rearguard during the first part of the subsequent **retreat to Corunna (25 December 1808–11 January 1809)**, and kept his brigade together by rigid discipline.

Craufurd was re-appointed to a light infantry brigade and returned to Portugal with it in 1809. Learning of the engagement at **Talavera (27–28 July 1809)**, he marched his men 43 miles in twenty-two hours and reached the battlefield on 29 July 1809. With the veteran Major General John Mackenzie having been killed in the battle, Craufurd was given the vacant command of the 3rd Division, where he remained until 22 February 1810. He was then appointed to the newly-formed Light Division, composed of his original light infantry brigade and two battalions of Portuguese cacadores (riflemen). Impulsive in action but methodical in character, Craufurd issued a code of divisional standing orders for every kind of activity. At first heartily disliked, especially when enforced by severe punishment, this code raised divisional *esprit de corps* to a high level and enabled the division to assemble under arms in seven minutes from an alarm, even at night, and to be ready to move within fifteen minutes.

During the first half of 1810, Craufurd held the line of the Coa from the Douro southwards to the Serra da Estrela, effectively screening Wellington's army from French patrols. In July 1810, when Marshal Ney advanced into Portugal from Ciudad Rodrigo, Craufurd 'as enamoured with his separate command as any youth with his mistress' according to one of his officers, held his position too long, despite explicit warnings from Wellington and was almost trapped. At the combat of the Coa (24 July 1810) the Light Division escaped across the only bridge under heavy fire and suffered over 300 casualties, twenty-eight officers among them. Wellington refused to blame Craufurd for this episode, which was, he said, a fault of judgement, not intention. At **Busaco (27 September 1810)** Craufurd called on his men to avenge the death of Sir John Moore, under whom many of them had been trained. From there, they covered Wellington's withdrawal to the Lines of Torres Vedras, reached on 10 October 1810. When the French retreated to Santarem in mid-November, the Light and 6th Divisions were ordered to follow, and on both 16 and 17 November Craufurd was only prevented from launching over-hasty attacks by Wellington's personal intervention. On the night of 18 November, leading a three-man patrol, he was shot at by a French sentry and, by ordering his men to return fire, aroused an entire French division.

With operations at a standstill for the winter, Craufurd went on leave to the United Kingdom in February 1811. His request for leave was rather grudgingly allowed by Wellington, who said that general officers must be presumed to know best whether their business obliged them to leave the field, but that with several major generals to be found employment, it had not been an easy task to keep Craufurd (still a substantive colonel) in post as a brigadier general and he should not count on retaining his command. Nevertheless Craufurd rejoined his division during the battle of **Fuentes d'Onoro (3–5 May 1811)**, greeted with cheers by the men he had so often had flogged. Portuguese cacadores were heard shouting '*Viva* General Craufurd, who takes care of our bellies.' He was promoted to local major general (Spain and Portugal) on 4 June 1811.

In August 1811 Wellington reached Ciudad Rodrigo, but the arrival of French reinforcements obliged him to fall back, leaving only the 3rd and Light Divisions near the city. When the French attacked the 3rd Division at El Bodon (25 September 1811) Wellington ordered his army to concentrate at nearby Fuente Guinaldo but the late arrival of Craufurd's division, attributable in part to the French presence and in part to Craufurd's habitual reluctance to leave a separate position, caused Wellington some irritation. 'I am glad to see you safe,' he said when Craufurd at last arrived. 'I was in no danger, I assure you,' Craufurd replied, only to be told, 'No, but I was, through your conduct.' Unabashed, Craufurd responded, under his breath, 'He's damned crusty today'. In the New Year, Wellington made a surprise advance and stormed **Ciudad Rodrigo (19 January 1812)** in a night attack. As they waited under the shelter of a convent wall, Craufurd addressed his division's storming parties, saying 'Soldiers! The eyes of your country are upon you' and telling them that as soon as they had taken the wall, their first task was to clear the ramparts, keeping together as they did so. Leading his division forward into a hail of fire, Craufurd was among the first to fall, shot through the spine and lower body. He died of wounds on 24 January and was buried at the foot of the Lesser Breach, the objective that his men had taken. As his funeral cortège passed a working party coming out of flooded trenches, the men, following the drills he had taught them, deliberately marched through the water rather than breaking formation to find a drier passage.

A memorial to him was placed in St Paul's Cathedral, London. Although the Light Division went on to other achievements under his successor, Alten [1], it is Craufurd who is remembered in the British Army as its most famous trainer of light infantry, second only to Sir John Moore himself. Unlike Moore, he was prone to violent outbursts of temper and was the subject of numerous complaints about excessive harshness to his men. His sharp tongue brought him enemies in the Army just as it had in Parliament, but Wellington always treated him with greater consideration than any of his other generals, possibly in recognition of his age and experience.

DALHOUSIE, EARL OF, *see* **RAMSAY,** GEORGE, 9th Earl of Dalhousie [34]

DICKSON, Major General Sir ALEXANDER, GCB, KCH (1777–1840) [13]

Alexander Dickson, the third son of Admiral Sir William Dickson, was born at Sydenham House, Roxburghshire, on 3 June 1777. He was appointed a gentleman cadet at the Royal Military Academy, Woolwich, on 5 April 1793, a few weeks after the outbreak of the French Revolutionary War, and was promoted in the Royal Artillery to second lieutenant on 6 November 1794 and lieutenant on 6 March 1795. Spain, originally an ally in the coalition against revolutionary France, declared war on the United Kingdom in 1795 and Dickson's first campaign was the capture of Minorca in November 1798. During 1800 he was in the British expedition to Malta (seized from the Knights of St John by Bonaparte on his way to Egypt) and served as an engineer in operations against Valletta, where the French garrison was starved into surrender in September 1800. He was promoted to captain-lieutenant on 14 October 1801. Dickson married Eulalia, the daughter of Don Stefano Briones of Minorca, on 19 September 1802, and later had with her a family of two sons (one of whom would join the Royal Artillery and be awarded the Victoria Cross) and two daughters. He was promoted to captain on 10 April 1805 and, early in 1807, became the senior artillery officer in the army on the **River Plate (June 1806–July 1807)**, where he served at the siege and capture of Montevideo.

In April 1809 Dickson joined Wellington in the Peninsula, where he served as brigade-major of artillery in the advance to Oporto, the **passage of the Douro (12 May 1809)** and the subsequent campaign that drove the French from Portugal. When the Portuguese Army was re-organised by Beresford [3], many British officers were appointed to it and Dickson joined the Portuguese artillery, with subsequent promotion to major and lieutenant colonel in that service. He commanded the Portuguese artillery at **Busaco (27 September 1810)**, Campo Mayor (March 1811), the siege and taking of Olivenza (11–15 April 1811) and **Albuera (16 May 1811)**. Dickson directed the artillery at the first siege of Badajoz (5–13 May 1811), the second siege of **Badajoz (19 May–10 June 1811)** and the siege of **Ciudad Rodrigo (7–19 January 1812)**. Noticed by Wellington, he was promoted to major in the Army on 6 February 1812 and directed the third siege of **Badajoz (17 March–6 April 1812)**. He became a lieutenant colonel in the Army on 27 April 1812, took part in the operations leading to the capture of Almaraz (19–20 May 1812) and commanded the artillery reserve at **Salamanca (22 July 1812)** and the first liberation of Madrid.

Dickson was with Wellington at the siege of **Burgos (16 September–21 October 1812)** and in the **retreat from Burgos (21 October–19 November 1812)**. In May 1813 Wellington, critical of more senior gunner officers, arranged for him to be appointed commander of all the artillery in his field army. Dickson, still a regimental captain and as such junior to several other Royal Artillery officers in the Peninsula, handled the situation with great tact and continued to wear his Portuguese uniform. He commanded the artillery at **Vitoria (21 June 1813)**, where he massed some seventy field guns with devastating effect; **San Sebastian (29 June–8 September 1813)**; the **passage of the Bidasoa (7 October 1813)**; the

passage of the Nivelle (10 November 1813); the **passage of the Nive (10–13 December 1813)** and **Toulouse (10 April 1814)**. At the end of the Peninsular War, he commanded over 8,000 men, 4,000 draught, riding and pack horses (the latter including those of the mountain train in the Pyrenees), and 200 guns.

After Napoleon's abdication, Dickson was sent with many of Wellington's veterans to the American War of 1812, where he commanded the British artillery at the battle of New Orleans (8 January 1815) and the siege and capture of Fort Bowyer, Mobile Bay (8–12 February 1815), both actions fought before news came that hostilities with the USA had already ended. At the beginning of the Hundred Days, when Napoleon escaped from Elba, Dickson was captain of a troop in the Royal Horse Artillery. On cordial terms with Wellington, he wrote asking for an appointment in the Allied army being formed in Belgium. Wellington replied that he would welcome his services but that the best position in his gift was command of the battering train. Dickson served at Quatre Bras (16 June 1815) and **Waterloo (18 June 1815)** as second captain of an artillery company. Afterwards, as Wellington had promised, he was given command of the siege artillery, with which during July and August 1815 he supported Prussian operations against the French fortresses of Maubeuge, Landrecies, Philipville, Marienburg and Rocroy. In 1817 he was awarded the KCH.

Sir Alexander Dickson was appointed inspector of artillery at the Royal Gun Factory, Woolwich, in April 1822 and became a major in the Royal Artillery on 26 June 1823. He was promoted to lieutenant colonel in the regiment on 2 April 1825, colonel in the Army on 27 May 1825, with the award of the KCB in the same year, and was appointed Deputy Adjutant-General, Royal Artillery, on 10 April 1827. Eulalia, Lady Dickson, died in July 1830 but in the following December Dickson married the widowed Harriet Maria Meadows, formerly of Conholt Park, near Andover, Hampshire. He became Master Gunner, St James's Park, in January 1833, colonel in the Royal Artillery on 1 July 1836 and major general on 10 January 1837. He was appointed Director-General, Royal Artillery, on 14 March 1838, with the award of the GCB, and held this post until his death, at his house in Berkeley Square, London, on 22 April 1840. Dickson was buried in the churchyard of the ancient parish church of St Nicholas, Plumstead, near Woolwich, Kent. An impressive memorial to him was erected at the Royal Artillery Repository, Woolwich, and moved first to the front of the main parade ground in 1911, and then to Larkhill, Wiltshire, when the Royal Artillery Depot was relocated there in 2007. A popular and much admired officer, Dickson was the foremost British artilleryman of his day and the notebooks that he kept up in meticulous detail from his days as a gentleman cadet until a few months before his death provide a valuable record of his many campaigns.

DUNLOP, Lieutenant General JAMES WALLACE of that ilk (1759–1832) [14]

James Dunlop was born in East Ayrshire on 19 June 1759, the fifth son of John Dunlop of that ilk, and his wife Frances Anna, daughter of Sir Thomas Wallace of Craigie, South Ayrshire. He entered the Army on 16 December 1777 as an ensign in the 82nd Foot, newly-raised by the Duke of Hamilton from his estates in the Scottish Lowlands for service in the American War of Independence. Dunlop was promoted to lieutenant on 11 January 1778 and went with his regiment to Nova Scotia. Early in 1779 they were sent to reinforce the British garrison of New York but their ship was wrecked on the coast of New Jersey. Most of his company perished and Dunlop, with the other survivors, was taken prisoner. After being exchanged, he joined the 80th Foot (a Lowland regiment raised at the same time as his own) in New York and later served with it on operations in Virginia. In April 1781 he was sent with despatches to Lord Cornwallis's army at Charleston, South Carolina, and then joined a force detached to hold Cape Fear, Wilmington, North Carolina. He commanded a troop of infantrymen, mounted as dragoons, until the garrison at Wilmington withdrew to Charleston following Cornwallis's surrender at Yorktown, Virginia (19 October 1781) and then rejoined the 82nd at Halifax, Nova Scotia, with promotion to captain on 6 May 1782. With hostilities ended, the 82nd sailed for home in 1783 but their troopship sprang a leak and was driven to Antigua, in the Leeward Islands. After finally reaching Scotland, the regiment was disbanded in 1784 in the usual post-war reductions and Dunlop went onto the half-pay list. His father transferred the estates at Dunlop to him, so that he became the 21st Dunlop of that ilk.

In 1787 the Board of Control for the Affairs of India, the ministry set up to oversee the East India Company, decided that four new regiments, the 74th, 75th, 76th and 77th Foot, should be raised for service in India. The Company's Court of Directors protested at being made to pay for British troops it did not want and refused them passage on its ships. It was eventually overruled, with the compromise that the regiments' officers would be drawn equally from those on the British half-pay and from the Company's own unemployed officers. On 25 December 1787 Dunlop was restored to full-pay as captain of a company of the 77th Foot, largely recruited from his family's

Ayrshire estates. He served in the Third Mysore War (1789–1792) against Tipu Sultan, ruler of Mysore, in southern India, and was appointed deputy paymaster-general of the British element of the East India Company's Bombay Army before becoming military secretary to the Government of Bombay. Dunlop was promoted to major in the Army on 1 March 1794, major in his regiment on 15 September 1795 and lieutenant colonel in the regiment on 12 December 1795. He returned to regimental duty late in 1796, when the news of his promotions reached India, and commanded the 77th in successful operations in Malabar before becoming senior officer at Cochin (Kochi), Kerala.

During the Fourth Mysore War (1798–99) Dunlop commanded an infantry brigade, composed of the 75th and 77th Foot and the 1st Bombay European Regiment, and served at Seedaseer (Siddeshwara) on 6 March 1799, where the advancing Bombay troops fought off a determined attack by Tipu Sultan's forces. In the subsequent storm of Seringapatam (Srirangapattana) on 4 May 1799, where Tipu fell fighting, he led the left column and was badly wounded by a sword cut. During the subsequent redistribution of Tipu's dominions, Dunlop took part in minor operations establishing British control over Canara (Kanara), on the west coast of the Carnatic (Karnataka), after which he sailed for home in 1800. On 20 July 1802, he married Julia Baillie, the daughter of a landholder in Monkton, South Ayrshire and later had with her a family of three sons and two daughters.

The treaty of Amiens (25 March 1802) brought a general peace but war with France was renewed in May 1803. Dunlop was promoted to colonel in the Army on 25 September 1803 and given command of a garrison battalion in the Army of Reserve, a force raised for full-time home defence in much the same way as the Militia. On 31 March 1804 he exchanged from the 77th to the 59th Foot, stationed on the coast of Kent against the threat of a French invasion. He was given command of a brigade in Cornwall on 11 February 1805 and subsequently moved to Colchester, Essex, to command a brigade of Highlanders.

Dunlop was promoted to major general on 25 July 1810 and joined Wellington's army in the Peninsula, where on 5 November 1810 he was given command of a newly-formed brigade in the 5th Division under Leith [26].When Leith went home in February 1811, command of the division passed briefly to Erskine [16], who was succeeded by Dunlop on 7 March 1811. Dunlop led the 5th Division at **Fuentes d'Onoro (3–5 May 1811)** and remained in the field until Wellington withdrew to Portugal during October 1811. He then returned home, considering himself too old and unfit for active service, though Wellington reported his departure as 'a real loss'.

Dunlop then took up a political career and in 1812 was elected Member of Parliament for the stewartry (county) of Kirkcudbright, in which he held part of his estates. He supported the Tory government led by Lord Liverpool and, when the twenty–year renewal of the East India Company's Charter was under consideration in 1813, argued strongly against new provisions that obliged the Company to admit missionaries into its territories. He was promoted to lieutenant general on 4 June 1814. In the general election of 1826, when the Tories increased their majority in the country as a whole for a third time, Dunlop himself was narrowly defeated. He became colonel of the 75th Foot (Stirlingshire Regiment) on 10 November 1827, and died at his family home, Newfield, Southwick, Kirkcudbrightshire, on 30 March 1832.

ELPHINSTONE, Major General Sir HOWARD, baronet (1773–1846) [15]

Howard Elphinstone was born on 4 March 1773, the sixth son of John Elphinstone, a Scot who, after serving as a captain in the Royal Navy, became a vice-admiral in the Russian Navy. He entered the Army as a gentleman cadet at the Royal Military Academy, Woolwich, from where, just after the beginning of the French Revolutionary War, he was promoted to second lieutenant in the Royal Artillery on 24 April 1793 and transferred to the Royal Engineers on 17 October 1793. Elphinstone served in the capture of the Dutch colony of the Cape of Good Hope in August–September 1795, after the Netherlands, renamed the Batavian Republic, had become a French satellite, and was promoted to lieutenant on 5 February 1796. He became a captain-lieutenant on 1 July 1800 and served in **Egypt (March–October 1801)** as commanding Royal Engineer of the force sent from Bombay under Sir David Baird. The treaty of Amiens (25 March 1802) brought a general peace and Elphinstone returned home, where on 14 February 1803 he married his cousin Frances, the daughter of John Warburton of Parliament Street, Westminster, and later had with her a family of one son and three daughters.

War with France was renewed in May 1803. Elphinstone's rank was re-designated 2nd captain on 19 July 1804, and he was promoted to captain on 1 March 1805. In August 1806, when Napoleon threatened to invade Portugal if it continued to trade with the United Kingdom, Elphinstone was one of a team of military experts sent with a new ambassador, the Earl of Rosslyn (supported by a British fleet in the Tagus) to advise on the defences of Lisbon. Napoleon's attack on Prussia in October 1806 convinced the

Portuguese that the threat of invasion was over so that, hoping to stay neutral, they asked the British advisors to leave. In March 1807 Elphinstone was sent to the **River Plate (June 1806–July 1807)** as the senior of the seven Royal Engineers there.

The French invaded Portugal with little opposition in November 1807. When, in the following summer, Portuguese and Spanish patriots rose against French occupation, the British Cabinet decided to support them, and Elphinstone returned to Portugal on 24 July 1808 as commanding Royal Engineer of the army landed under Sir Arthur Wellesley. At **Rolica (17 August 1808)** he was badly wounded in the mouth by a musket ball with three teeth and a fragment of jawbone driven down his throat and only dislodged later by a violent bout of motion sickness as he was shipped back to England. He was promoted to major in the Army on 1 January 1812 and returned to Portugal, where he served at Lisbon, with promotion to lieutenant colonel on 21 July 1813, until Lieutenant Colonel Sir Richard Fletcher [17], the commanding Royal Engineer in Wellington's field army, was killed in action during the siege of **San Sebastian (29 June–8 September 1813)**. Wellington wished Fletcher's successor to be Lieutenant Colonel John Fox Burgoyne, who had served in all his campaigns since April 1809, and who was fifteen months senior to Elphinstone as a lieutenant colonel in the Army. Elphinstone, however, was senior in the Royal Engineers to Burgoyne, who was still only a regimental captain. Elphinstone insisted on taking Fletcher's place and was therefore the commanding Royal Engineer at the **passage of the Nivelle (10 November 1813)**, the **passage of the Nive (10–13 December 1813)** and the passage of the Adour (23–25 February 1814), where he constructed a bridge of coastal vessels and fishing boats, as the water was too rough for ordinary pontoons. He then directed the siege of Bayonne (27 February–27 April 1814), which held out until the war ended with Napoleon's abdication.

In the post-war awards Elphinstone was given the CB and the Army Gold Medal with the clasp for Rolica. He became a baronet on 25 May 1816. Sir Howard Elphinstone became a colonel on 2 December 1824, a colonel commandant of Royal Engineers on 7 July 1834 and a major general on 10 January 1837. He died at his home, Ore Place, Hastings, Sussex, on 28 April 1846.

ERSKINE, Major General Sir WILLIAM, baronet (1769–1813) [16]

William Erskine was born in 1769, the eldest son of the then Lieutenant Colonel (later Lieutenant General) Sir William Erskine, knight (later baronet), of Torry, Flintshire, Clwyd. The young Erskine joined the Army as a second lieutenant in the 23rd Royal Welsh Fusiliers on 28 September 1785, was promoted to lieutenant in the 5th Dragoons on 14 November 1787 and transferred to the 13th Light Dragoons on 28 February 1788. He became a captain on 28 February 1791 and, after the outbreak of the French Revolutionary War in February 1793, commanded a troop of the 15th Light Dragoons in the **Low Countries (March 1793–April 1795)**. At Villars en Cauchies (24 April 1794) his regiment, together with the Leopold Hussars of the Austrian Army, found itself unsupported, but made a charge that routed their French opponents. Eight officers of the regiment were decorated by their Austrian allies for their gallantry in this episode, but Erskine was not among them, and it is probable that he was with his father, the British cavalry commander, whose aide-de-camp he then was. Erskine became a major on 1 March 1793 and lieutenant colonel on 14 December 1794 and led his regiment creditably in the British retreat into north-west Germany during the winter of 1794–95. He succeeded to his father's baronetcy during 1795 and served as Member of Parliament for Fife from 1796 to 1806. In 1796 he transferred to the half-pay list as lieutenant colonel in the 133rd Foot, raised in 1794 and disbanded in 1796. Erskine was promoted to colonel on the half-pay list on 1 January 1801 and became colonel on 9 July 1803 of the 14th Battalion of the Reserve Army (later the 14th Garrison Battalion), raised for full-time home defence in much the same way as the Militia. He became a brigadier in February 1804 and was promoted to major general on 25 April 1808.

Erskine was then given command of an infantry brigade in the Peninsular War, where he was with the rearguard during the first part of Sir John Moore's **retreat to Corunna (25 December 1808–11 January 1809)** before being evacuated through Vigo on 13 January 1809. He commanded an infantry brigade at **Walcheren (August–December 1809)** and the following year was sent to the Peninsula in response to Wellington's request for replacements of casualties among his general officers. Sir David Dundas (C-in-C of the British Army during the temporary retirement of the Duke of York) had served with Erskine in the **Low Countries (March 1793–April 1795)** and thought highly of him, though Colonel Henry Torrens, Dundas's Military Secretary, warned Wellington that Erskine 'is sometimes a little mad but in his lucid intervals he is an uncommonly clever fellow; and I trust he may have no fit during the campaign, though he looked a little wild before he embarked'.

On 6 October, commanding a newly-arrived infantry brigade, Erskine joined the 1st Division under Spencer [38]. In February 1811, with the

French advance on Lisbon halted by the Lines of Torres Vedras, he commanded the 5th Division while Leith [26] was on leave in England. A month later, Erskine was given command of both the Cavalry Division and the Light Division, in the absence on leave of Cotton [11] and Craufurd [12] respectively, and led these as Wellington's advance-guard when the French withdrew northwards from Santarem. He encountered the French rearguard under Marshal Ney at Pombal (11 March 1811) and Rodinha (12 March 1811), where he launched a series of rash attacks, incurring needless casualties and becoming increasingly unpopular. At Sabugal (1 April 1811) he was criticised for advancing before the morning mist had cleared. Erskine's eyesight as well as his judgement was questioned by Captain Harry Smith, an officer in the Light Division, who described him as 'a short-sighted ass'. At **Fuentes d'Onoro (3–5 May 1811)** Craufurd's return to resume command of the Light Division on 4 May was greeted by his men with open rejoicing.

A week later Erskine was tasked with deploying the 5th and 6th Divisions to prevent the escape of the French garrison of Almeida. It was said that he wrote out his orders, put them in his pocket with his snuff box, but forgot to send them, so that they did not reach their intended recipients in time. The failure to intercept the retreating French was described by Wellington as the most disgraceful military event of the campaign thus far. The commanding officer of the 4th Foot, which arrived at the unguarded bridge of Barba del Puerco after the French had passed, was ordered to be court-martialled, but shot himself rather than face this reproach and many felt he had been sacrificed to save Erskine. Wellington described the affair as yet another example of his officers, despite their personal gallantry, failing every time he was not there to supervise an operation in person.

Erskine was given command of the 2nd Cavalry Division (an administrative rather than a combat formation) when this was formed in June 1811 and he was promoted to local lieutenant general (Spain and Portugal) on 6 September 1811. Commanding all the cavalry south of the Tagus, he then took part in the successful raid by Hill [21] on Arroyo Molinos (28–29 October 1811) and the operations leading to Hill's capture of Almaraz (19–20 May 1812). In Wellington's retreat to Portugal during November 1812, he ordered a brigade of the hard-pressed Light Division to hold the crossing of the Huebra, until all his cavalry had passed. Alten [1], the divisional commander, protested and Wellington, appearing on the scene, retrieved the situation by ordering the infantry to retreat across the river at the double.

By early 1813 Wellington had formed the view that Erskine, along with his two brigadiers, Major Generals John Slade [37] and Robert Long, were all useless and should be sent home but, in Erskine's case, his political connections made this impossible. Erskine's eyesight and mental health remained subjects for general comment, with Long describing him as 'as blind as a beetle' and there was concern that, if Cotton became a casualty, command of the cavalry would devolve on either Erskine or Slade. Erskine, a heavy drinker and suffering from fever, was invalided to Lisbon, where on 14 May 1813, shortly after a perfectly rational conversation with his physician, he suddenly rose from his sickbed and jumped out of a window. Still conscious when picked up, he was unable to explain his action and admitted its stupidity. He died the following day and, as he was unmarried, his baronetcy was inherited in turn by his two younger brothers.

FLETCHER, Lieutenant Colonel Sir RICHARD, baronet (1768–1813) **[17]**

Richard Fletcher, the son of a clergyman, was born in 1768 and entered the Royal Military Academy, Woolwich, as a gentleman cadet on 7 October 1782. He was promoted to second lieutenant in the Royal Artillery on 9 July 1788, transferred to the Royal Engineers on 29 June 1790 and became a lieutenant on 16 January 1793, shortly before the outbreak of the French Revolutionary War. He took part in the subsequent campaign against the French colonies in the West Indies and was at the capture of Martinique (February–March 1794), Guadeloupe, and **St Lucia (April 1794)** where he was wounded by a musket ball. After serving as chief engineer in the neighbouring British island of Dominica, Fletcher returned to England late in 1796, where he was appointed adjutant of the Portsmouth companies of the Royal Military Artificers, the corps that provided skilled military labour for the Royal Engineers. At Plymouth, on 27 November 1796 he married Elizabeth Mudge, the daughter of a physician, and later had with her a family of two sons and three daughters. He was promoted to captain-lieutenant on 18 August 1797.

Fletcher remained at Portsmouth until December 1798, when he was sent as a military advisor to the Ottoman government, which had declared war on France in September 1798, following Bonaparte's invasion of Egypt and Nelson's victory at the Battle of the Nile (1–2 August 1798). Travelling via Hanover, he was shipwrecked off the mouth of the Elbe and had to cross 2 miles of ice before reaching land. From there he proceeded through Austria to the Ottoman provinces in the Balkans and arrived at Constantinople (Istanbul) on 29 March 1799. In June 1799 he served with the Ottoman forces whose advance into Syria obliged Bonaparte to abandon the siege of Acre

(Akka) and retreat through Palestine back towards Egypt. Fletcher then returned to Constantinople (Istanbul), where he advised on modernising the fortifications of the Turkish Straits. He subsequently served with the Ottoman garrison in Cyprus and returned to Syria in June 1800 to supervise the reconstruction of the fortifications of Jaffa and El Arish.

At the end of December 1800 Fletcher joined a British expedition under Sir Ralph Abercromby at Marmaris Bay, as it practised beach landings for the campaign in **Egypt (March–October 1801)**. He was then sent to the coast of Alexandria in the frigate *Peterel* to select a suitable area for disembarkation but, after going ashore for night reconnaissance, was intercepted by a French patrol vessel as he returned to his ship. He spent the rest of the campaign as a prisoner of war inside Alexandria until the French surrendered on 2 September 1801. Fletcher was promoted to captain on 18 April 1801, while in captivity, and was repatriated to England when hostilities were ended by a general armistice in October 1801, leading to the treaty of Amiens (25 March 1802). Decorated by the Ottomans, Fletcher returned to Portsmouth where he was employed on improving the defences of Gosport following the renewal of hostilities with France in May 1803. He became a major in the Army on 2 April 1807 and then took part in the British attack on **Copenhagen (8 August–7 September 1807)**.

At the opening of the Peninsular War, Fletcher joined the army in Portugal late in August 1808 and moved with it to Lisbon when the city was evacuated by the French following the Convention of Cintra (Sintra). From there, as the commanding Royal Engineer, he accompanied Sir Arthur Wellesley's army into the field in 1809, with promotion to lieutenant colonel in the Army on 2 March 1809 and in the Royal Engineers on 24 June 1809, and was present at **Talavera (27–28 July 1809)**, where he was mentioned in despatches.

When Wellington prepared to retreat into Portugal, Fletcher became responsible for one of the most famous feats of military engineering in the history of the British Army, the construction of the Lines of Torres Vedras for the defence of Lisbon. Built across a long narrow peninsula between the Tagus and the Atlantic, these consisted of three lines, with the outermost sited 6 miles in advance of the principal one, and an inner one 20 miles behind it, intended to reassure the army that, if the need arose, there would always be a way back to the ships waiting for them. Fletcher received his orders on 20 October 1809 and began work, using Portuguese civil and military labour, on over 50 miles of defences. Rocky hillsides, difficult enough in their natural state, were turned into impassable precipices. Every defile was blocked by obstacles and field fortifications. Orchards and woods were cut down and cleared of anything that might give cover. Streams were dammed to form swamps. Buildings were pulled down or converted into blockhouses. Earthworks, ramparts and stockades guarded every approach, while batteries crowned every height and a chain of visual telegraph stations provided rapid communication along the line. Roads were built across the grain of the country, allowing the field army to be kept concentrated and moved rapidly to any threatened point, while the fixed defences were manned only by artillerymen and militia. In July 1810, with the works nearing completion, Fletcher rejoined Wellington in the field and was mentioned in despatches at **Busaco (27 September 1810)**.

Wellington retired behind the Lines of Torres Vedras early in October. Despite their extensive nature, and the whole year during which they had been under construction, their existence took Marshal Massena and his Army of Portugal completely by surprise. When Portuguese renegades, who had assured him that the road to Lisbon was easy, declared that Fletcher had secretly made it impassable, he turned on them with an oath and 'he didn't build those mountains'. After a probing attack on 18 October 1810 Massena retired to Santarem, from where in March 1811, with his troops having exhausted all available supplies, he began to retreat northwards. In the following campaign Fletcher served at Sabugal (2 April 1811) and **Fuentes d'Onoro (3–5 May 1811)** and at the occupation of the Portuguese border fortress of Almeida, evacuated by the French on 10 May 1811. He was chief engineer at the second siege of **Badajoz (19 May –10 June 1811)** where he was again mentioned in despatches, the siege of **Ciudad Rodrigo (7–19 January 1812)** and the third siege of **Badajoz (17 March–6 April 1812)**, where he was hit in the groin by a musket ball during an enemy sortie on 19 March. A silver dollar in his pocket took most of the impact, but he was effectively immobilised so that Wellington, desperately short of siege engineers, came to his tent every morning for specialist advice. Fletcher then returned home on sick leave, and was awarded a pension of £1 *per diem*. He was also awarded the Portuguese Order of the Tower and Sword and was created a baronet in December 1812.

Sir Richard Fletcher rejoined Wellington in 1813 and was present at **Vitoria (21 June 1813)** where he was once more mentioned in despatches. In the Allied advance towards the Pyrenees, Fletcher was responsible for organising the blockade of Pamplona, which was finally starved into surrender on 31 October 1813. His final action was the siege of **San Sebastian (29 June–8 September 1813)**, where he was killed by a musket ball when the city was stormed on 31 August. He was buried outside the walls and a monument to him, funded by the Royal Engineers, was put up in Westminster Abbey.

GORDON, General the Right Honourable Sir JAMES WILLOUGHBY, baronet, GCB, GCH (1772–1851) **[18]**

James Gordon was born on 21 October 1772, the son of Captain Francis Grant, a sea officer who changed his name to Gordon on coming into an inheritance, and his wife Mary, sister of Sir Willoughby Aston, baronet. He entered the Army on 17 October 1783, just before his eleventh birthday, as an ensign in the 66th Foot, stationed in Ireland. Between 1786 and 1793 he served with his regiment in the West Indies, with promotion to lieutenant on 5 March 1789. The 66th moved to Gibraltar in 1793, from where, following the outbreak of the French Revolutionary War in February 1793, Gordon served as a volunteer at **Toulon (August–December 1793)**. He was promoted to captain on 2 September 1795 and, when the 66th sailed to French San Domingo (Haiti) later that year, became assistant adjutant-general in Ireland. At the end of December 1796 he was with the troops called out from Cork to counter the threat of a landing in Bantry Bay by a French invasion force under General Lazare Hoche, only to see this driven away by a violent storm. Gordon was promoted to major in his regiment on 9 November 1797 and in 1798 became military secretary, British North America, based at Halifax, Nova Scotia. He returned home on promotion to lieutenant colonel in the 85th Light Infantry on 21 May 1801.

Following the brief 'War of the Oranges' when Spain, under French influence, obliged Portugal to close its ports to British trade, a British expedition occupied the Portuguese island of Madeira in July 1801. Gordon commanded the 1st Battalion, 85th Light Infantry, in Madeira before going back to the West Indies later in the year as deputy adjutant-general. He remained there during the brief period of peace with France from March 1802 until May 1803, when he returned to England to become, initially, assistant quartermaster-general, Southern District, based at Chatham, and then deputy barrackmaster-general. He transferred to the 92nd Foot as lieutenant colonel on 4 August 1804 and became military secretary to the Duke of York, C-in-C of the British Army. On 15 October 1805, Gordon married Julia Lavinia Bennet, the daughter of a landholder in Beckenham, Kent, and later had with her a son and a daughter. He became lieutenant colonel commandant of the Royal African Corps (raised mostly from British military criminals pardoned in return for serving in Africa) on 13 June 1808.

In January 1809, Colonel Gwyllym Wardle, an opposition MP, alleged in the House of Commons that the Duke of York's mistress, Mary Anne Clarke, had taken bribes in return for recommending promotions. Gordon who, as military secretary, dealt with officers' appointments, was among those called to give evidence to the subsequent parliamentary enquiry (where most of those attending did so mainly to admire Mrs Clarke, whose spirited performance brought her some sympathy at ministerial expense). Responding to allegations about the improper promotion of a junior officer in the Royal African Corps, Gordon outlined his own extensive record of service at home and overseas, including command appointments for which he had received the thanks of his superiors and a prize sword, and staff appointments in every level and branch open to him. He robustly defended his royal chief and pointed out all the regulations the latter had introduced to prevent the very abuses of which he stood accused. Nevertheless, only the Government's majority saved York from a vote of censure and he was obliged to resign in February 1809. Gordon left office as military secretary in October 1809 and published his *Military Transactions of the British Empire 1803–07* in the same year. He then became Commissary-in-Chief to the Forces, with promotion on 25 July 1810 to colonel in the Army and colonel commandant of the Royal African Corps.

In May 1812, when Murray [28], Wellington's quartermaster-general, was given an appointment in Ireland, Gordon was sent to the Peninsula in his place. Colonel Henry Torrens, who had been Gordon's assistant on the C-in-C's staff and succeeded him as military secretary in October 1809, assured Wellington that Gordon was one of the ablest staff officers available. Wellington, however, was displeased at losing Murray, whom he had come to trust, and suspicious of Gordon's friendships with the Prince of Wales and members of the Whig opposition party in Parliament. Gordon had openly promised to write to the Whig leader, Earl Grey, about the campaign and in November 1812 opposition newspapers published reports containing information that could only have come from Wellington's confidential despatches. Neither Wellington nor Earl Bathurst, the newly-appointed Secretary of State for War and the Colonies, could find the source of the leak, but both believed that it could only have been Gordon, and Bathurst had forecast that Gordon's appointment would mean trouble. Gordon himself wished to be made chief of staff and said that unless formally appointed to this position he would return home. The proposal was given some consideration by the Duke of York (who had been reinstated as Commander-in-Chief of the Army in May 1811) but was ultimately rejected.

Meanwhile, in the Peninsula, there were many allegations about Gordon's incompetence, especially during the **retreat from Burgos (21 October–19 November 1812)**. When Wellington sought Gordon's recall, the Duke of York asked for firm evidence to justify it. Wellington was convinced that Murray had been moved to make room for Gordon, one of the Prince of

Wales's favourites, but could scarcely say as much to York (whom he suspected of having made these arrangements to oblige his royal brother). Instead, he suggested that Gordon be found a new appointment on York's own staff. In reply, Torrens told him that, if given a definite reason to recall Gordon, the Duke of York would act on it and take full responsibility for the decision, but there could be no question of appointing officers to senior posts only to spare their feelings. At the end of 1812 Gordon went back to the United Kingdom on medical grounds and Wellington informed Torrens that he was not sorry to lose him. Gordon's doctors solved the problem by declaring that he needed major surgery, which would leave him unfit for duty for many months. 'He will not go out again' wrote Torrens, adding that Gordon himself seemed genuinely concerned that Wellington would be disappointed at this decision.

In 1813, Gordon became Quartermaster-General to the Forces, a post that he retained until his death nearly forty years later, including the periods when Wellington was C-in-C of the British Army. He was promoted to major general on 4 June 1813 and was appointed colonel of his old regiment, the 85th Light Infantry, on 27 November 1815. Sir James Gordon was created a baronet on 5 December 1818, and became colonel of the 23rd Royal Welsh Fusiliers on 23 April 1823. He was promoted to lieutenant general on 27 May 1825, with the award of the GCH. In 1830 he was sworn in as a member of the Privy Council, followed by the award of the GCB on 13 September 1831 and promotion to general on 23 November 1841. He died at his home near the Royal Hospital, Chelsea, on 4 January 1851.

GRAHAM, General Sir THOMAS, Baron Lynedoch, GCB, GCMG (1748–1843) **[19]**

Thomas Graham was born on 19 October 1748 at Blairgowrie, Perthshire, the third son and only surviving child of Thomas Graeme of Blairgowrie and his wife Lady Christian Hope, a daughter of the 1st Earl of Hopetoun. He was thus a distant relative of Hope **[23]**, the future 4th Earl. Educated privately and at Christ Church, Oxford, he inherited his father's estate in 1767 and made the grand tour of Europe between 1768 and 1771. In 1772 he contested the parliamentary constituency of Perthshire, but was defeated by a brother of the Duke of Atholl, who controlled the local electors. For the next eighteen years he lived the life of a wealthy country gentleman, spending much of his time in Edinburgh or London and taking a keen interest in cricket, hunting and other outdoor sports as well as in the improvement of his estate and the welfare of his tenants. A fit and active man, he dealt with a gang of footpads who held up his coach in Park Lane by placing his lady passengers in a safe corner, drawing his dress sword, seizing one robber and putting the other two to flight. On 26 December 1774 he married the Honourable Mary Cathcart, second daughter of the 9th Lord Cathcart, in a combined wedding at which her eldest sister, the Honourable Jane Cathcart, married John Murray, the 4th Duke of Atholl. Their father noted that Jane married to please herself and Mary married for love. The Honourable Mary Graham, a great beauty, was twice painted by Gainsborough, and the couple, though childless, were devoted to each other, Graham on one occasion undertaking a 90-mile ride on relays of horses to fetch the jewellery she had left at home and wished to wear at an Edinburgh ball. Always of delicate health, she contracted tuberculosis, and died at sea off Hyeres, en route to the milder climate of Italy, on 26 June 1792.

Graham took her body ashore and set out for home overland. At Toulouse, a group of drunken Jacobins broke open the casket to search for smuggled arms, an insult to his dead wife that Graham, previously sympathetic to the principles of the Revolution, never forgave. Unable to settle at home, he sought distraction by again travelling abroad and, following the outbreak of the French Revolutionary War in February 1793, joined the multi-national force at **Toulon (August–December 1793)** as a volunteer interpreter. He took part in the defence of the city as aide-de-camp to the Earl of Mulgrave, one of the commanders of the British contingent, and was mentioned in general orders on 6 October 1793 for leading a successful charge in which he was wounded.

After returning home, Graham was elected MP for Perthshire in 1794 but, having at the age of 43 discovered an aptitude for soldiering, raised a regiment, the Perthshire Volunteers (later the 90th Foot), at his own expense and appointed Captain Rowland Hill [21] with whom he had served at Toulon, as one of its majors. Graham's first commission was dated 10 February 1794, as lieutenant colonel commandant of the 90th. He subsequently raised a second battalion and commanded the 1st Battalion, 90th Foot, in southern England, from where in 1795 he took part in an unsuccessful expedition to support the French Royalists in the Ile de Yeu, Quiberon.

He decided against going to Gibraltar with his regiment and instead obtained an appointment in the British military mission with the Austrian army in northern Italy, a post for which his extensive continental travels and grasp of foreign languages made him well qualified. Following Bonaparte's victories in Italy in May 1796, Graham was besieged inside the fortress of

Mantua. Between 24 December 1796 and 4 January 1797 he made his way through enemy lines to the nearest Austrian troops, 50 miles away at Bassano, to stress the urgent need for yet another attempt at relief. The attempt was stopped at Rivoli (14–15 January 1797), the last and greatest of Bonaparte's victories in his Lombardy campaign and Mantua surrendered a fortnight later. During this period Graham's applications for a commission as colonel of his regiment were repeatedly rejected by the C-in-C, the Duke of York, who was opposed to regimental colonels being appointed without first serving as junior officers, but he was given promotion to colonel in the Army on 26 January 1797.

After returning to the 90th, Graham served as second-in-command to Lieutenant General Sir Charles Stuart in the British capture of Minorca (7–15 November 1798). From there he accompanied Stuart to Sicily and commanded the British troops at Messina until they were sent to join the blockade of the French garrison left in Malta by Bonaparte on his way to Egypt. Graham, at the head of a brigade formed by both battalions of the 90th, commanded at the siege of Valletta until the French were starved into surrender on 5 September 1800. Rather than return to regimental duty, he went home early in 1801, thereby missing the chance of leading the 90th in **Egypt (March–October 1801)** and only reaching Egypt when the campaign was almost over.

Graham journeyed home via Constantinople (Istanbul), Vienna and, following the restoration of peace by the treaty of Amiens (25 March 1802), Paris. Resisting pressure from the Duke of York for his resignation, Graham took up his parliamentary duties and, after the war with France was renewed in May 1803, the 90th served in Ireland and the West Indies without him. In the Commons, he opposed the Tory administrations led by Addington and Pitt the Younger and supported the Whig 'Ministry of all the Talents', formed in 1806, until it fell in March 1807 over the question of catholic emancipation, a cause that Graham supported. He did not stand in the general election that followed, as he was again out of favour with the Duke of Atholl, and instead resumed military duty as an aide-de-camp to Sir John Moore in the **Baltic (May–June 1808)**.

Graham was Moore's senior aide-de-camp throughout the Peninsular campaign that began later in 1808 and acted as Moore's link to the Spanish Junta in Madrid when the British advanced to support the patriot forces there. When Castilian generals at Moore's headquarters insisted that, despite previous defeats, their armies would prevent Napoleon from reaching Madrid, it was Graham who arrived on 2 December 1808 to report that the French were already there. Undertaking all the hard riding required of an aide-de-camp in the field, Graham remained with Moore during the subsequent **retreat to Corunna (25 December 1808–11 January 1809)**. In the final battle of **Corunna (16 January 1809)**, he was beside Moore when the latter was mortally wounded. In March 1809, Graham was granted his regimental colonelcy in accordance with one of Moore's dying requests, relayed to the Duke of York by Graham's cousin Hope, who assumed command when Moore fell (though it is not clear that Moore actually had remembered Graham in this way). In recognition of his services, his commission as colonel was backdated to the establishment of his regiment in 1794 and he therefore immediately became major general by seniority, with effect from 25 September 1803.

Graham commanded first a brigade and then a division at **Walcheren (August–December 1809)**, from where he was invalided home after contracting malaria. On 19 February 1810, in recognition of his diplomatic as well as his military skills, he was given command of the Anglo-Portuguese element in the garrison of Cadiz, the seat of the Spanish provisional government, then under siege by the French. He was promoted to local lieutenant general (Spain and Portugal) on 21 February 1810, later made substantive with seniority from 25 July 1810. When the French force besieging Cadiz was weakened by the demands of other fronts, Graham proposed using Allied naval supremacy to make a landing behind the French lines in conjunction with a sortie from the city. Repeated changes of plan by the local Spanish commander, General La Pena, left Graham to fight superior numbers of the French unaided at Barossa (5 March 1811), where he was wounded. He achieved a victory but afterwards, angry and exasperated at being abandoned by his Spanish allies, withdrew back into Cadiz. To soothe his feelings, he was offered the rank of a grandee of Spain, an honour that he declined. La Pena (called 'Donna Manuela' by his own men) was court-martialled for his conduct and, although acquitted, was removed from command.

Graham had kindlier feelings for a young Andalusian dog, found on the field of Barossa beside the body of the French General Rousseau, who had fallen in the battle. The dog would at first not leave its dead master, but Graham, hearing of the case, had it brought in and made a companion of it. He later sent it to Balgowen, in the care of an officer going home on leave, with instructions that it was to be treated as a house dog and not kept in kennels. Despite his hatred of the French, Graham behaved chivalrously to the officers taken prisoner, sending food from his own table to the dangerously wounded General Ruffin and placing his purse at the disposal of Colonel Vigo-Rousillon, who unaware of his identity, had nearly killed him in the battle. He promised to have the colonel exchanged as soon as possible or, failing that, to entertain him at Balgowen. Graham's victory made him the hero of the hour at home, but he had come to regard Cadiz as little better than 'a loathsome prison' and was glad to leave it in June 1811 and join Wellington in Portugal.

Wellington and Graham had not previously served together and Graham had originally shared the Whig view that Wellington owed his command to Tory influence. Wellington, however, had especially asked for him as a replacement for his second-in-command, the ailing Sherbrooke [36], at the end of 1809, an appointment only delayed by the needs of the Cadiz command. The two men came to admire and respect each other and rode to hounds together during the Portuguese winter. Graham succeeded Spencer [38] as commander of the 1st Division on 9 August 1811 and Wellington, though short of competent general officers, asked that none senior to Graham should thereafter be sent to him. Graham renewed his friendship with Hill, who shared his interest in field sports and sent Graham setters and pointers from his own Shropshire estates. After leading the 1st Division at **Ciudad Rodrigo (7–19 January 1812)**, Graham was awarded the KB in March 1812. Sir Thomas Graham's eyesight had been damaged by a combination of using his field telescope by day in the bright Spanish sunshine and dealing with his correspondence at night by candlelight. On 3 June 1812, Dr McGrigor [27], Wellington's senior medical officer, ordered him home where Graham stood once more for the Perthshire constituency, only to be defeated by seven votes.

At the end of 1812, with his eyes improved, Graham was urged both by Wellington and the Duke of York to return to the Peninsula. He did so in April 1813 and commanded the northern part of Wellington's army in the advance through Spain to **Vitoria (21 June 1813)**, where he led the attack on the French right flank. While Wellington took the main army towards the Pyrenees, Graham marched to intercept a French force approaching from Bilbao. At Tolosa (25 June 1813) he was hit on the hip by a bullet, but escaped with severe bruising.

On 13 July 1813 Graham was given charge of the siege of **San Sebastian (29 June–8 September 1813)**, which held out for fifty-five days. After the city was stormed on 31 August 1813 the French garrison retreated into a castle outside the walls and asked for terms. Graham invited the French commandant to write them himself, in recognition of the valiant defence, and handed him his own pen for the purpose. His opponent, with equal chivalry, asked only that his officers should retain their swords and his men march out with the honours of war. Graham commanded Wellington's left flank at the **passage of the Bidasoa (7 October 1813)** and then, having reached France and considering himself too old and unfit for further active service, returned home, awarded the Portuguese Order of the Tower and Sword and the Spanish Order of St Ferdinand.

Six weeks later, despite his protests, he was selected to lead a British army to the Netherlands, where Dutch patriots had risen against the Napoleonic regime and declared the restoration of the House of Orange. In co-operation with Prussian and Russian forces, he reached the outskirts of Antwerp, but his allies then switched their troops to support the armies invading north-eastern France from Germany. The British fought their way into the fortress of Bergen-op-Zoom (8 March 1814), only to be driven out with heavy losses. Graham's own conduct was praised by the Prince Regent, and even Napoleon described it as an affair that did honour to him and his men. Following Napoleon's abdication on 11 April 1814, Graham, greatly reinforced and appointed C-in-C of all the Allied forces in Belgium, was granted a peerage as Baron Lynedoch. At Brussels he became a social lion and entertained British travellers to the Continent until, on 16 August 1814, he handed over command to the young Prince of Orange and returned to Scotland for a hero's welcome. His KB was converted to GCB on the reconstitution of the Order of the Bath in January 1815.

Lord Lynedoch took no part in the Hundred Days' campaign, when Napoleon returned from Elba, but continued active in military and social affairs. After the war he supported the formation of the United Service Club in London, despite objections that military clubs were a threat to the constitution, and in 1817 became its first chairman. In May 1821, through the patronage of his old comrade Hill (by this time commanding the British Army), he was appointed governor of Dumbarton Castle. Lynedoch was promoted to general on 19 July 1821. On 2 May 1822 he acted as second to his friend the 8th Duke of Bedford in a duel with the newly-created Duke of Buckingham. Shots were fired but, through an arrangement between the seconds, neither party was injured and the affair ended with a handshake. Graham was appointed successively colonel of the 58th Foot in 1823, the 14th Foot in 1826, and the 1st Foot (the Royal Scots) in 1834. He travelled extensively on the Continent, hunted regularly in Leicestershire, and spoke in the Lords in support of catholic emancipation and parliamentary reform. In 1833, after the British and French had intervened in Portugal in the civil war between Donna Maria Gloria and her uncle, the absolutist Dom Miguel, he was offered command of her Army, but declined.

Lynedoch was awarded the GCMG in May 1837, in Queen Victoria's coronation honours. In his old age, fearing that blindness would prevent him from continuing to hunt, he underwent surgery for cataracts. He died at his

London house in Stratton Street, Piccadilly, on 18 December 1843 and was buried beside his mother and his wife in a mausoleum of his own design at Methven, Perthshire.

HAY, Major General ANDREW (1762–1814) [20]

Andrew Hay of Mountblairy, the son of a Banffshire laird, entered the Army during the American War of Independence as an ensign in the 1st Foot on 6 December 1779. He was promoted to lieutenant in that regiment on 21 July 1781 and became a captain in the 88th Foot on 24 January 1783. When the 88th was disbanded in the usual post-war reductions, Hay returned to the 1st Foot as a captain, with seniority in the regiment from 17 April 1784. At Banff parish church on 2 April 1784, he married Elizabeth Robinson, the 22-year-old daughter of a deceased tweed manufacturer and later had with her a family of four daughters and two sons. In 1787 Hay went onto the half-pay list as a captain in the disbanded 72nd Foot. After the outbreak of the French Revolutionary War in February 1793, he continued to appear in the Army List as a half-pay captain in the disbanded 72nd with promotion to major in the Army on 1 September 1794, until restored to the full-pay list as a major in the 93rd Foot, a newly-raised Scottish regiment, on 9 December 1795. He served with this in the West Indies until 1797 when it was disbanded. On 29 December 1798 Hay was appointed colonel of the Banffshire Fencibles, a full-time home defence regiment raised mostly in his family's estates. In 1801 he sold his Banffshire home and bought Packham House, Fordingbridge, Hampshire, while commanding his regiment in the Channel Islands. In 1802, after the restoration of peace by the treaty of Amiens (25 March 1802), the Fencibles were disbanded.

On the renewal of hostilities with France in May 1803, Hay was given command of another Scottish-recruited unit, the 16th Battalion of the Army of Reserve, a home service force raised in much the same way as the Militia, in July 1803. Its units were encouraged to transfer to the Regular Army as second battalions of Line regiments and Hay joined the 2nd Battalion, 72nd Foot (Highlanders), as a lieutenant colonel in that regiment on 1 December 1804. On 19 March 1807 he became the commanding officer of the 3rd Battalion, 1st Foot, in Ireland and was promoted to colonel in the Army on 25 April 1808.

After the British Cabinet decided to support the patriots of Spain and Portugal in their rising against French occupation, Hay's battalion reached Corunna on 14 October 1808 with the troops, under Sir David Baird, sent to reinforce Sir John Moore's army in the Peninsula. Moore concentrated his forces on 20 December 1808 and moved towards Madrid, only to learn that a large French force, led by Napoleon himself, was marching against him. Hay served in the subsequent **retreat to Corunna (25 December 1808– 11 January 1809)** and battle of **Corunna (16 January 1809)** and then returned to the United Kingdom with the survivors of Moore's command. After commanding a brigade at **Walcheren (August–December 1809)**, Hay returned to the Peninsula in July 1810 with the 3rd Battalion, 1st Foot, and was given command of the battalion on 4 August 1810, followed by that of a brigade in the 5th Division on 30 September 1810. He served at **Busaco (27 September 1810)** and was promoted to major general on 4 June 1811. Hay was present at **Salamanca (22 July 1812)**, commanded the 5th Division from January to April 1813, was with his brigade at **Vitoria (21 June 1813)** where his son, Captain George Hay of the 1st Foot (the Royal Scots) was mortally wounded serving as his aide-de-camp, and at **San Sebastian (29 June–8 September 1813)**. With the two senior officers of the 5th Division (Leith [26] and Oswald [29]) both having become casualties during the storming of San Sebastian, command reverted to Hay, who led the division at the **passage of the Bidasoa (7 October 1813)**, and the **passage of the Nive (10–13 December 1813)**.

After being superseded by Colville [10] at the end of 1813, Hay returned to his brigade and served with it at the passage of the Adour (23–25 February 1814) and the siege of Bayonne (27 February–27 April 1814). On 13 April 1814 news came of Napoleon's abdication and Hay, as general officer of the day, made his round of the trenches, telling the soldiers that the war was over and they would soon be home with their wives and sweethearts. In the early hours of 14 April 1814, the French governor of Bayonne made a useless and wanton sortie, well meriting Wellington's description of him as a 'blackguard'. Hay was killed encouraging his men to fight to the last as they defended the church of St Etienne, in the last engagement of the Peninsular War. The officers of the 3rd Battalion, 1st Foot, placed a memorial to him at St Etienne, and a grander one, funded by Parliament, was installed in St Paul's Cathedral. His widow erected a monument to him in the parish church of St Mary the Virgin, Fordingbridge.

HILL, General Sir ROWLAND, 1st Viscount Hill, GCB, GCH (1772–1842) **[21]**

Rowland 'Daddy' Hill was born at Prees Hall, Hawkestone, near Shrewsbury, Shropshire, on 11 August 1772. He was the second son and the fourth of sixteen children of a well-connected country gentleman, John Hill, later third baronet, six of whose sons would bear arms during the Napoleonic Wars. After attending school at Chester, Rowland Hill was intended for a career in the law, but insisted on following his eldest brother into the Army and became an ensign in the 38th Foot on 31 July 1790. He studied at a military academy in Strasbourg and was promoted to lieutenant on 24 January 1791 before returning home to regimental duty after transferring to the 53rd Foot (Shropshire Regiment) in January 1792. With the expansion of the Army following the outbreak of the French Revolutionary War in February 1793, individuals were granted commissions according to the number of recruits they raised, allowing Hill to become captain of an independent company of Foot on 23 March 1793. In July 1793 he was appointed assistant secretary to the diplomat Francis Drake, newly-appointed British envoy to the Republic of Genoa, where revolutionary ideas were spreading from France into Italy. Hill rejoined the 53rd in the multi-national force at **Toulon (August–December 1793)** where he served as aide-de-camp to three successive British commanders and was slightly wounded. Sent home with the despatches as a mark of distinction, he joined Cuyler's Shropshire Volunteers, a newly-raised corps that soon became the 86th Foot and was then invited by Graham **[19]**, with whom he had become friends during the defence of Toulon, to help raise the 90th Foot (Perthshire Volunteers), with promotion to major. Hill was at first denied leave to recruit the number of men required for his majority, but this was eventually granted and he became a major in the 90th on 10 February 1794 and lieutenant colonel, commanding the 1st Battalion, 90th Foot, on 13 May 1794.

Hill was promoted to colonel in the Army on 1 January 1800. From garrison duty at Gibraltar he again joined a diplomatic mission under Drake, but left in order to command the 90th in **Egypt (March–October 1801)**. On 13 March, during Sir Ralph Abercromby's advance from Aboukir (Abu Qir) to Alexandria, he was wounded in the head but his life was saved by the light infantry pattern helmet worn, contrary to the dress regulations, by the 90th, which was not a Light Infantry corps, though it trained as such. With the end of hostilities, he moved to Malta where, despite the terms of the peace treaty of Amiens (25 March 1802), the British remained pending an international settlement of the island's future. When, largely over this question, the war was renewed in May 1803, Hill was on leave with his family at Hawkestone. He was ordered to Belfast, where he was employed on preparations against a possible French invasion, a threat that was ended by Nelson's victory at Trafalgar in October 1805. Promoted to major general on 30 October 1806, Hill organised the embarkation of the British expedition to **Hanover (8 November 1805–15 February 1806)** and served with it in Germany.

On returning to England he briefly joined Sir John Moore in Kent and followed his example of treating soldiers as individuals capable of thinking for themselves. Throughout his career, he displayed a paternal care towards the officers and men serving under him and thereby gained the soubriquet 'Daddy' Hill from the troops. Serving in Ireland from 1807, Hill was selected to join Sir Arthur Wellesley at Cork in an expedition intended against the Spanish colony of Venezuela. At the last moment, the patriot rising in Spain led to the troops being re-assigned to the Peninsula, and Hill organised both their embarkation and the beach landing at Mondego Bay, Portugal, during the first week of August 1808. He commanded a brigade at **Rolica (17 August 1808)** and **Vimiero (21 August 1808)**, where he arrived with a regiment of his own brigade to steady the 39th Foot, in disorder after its commanding officer had been killed leading a hasty attack. He took part in the British advance into Spain in October 1808 and the subsequent **retreat to Corunna (25 December 1808–11 January 1809)**, followed by the battle of **Corunna (16 January 1809)** where his brigade was deployed on the flank and helped cover the British embarkation the next day. In February 1809 he was appointed colonel of the 3rd Garrison Battalion, raised for full-time home defence in much the same way as the Militia.

Hill went back to Portugal with reinforcements for the British force left at Lisbon, where Wellesley took over in April 1809, and was given command of a brigade. In the advance from Coimbra (Quimbra) to Oporto he commanded a division of two brigades and was present at the **passage of the Douro (12 May 1809)**, where he became the senior officer in the fighting inside Oporto after Paget [30] was wounded. On the organisation of Wellington's army into permanent divisions in June 1809, Hill's command became the 2nd Division.

At **Talavera (27–28 July 1809)** Hill was returning to his division after dining in the town when he heard firing, and supposed it was 'the old Buffs' (3rd Foot) making some kind of blunder in the gathering dusk. He then found a Frenchman's hand on his bridle as his brigade-major was shot dead beside him. Breaking free, he rallied the 29th Foot, led a successful counter-attack and occupied his appointed position on the Cerro de Medellin before the French launched their main attack at dawn. As the French advanced, the

British skirmishers fell back slowly, keeping their intervals as they had been taught in Moore's light infantry camp at Shorncliffe, Kent, but causing Hill to shout '* * * * their filing! Let them come in anyhow!' (one of the only two occasions when he was heard to use bad language). He was wounded by a musket ball, but remained fit enough for Wellington to entrust him with a corps of two divisions for the defence of Portugal south of the Tagus, when the army went into winter quarters.

In response to Marshal Massena's invasion of Portugal, Hill's corps made a rapid march to **Busaco (27 September 1810)** and then retreated with Wellington to the Lines of Torres Vedras. When Massena, checked by these impassable defences, fell back towards Santarem on 15 November 1810, Hill was ordered to follow him, but bad weather and the discovery that Massena had no intention of retreating further checked the pursuit and the British withdrew to their lines for the winter. Hill, affected by fever, went back first to Lisbon and then home to recover. When Wellington took the offensive in 1811, command of the southern front was, in Hill's absence, given to Beresford [3].

Hill returned on 1 June 1811, two weeks after Beresford's Pyrrhic victory at **Albuera (16 May 1811)**, and, with his numbers increased to 16,000 men, was ordered across the Portuguese frontier to Portalegre, tasked with watching the French 5th Corps in Estremadura (Extremadura). While he watched, he entertained his officers and visitors to meals served on silver brought out from England and, in Wellington's opinion, gave the best dinners in the army after Cole [9].

By 22 October 1811, with the French concentrating troops to deal with Wellington's threat to Ciudad Rodrigo, their garrison in Estremadura had been sufficiently weakened for Hill to take the offensive. Marching over mountain tracks, in co-operation with Spanish regular troops and guerrillas, he surprised a French division at Arroyo Molinos (28–29 October 1811) and inflicted heavy casualties at minimal loss to his own troops. He was then recalled to Portalegre, but the raid was a great propaganda victory, and the whole army took pleasure in Hill's success. 'The man seems to be beloved by all', noted an officer of the King's German Legion. He was promoted to lieutenant general on 1 January 1812 and was made a KB on 22 February 1812. Later that year Sir Rowland Hill was elected Member of Parliament for Shrewsbury, a seat owned by his family.

While Wellington led his main army south from **Ciudad Rodrigo (7–19 January 1812)** to **Badajoz (17 March–6 April 1812)**, Hill surprised the French at Almaraz (19–20 May 1812) and destroyed its strategically important bridge over the Tagus. During Wellington's subsequent operations, including **Salamanca (22 July 1812)** and the first liberation of Madrid (12 August 1812), Hill remained mostly at Zafra, in southern Estremadura, under orders to avoid a major engagement. During September 1812 he was called north to strengthen the Allied position in central Spain. Retreating north-westwards before a French counter-offensive, Hill gathered the British troops holding Madrid, joined forces with Wellington at Alba de Tormes in early November 1812 and remained with him during the rest of the **retreat from Burgos (21 October–19 November 1812).**

Advancing again into Spain in May 1813, Wellington initially sent most of his army northwards under Graham, through the Tras-os-Montes, while going himself with Hill and the remainder to reach Salamanca on 25 May. He then left Hill and joined Graham, outflanking the French defences on the Douro and concentrating the two wings of his army on 4 June 1813. Hill, with the 2nd Division under William Stewart [39] and a Spanish division under General Pablo Morillo, commanded Wellington's right flank at **Vitoria (21 June 1813)** and was subsequently tasked with the blockade of Pamplona.

On reaching the Pyrenees, Wellington established an advanced line under Hill, to hold the Maya and Roncesvalles passes. In the subsequent battles of the **Pyrenees (25 July–1 August 1813),** when the French attacked on 25 July 1813, Maya was held but Hill, who arrived at the scene after learning that Cole [9] had retreated from Roncesvalles, ordered that it should be abandoned in order to straighten the line. He then led his corps to support Wellington at Sorauren (28–30 July 1813). After Wellington resumed the offensive, Hill was at the **passage of the Nivelle (10 November 1813)** and the **passage of the Nive (10–13 December 1813),** where at St Pierre d'Irube his corps took the brunt of the final French counter-offensive. Credit for the victory in this sector was acknowledged to be Hill's alone, from his decision to commit his reserve early in the fight and from the way in which he personally rallied the 71st Foot (the only occasion apart from Talavera when he was heard to swear). In the final battles of the war, he was present at **Orthez (27 February 1814)** and **Toulouse (10 April 1814)** where Wellington, on leaving for Paris in the armistice that followed the fall of Napoleon, left him in command of the army. Sir Rowland Hill was raised to the peerage in May 1814 as Baron Hill of Almaraz and Hawkestone and became a GCB on 2 January 1815.

At the time of Napoleon's return to France in March 1815, the senior-ranking officer at Brussels in both the British and Dutch-Belgian Armies was the 22–year-old Prince of Orange, who had served on Wellington's staff at the end of the Peninsular War. This prince welcomed the arrival of his old comrades from that campaign with such enthusiasm that his royal father warned him against offending his own officers. When the prince spoke of leading an offensive against Napoleon, Hill was sent urgently to Brussels to persuade him to wait for Wellington. He arrived on 1 April 1815 and his fatherly manner exerted a calming influence until Wellington took command a few days later. When Wellington subsequently divided his army into three Corps, Hill was given the second, composed of the 2nd and 4th British Divisions under Clinton [8] and Sir John Colville respectively, and the 1st Netherlands Division with an additional Netherlands brigade. Before **Waterloo (18 June 1815)**, Hill was placed at Hal, 10 miles on Wellington's right, to guard against any attempt by Napoleon to reach Brussels by an outflanking movement. When it became clear that this threat did not exist, he led some of his troops to reinforce the main battle, where his horse was shot under him and his staff for a time feared he was missing.

In the post-war honours, Hill was decorated by the Allied sovereigns and was awarded the GCH in 1816. He was Wellington's second-in-command in the Army of Occupation, based at Cambrai, until 1818, and then returned to Shropshire, where in 1809 he had inherited Hardwick Grange from an uncle. Hill was colonel of the 53rd Foot, long associated with Shropshire, between 1817 and 1830, was promoted to general on 27 May 1825 and became governor of Plymouth castle in 1830. He declined offers of appointment as C-in-C, India, and Master-General of the Ordnance, pleading that the environment in Calcutta and London respectively would not agree with him. In January 1828, when Wellington resigned as C-in-C of the British Army on becoming Prime Minister, Hill succeeded him as commander of the forces and general on the staff, a title adopted in order to pre-empt claims on the post of C-in-C by officers senior to him.

While Wellington lived, no-one dared seek major reforms of the Army he had led to victory, and Hill contented himself with improvements in the soldiers' welfare. He succeeded in reducing the time taken up by visits from widows presenting claims for pensions by receiving them in a room with only one chair, which convention required him to offer them. 'Then they are sorry to see me standing, so they do not stay very long.' His early years as C-in-C coincided with widespread agitation for parliamentary reform, but he kept the Army outside politics and held it ready to support the civil power. Though on his rare attendances in the House of Lords he had continued his family's support for the Tories, he now remained neutral and withstood pressure from William IV to vote against the Reform Bill (eventually carried in 1832). His dependability and sense of duty, key features of his character, kept him in office first under the Tories from 1828 to November 1830, then the Whigs from November 1830 to December 1834, the Tories (renamed the Conservatives) from then until April 1835, the Whigs again from April 1835 to September 1841, and finally the Conservatives from September 1841. He came under attack from Radical MPs in 1837, when several hundred officers, selected strictly by seniority, were given extra-regimental promotion to mark the accession of Queen Victoria. Complaining that Hill had used his patronage to favour Tories, the Radicals attempted to reduce his salary and the size of the Army, already affected by the usual peace-time reductions.

As Hill passed his eightieth birthday, his health declined and he resigned office on 9 August 1842. He was created a viscount on 22 September 1842, with a remainder in favour of his nephew, as he never married and had no offspring. He died at Hardwick Grange on 10 December 1842 and was buried in the nearby parish church of St Mary Magdalene, Handball, Shropshire. Among his bequests was a sum for the maintenance of a memorial column 133 feet high, erected in his honour at Shrewsbury. Wellington trusted Hill more than all his other generals, saying that he always knew where he could find him, and their correspondence was the most informal of any, with Wellington writing to him as 'My dear Hill' and Hill writing to Wellington as 'My dear Lord'.

HOPE, Lieutenant General Sir JOHN, knight, GCH (1765–1836) [22]

John Hope was born on 15 July 1765, son of John Hope, a Scottish politician and writer, and his wife Mary. Mary Hope died by her own hand in June 1767, leaving her husband with three infant sons, of whom one later became head of the judiciary in Scotland, and another became a vice-admiral. John Hope entered the military in November 1778 as a cadet in Houston's Regiment of the Scots Brigade in the Army of the United Provinces (the Dutch Netherlands) in which, after serving successively as corporal and sergeant, he became an ensign in December 1779. During the American War of Independence (1776–83) the Dutch openly sympathised with the revolutionary (or patriot) cause and the British declared war on the United Provinces in 1780. In 1782 the Scots Brigade was ordered to change its British-based procedures to those used by the rest of the Netherlands Army, and to repudiate any allegiance to a British sovereign. Hope returned from home leave, with promotion to captain on 26 April 1782, to find that the officers of the Scots Brigade had declined to accept these terms. Many of the men by this time were actually Dutch or Germans but the remainder then returned with their officers to Scotland.

After a period of half-pay, Hope became a captain in the 60th Foot (Royal American Regiment) on 29 September 1787, and transferred to the 13th Light Dragoons on 30 June 1788. Following the outbreak of the French Revolutionary War in February 1793, he served in the **Low Countries (March 1793–April 1795)** as aide-de-camp to the veteran Lieutenant General Sir William Erskine until the latter's death on 19 March 1795. Hope became a major in the 28th Light Dragoons when this was raised in Scotland on 25 March 1795 and was promoted to lieutenant colonel on 20 February 1796. This regiment was sent to reinforce the British garrison at the Cape of Good Hope (seized from the Dutch East India Company in September 1795 after the United Provinces, renamed the Batavian Republic, came under French Revolutionary control) and took part in repulsing a Dutch attempt to recover it in August 1796. Hope returned home with his regiment and on 19 April 1799 transferred to the 37th Foot, which in March 1800 sailed from Gibraltar for the West Indies. After the brief period of peace with France between March 1801 and May 1802, he returned to the 60th Foot as a lieutenant colonel on 30 June 1804, and served as assistant adjutant-general in Scotland. He was promoted to colonel in the Army on 1 January 1805 and was deputy adjutant-general in **Hanover (8 November 1805–15 February 1806)**. On 20 September 1806 he married Margaret Scott of Logie, Forfar, the heiress of a Scottish laird.

Hope was deputy adjutant-general at **Copenhagen (8 August– 7 September 1807)** and held various appointments on the staff in Scotland and South-West England, with promotion to major general on 25 July 1810. He joined Wellington in the Peninsula early in 1812, where he commanded a brigade until 2 May 1812, when he succeeded Alten [1] in command of the 7th Division. He was at **Salamanca (22 July 1812)** but on 23 September 1812 was obliged to go home on medical grounds, with Wellington reporting 'Major-General Hope I am sorry to lose, as he is very attentive to his duties.' In March 1813 Margaret Hope died, leaving her husband with three young daughters. With the coming of peace in Europe, he married again on 21 April 1814, to the 24-year-old Jane Hester Macdougall of Ardintriva, who gave him a second family of ten children, though only four survived infancy. Hope held successive commands in Ireland and Scotland, was promoted to lieutenant general on 12 August 1819 and became colonel of the 92nd Highlanders on 29 January 1820, with the award of the GCH in the same year. Sir John Hope was made a knight bachelor on 30 March 1821 and was appointed colonel of the 72nd Highlanders on 6 September 1823. He died at his home in Scotland in August 1836. In 1856, at the age of 66, his widow married the Reverend William Knight, the twice-widowed rector of

Steventon, north-east Hampshire, and nephew of the novelist Jane Austen. Having outlived both her husbands, she died at Brighton in 1880, and was buried at the parish church of St Michael, Steventon.

HOPE, General Sir JOHN, 4th Earl of Hopetoun, GCB (1765–1823) [23]

John Hope, son of the heir to a Scottish peerage and his second wife, was born at Hopetoun House, Abercorn, Linlithgowshire, on 17 August 1765. His mother died in 1767 and his father, after marrying for a third time, had other sons who later became generals in the British Army. The Honourable John Hope, as he became on his father's succession as 2nd Earl of Hopetoun in 1781, entered the Army as a cornet in the 10th Light Dragoons on 28 May 1784. He became a lieutenant on 24 December 1785 in the 100th Foot, a regiment that had just returned from India and was about to be disbanded in the usual post-war reductions. He moved to the 27th Foot on 26 April 1786 and was promoted to captain in the 17th Light Dragoons on 31 October 1789. In 1790 he was elected Tory Member of Parliament for Linlithgowshire, a seat owned by his family. Hope became a major in the 1st Foot during 1792 and moved to the 25th Foot with promotion to lieutenant colonel on 26 April 1793, shortly after the outbreak of the French Revolutionary War.

In the spring of 1793 the 25th embarked to serve as marines in the Mediterranean, with Hope remaining ashore in the depot at Plymouth while the regiment's 2nd Battalion was being recruited. In December 1794 he sailed with the 1st Battalion, 25th Foot, for the West Indies, but was invalided home after reaching Grenada on 30 March 1795 and returned the following year as adjutant-general with the large-scale reinforcements sent under Sir Ralph Abercromby. After dealing with a rising by slaves and Caribs in the British colonies, Abercromby recaptured the French colony of St Lucia (26 April–25 May 1796) and took the Spanish colony of Trinidad in February 1797. Hope was mentioned in despatches and returned home later in 1797. While overseas he had been re-elected by his Linlithgowshire constituency in 1796 (a seat he retained until 1800) and had been appointed on 3 May 1796 colonel of the North Lowland (Hope's) Fencible Infantry, one of the numerous fencible units (full-time regiments raised for home defence) formed in Scotland at this period. Many, like Hope's own corps, were raised by local noblemen or clan chieftains from the districts where their estates were located. On 17 August 1798 he married his cousin Elizabeth, youngest daughter of the Honourable Charles Hope-Weir of Craigiehall, near Edinburgh.

With his commission as a colonel in the Army dated from that of his rank in the fencibles, Hope rejoined Abercromby's staff as a deputy adjutant-general in **the Helder (August–October 1799)** where he was wounded in the ankle in the first landings in August 1799. He was sent back to England for treatment, but returned as adjutant-general when the Duke of York arrived to take over command on 12 September 1799, and served at Bergen (2 October 1799) and Kastrikum (6 October 1799). As a principal staff officer, Hope was part of the British delegation in negotiations with the French that achieved a local armistice allowing the Allied army to retreat to its ships.

Hope again served as Abercromby's adjutant-general in **Egypt (March–October 1801)**. At Alexandria (20–21 March 1801), Abercromby was mortally wounded and the command passed to Lieutenant General Sir John Hely-Hutchinson. Hope also was wounded but returned to duty and was given command of a brigade on 9 May 1800. He was delegated by Hutchinson to conduct the negotiations leading to the surrender of the French garrisons of Cairo and Alexandria and returned home after hostilities were ended by a general armistice in October 1801. His wife had died without offspring in March 1801, during his absence on this campaign. On 9 February 1803 he married Louisa Dorothea Wedderburn, the daughter of a Scottish baronet, and later had with her a family of nine sons and two daughters.

Hope was promoted to major general on 29 April 1802. After peace was restored by the treaty of Amiens (25 March 1802), the fencibles were disbanded in 1802 in the usual post-war reductions. Hostilities with France were renewed in May 1803 and Hope was given command of a brigade deployed against threat of an invasion in eastern England. In 1805 he became lieutenant-governor of Portsmouth and served in **Hanover (8 November 1805–15 February 1806)**. After a brief appointment as colonel commandant of a battalion of the 60th Foot (Royal American Regiment), Hope became colonel of the 92nd Foot, a Scottish regiment, on 3 January 1806. He was promoted to lieutenant general on 25 April 1808 and subsequently served as second-in-command to Sir John Moore in the **Baltic (May–June 1808)**.

Hope landed in Portugal in August 1808 with reinforcements for the army under Sir Arthur Wellesley sent to support the rising of Spanish and Portuguese patriots against French occupation. Although he stood several places higher than Wellesley in the Army List (both had been promoted to colonel, major general and lieutenant general in the same brevets, but Hope had four days seniority as a lieutenant colonel), he declined to take over command of the troops with which Wellesley had won the victories of **Rolica (17 August 1808)** and **Vimiero (21 August 1808)**. He was among the senior officers who assented to the Convention of Cintra (Sintra), by which the French were taken home from Portugal, in British troopships, with all their personal property (much of it plundered from the Portuguese), and was then placed in command at Lisbon, where he had to protect the departing French from indignant local citizens.

In Moore's subsequent advance into Spain, Hope was sent separately via Elvas and Badajoz with the cavalry, supply wagons and most of the artillery, escorted by 4,000 infantry, a move based on faulty information that this was the only route suitable for wheeled vehicles. He made contact with the Spanish patriots at Madrid but, as ordered, pressed on through appalling weather to join Moore near Salamanca on 4 December 1808. In the subsequent **retreat to Corunna (25 December 1808–11 January 1809)**, Hope commanded one of the four divisions into which Moore organised his army and at the battle of **Corunna (16 January 1809)** held the left of the British line. At the crisis of the battle, Moore's senior aide-de-camp, Hope's cousin Graham [19], arrived to say that Moore and his second-in-command had both been badly wounded (Moore mortally so) and that therefore the command had devolved upon Hope. Although the French, with the flooded River Mero behind them, were giving ground all along the line, Hope decided not to risk the army by attempting a pursuit at the end of the short winter day. He ordered the troops to embark on the waiting transports as Moore had planned and made a tour of the streets of Corunna himself before leaving Hill [21] and Beresford [3] to cover the final evacuation. After returning to England, he was voted the thanks of Parliament and awarded the KB.

Sir John Hope served in **Walcheren (August–December 1809)**, where he landed on South Beverland with 8,000 men on 1 August 1809 and captured the harbour of Batz, a few miles from Antwerp. His next appointment was in 1812, as commander of the forces in Ireland. In October 1813 he was invited to succeed Graham in command of the left wing of the Allied army in the western Pyrenees and declared his full readiness to serve under Wellington, who had superseded him by becoming a local general in the Peninsula on 21 July 1812 and a field marshal on 21 June 1813.

In Wellington's advance into France, Hope served at the **passage of the Nivelle (10 November 1813)** and the **passage of the Nive (10–13 December 1813)**, where, huge of stature and fighting with his habitual combination of courage and coolness, he first rallied his men and then joined the sharpshooters but, lacking their light infantry training, failed to take cover. His clothes and hat were pierced by several bullets and he was wounded in the ankle but refused to leave the field. Wellington noted that he, like everyone else, held a high opinion of Hope, whom he considered the most efficient officer in his army, but feared to lose him if he continued in this way, as no-one, even Wellington himself, liked to hint that he should take fewer risks in combat. Hope commanded at the passage of the Adour (23–25 February 1814) from where the Allied army began the siege of Bayonne (27 February–27 April 1814). On 14 April 1814, when despite being told that Napoleon had abdicated, the French governor made a pointless sortie, Hope, with his horse shot under him, was wounded and became a prisoner of war until the war ended two weeks later. He had been selected to lead an expedition to New Orleans in the American War of 1812, but his wounds kept him from being appointed and the command went instead to Pakenham [31].

In the victory honours Hope was created a baron in the peerage of the United Kingdom as Lord Niddry of Niddry Castle, Linlithgowshire, giving him a seat in the House of Lords in his own right. Lord Niddry succeeded his elder brother as the 4th Earl of Hopetoun on 29 May 1817 and was promoted to general on 12 August 1819. Lord Hopetoun remained colonel of the 92nd Foot until becoming colonel of the 42nd Royal Highlanders on 29 January 1820. He undertook the full range of ceremonial and civic duties appropriate to a great Scottish nobleman, and was widely respected for his experience and soldierly common sense. He died in Paris on 27 August 1823 and was buried in his family's vault at Abercorn, Linlithgow. Two great pillars, each almost 100 feet high, were erected to his memory in his estates on opposite sides of the Firth of Forth, one on the south side in the Garleton Hills near Haddington, and the other on the north side near Moonzie, Fife. A statue of him standing beside his charger was placed in St Andrew Square, Edinburgh, outside the head offices of the Royal Bank of Scotland, of which he had been a governor.

HOUSTON, General Sir WILLIAM, baronet, GCB, GCH (1766–1842) [24]

William Houston, only child of Andrew Houston of Calderhaugh, Renfrewshire, was born on 10 August 1766. He entered the Army, during the American War of Independence, as an ensign in the 31st Foot on 18 July 1781 and became lieutenant on 2 April 1782 in an unnumbered corps of Foot raised during the war as a provisional unit. Houston was promoted to captain on 13 March 1783 and after his regiment was disbanded in 1784 in the usual post-war reductions, joined the 19th Foot on 20 July 1785. He served with this unit in Jamaica until 1791 when he moved with it to Gibraltar, and thence to the United Kingdom. Following the outbreak of the French

Revolutionary War in February 1793, he was promoted to major on 30 May 1794 and served in the **Low Countries (March 1793–April 1795)**, where he commanded the 19th Foot. Houston became a lieutenant colonel in the Army on 18 March 1795 and in the 84th Foot on 21 March 1795, from which he transferred to the 58th Foot on 10 June 1795. He led the 58th at the capture of Minorca (7–15 November 1798) and at Aboukir (Abu Qir) on 20 March 1801 in the campaign in **Egypt (March–October 1801)**, where he went on to command a brigade in the sieges and capture of Rosetta (16–19 April 1801), Cairo (21–27 June 1801) and Alexandria (17 August–2 September 1801). In the subsequent distribution of honours, he was awarded the Order of the Crescent (second class) by his Ottoman allies.

With the war ended by the treaty of Amiens (25 March 1802), Houston was promoted to colonel on 29 April 1802 and served as a brigade commander first at Malta and then at Brighton, where invasion was feared after hostilities with France were renewed in May 1803. On 5 November 1808 he married a daughter of the 7th Earl of Lauderdale, Lady Jane Long (*nee* Maitland), whose first husband had died the previous year at the age of 61, leaving her with three young children. With her new husband, she later had two more sons. Houston commanded a brigade at **Walcheren (August–December 1809)** and was promoted to major general on 25 October 1809, after returning to Brighton with his surviving men.

At the end of 1809 Wellington reported that, during the year, seven out of his fifteen divisional or brigade commanders had become casualties. He asked for replacements, naming Houston among them, though with a *caveat* that he might not agree to come (perhaps because Lady Jane Houston had just presented him with their first child). Houston arrived in the Peninsula in January 1811, when he was given command of a brigade in the 4th Division. He became the first commander of the newly-formed 7th Division on 5 March 1811 and subsequently served at Sabugal (3 April 1811) where his raw troops were stationed in the rear of the army; **Fuentes d'Onoro (3–5 May 1811)** where he was for a time left isolated but, on rejoining the main body of the army, stopped a dangerous advance of the French cavalry by deploying his battalions behind rocks and stone walls; and **Badajoz (19 May–10 June 1811)** where he organised the forlorn hopes in the failed attacks of 6 and 9 June 1811. He was appointed colonel of the 4th Garrison Battalion, raised for full-time home defence in much the same way as the Militia, on 1 July 1811 and went home on medical grounds at the end of the same month.

Houston was then given command of South-Western District and though he later asked to return to the Peninsula, Wellington said he had nothing to offer him. He was promoted to lieutenant general on 4 June 1814 and, in the victory honours of January 1815, was awarded the KCB. Sir William Houston was appointed colonel of the 20th Foot on 5 April 1815 and was awarded the GCH in 1827. He was lieutenant-governor of Gibraltar between 8 April 1831 and 28 February 1835 and was created a baronet, as Sir William Houston of Calder Hall, Renfrewshire, in 1836. He became a general on 10 January 1837 and died at his home in Bromley Hill, Bromley, Kent, on 8 April 1842, from where he was buried in the West Norwood Cemetery, Carshalton.

HOWARD, General KENNETH ALEXANDER, 1st Earl of Effingham, GCB (1767–1845) **[25]**

Kenneth Howard was born on 29 November 1767 at Tower House, Arundel, Sussex, near to Arundel Castle, seat of the Dukes of Norfolk, to whose family he was related. His father was Captain Henry Howard, a descendant of the Elizabethan admiral, Charles, Lord Howard of Effingham and 1st Earl of Nottingham, a younger son of the 2nd Duke of Norfolk. Captain Henry Howard's father and brother were Lieutenant General Thomas Howard and Field Marshal Sir George Howard respectively and his second wife (Kenneth Howard's mother), *nee* the Honourable Maria Mackenzie, was a daughter and co-heiress of Colonel Kenneth Mackenzie, 1st Earl of Seaforth in the peerage of Ireland. The young Kenneth Howard thus had important military and social connections and, after appointment as a page of honour to George III, was first commissioned as an ensign in the Coldstream Guards on 21 April 1786. Following the outbreak of the French Revolutionary War in February 1793, he served in the **Low Countries (March 1793–April 1795)** where he was promoted to lieutenant in the regiment and captain in the Army on 25 April 1793. At St Amand (8 May 1793), the first significant engagement of the war, Howard was wounded while carrying the colours as an ensign. He was regimental adjutant from April 1793 to 30 December 1797, when he was promoted to captain-lieutenant in the regiment and lieutenant colonel in the Army, followed by appointment as brigade-major of Foot Guards on 17 April 1798 and active service in various counter-insurgency operations during the **Irish Rising (May–September 1798)**. He became a captain in his regiment on 25 July 1799 and served at **the Helder (August–October 1799)**, where he was present at every major action.

Howard subsequently became successively deputy inspector-general, inspector-general and depot commandant of the regiments of foreign troops in the British Army. On 27 May 1800, at St George's, Hanover Square, London, he married the 22-year-old Lady Charlotte Primrose, daughter of a Scottish peer, the 3rd Earl of Rosebery, and later had with her a family of five sons and four daughters. On 1 January 1805 he became a colonel in the Army and aide-de-camp to the King, followed by promotion to 2nd major in the Coldstream Guards on 4 August 1808 and major general on 25 July 1810.

Howard joined Wellington in the Peninsula with command of a brigade in the 1st Division on 6 February 1811. In June 1811, this brigade was transferred to the 2nd Division to replace the heavy casualties suffered at **Albuera (16 May 1811)** and subsequently served at Arroyo Molinos (28–29 October 1811) where Howard was mentioned in despatches and at Almaraz (19–20 May 1812). On 10 November 1812 he returned to the 1st Division to command a newly-arrived Guards brigade and in March 1813 succeeded William Stewart **[39]** as acting divisional commander, when the Foot Guards insisted on the convention that they should only serve under fellow-Guardsmen. During Wellington's subsequent advance into Spain, Howard commanded the 1st Division as part of the army's northern wing under Graham **[19]** and served at **Vitoria (21 June 1813)**. After Graham's departure on medical grounds, he remained as acting divisional commander under Hope **[23]** and was at the **passage of the Bidasoa (7 October 1813)**, the **passage of the Nive (10–13 December 1813)** and the siege of Bayonne (27 February–27 April 1814). When Hope was wounded and captured on 14 April 1814, in a pointless sortie from Bayonne after Napoleon had abdicated, Howard was formally appointed to command of the 1st Division in his place and remained in post until the army was broken up a few weeks later. He was awarded the Portuguese Order of the Tower and Sword and the Army Gold Medal for Vitoria, with a clasp for the passage of the Nive and became a KCB on 5 January 1815. After returning home, Sir Kenneth Howard was given command of the South-Western District, with the appointment of lieutenant-governor of Portsmouth. Following Napoleon's defeat at Waterloo, Howard commanded the British 1st Division in the Army of Occupation, while retaining his appointment at Portsmouth, and became colonel of the 70th Foot (The Glasgow Lowland Regiment) on 24 October 1816.

On 11 December 1816 Howard's distant cousin Richard, 4th Earl of Effingham and 11th Lord Howard of Effingham, died without offspring and the earldom became extinct. The barony of Howard of Effingham, created in Elizabethan times, survived through a cadet line and Sir Kenneth Howard thus succeeded to the peerage as 12th Lord Howard of Effingham. He was promoted to lieutenant general on 12 August 1819 and became a GCB on

17 March 1820. At George IV's coronation on 19 July 1821, through his family connection to the Duke of Norfolk, hereditary Earl Marshal of England, Howard was appointed deputy earl marshal, and was one of the high officers of state who rode into Westminster Hall as part of the coronation banquet ceremonies. At least one other of the participants had taken the precaution of hiring a horse from Astley's Circus, to ensure he had an animal that was used to crowds and noise in a confined space. Howard was reported to have done the same, but had difficulty controlling his mount and swore at it in language clearly heard throughout the hall. The horse, trained to circus tricks, tried to rear up rather than back out as protocol demanded, and eventually had to be pulled out by its tail.

Howard was appointed colonel of the 3rd Foot (The Buffs) on 30 January 1832 and was promoted to general on 10 January 1837. In the House of Lords he supported the Whigs, but did not play an active part in political life. On 27 January 1837, with the Whig Lord Melbourne in office as Prime Minister for the second time, Howard was advanced in the peerage to become 1st Earl of Effingham in the second creation of this title. He died at Brighton, Sussex, on 13 February 1845 and was buried in the Effingham family vault at the parish church of All Saints, Rotherham, (later Rotherham Minster), South Yorkshire, where he had inherited the extensive estates of the 4th Earl.

LEITH, Lieutenant General Sir JAMES, GCB (1763–1816) **[26]**

James Leith, third son of John Leith, a Scottish laird, was born at Leith Hall, Kennethmont, Aberdeenshire, on 8 August 1763. After attending Marischal College, Aberdeen and a military academy at Lille, he joined the 21st Foot (Royal North British Fusiliers) as a second lieutenant on 13 March 1780, during the American War of Independence. He transferred to the 81st Highlanders, raised in 1777 for service in Ireland, with promotion to lieutenant on 4 August 1781 and became a captain on 23 November 1782. This regiment was disbanded in 1783 in the usual post-war reductions and Leith went onto the half-pay list until joining the 50th Foot on 25 June 1784, two months before it was posted to Gibraltar. From there, after the outbreak of the French Revolutionary War in February 1793, he served at **Toulon (August–December 1793)**, where he was an aide-de-camp to successive commanders of the British contingent.

Leith was promoted to major in the Army on 1 March 1794 and exchanged, as a regimental captain, to an independent company of foot in Scotland. He then raised the Princess of Wales's Aberdeenshire Fencibles, a full-time home defence regiment of which he was appointed colonel on 25 October 1794. This later provided drafts to form the 13th Garrison Battalion (Leith's) in the Army of Reserve, a force raised for full-time home defence in much the same way as the Militia, allowing Leith to become a colonel in the Army on 1 January 1801. Leith commanded this unit in Ireland until it was disbanded following the restoration of peace by the treaty of Amiens (25 March 1802), with its officers being placed on the Irish half-pay list. After the renewal of hostilities with France in May 1803, Leith served on the staff in Ireland and was appointed a brigade commander in 1804. Still regimentally on the Irish half-pay, he was promoted to major general on 25 April 1808.

In August 1808 Leith was sent to the Asturias in north-western Spain to take control of the British military advisers despatched there in response to appeals from the local patriots at the beginning of the Peninsular War. He condemned the way in which these officers had encouraged a premature rising in the Spanish province of Biscaya and had distributed British funds on a lavish scale without keeping proper accounts. A proposal to land British troops in northern Spain came to nothing when the patriot leaders explained that they had enough men and wanted only money and equipment. Leith was transferred to Portugal, where in October 1808 he commanded a brigade in Sir John Moore's advance into Spain and **retreat to Corunna (25 December 1808–11 January 1809)** during which he personally led a charge of the 59th Foot against the pursuing French at Lugo (7 January 1809). At the battle of **Corunna (16 January 1809)** Leith's brigade held the centre of the British line.

After being evacuated to the United Kingdom with the rest of Moore's army, Leith commanded a brigade at **Walcheren (August–December 1809)**, where he contracted malaria. In December 1809 Wellington included Leith's name among the general officers for whom he was asking as replacements for the casualties he had suffered in the Peninsula, and said that he had personal experience of his efficiency (probably from Wellington's time at Dublin Castle as Chief Secretary for Ireland). Leith commanded a brigade in the 2nd Division from 20 June to 8 August 1810, when he was succeeded by William Stewart [39]. He was then given command of the new 5th Division, which he led at **Busaco (27 September 1810)** and in the subsequent retreat to the Lines of Torres Vedras, after which a recurrence of malaria obliged him to return home in February 1811.

Leith returned to the regimental full-pay list on being appointed colonel of the 4th West India Regiment on 19 July 1811 and was promoted to lieutenant general on 6 September 1811. After resuming command of the 5th Division at the end of November 1811, he rejoined Wellington following the siege of **Ciudad Rodrigo (7–19 January 1812)** and served in the subsequent advance into Spain and at the final siege of **Badajoz (17 March–6 April 1812)**. Leith commanded the 5th Division at **Salamanca (22 July 1812)** where he ordered his men to lie down as they held their position under heavy artillery fire, while he rode slowly up and down their front to steady them. They then advanced in good order, Wellington riding in their midst, and made a charge that routed the French division opposed to them, but Leith was severely wounded and invalided home. He was promoted to substantive lieutenant general on 4 June 1813 and was awarded the KB, an augmentation to his armorial bearings, and the Portuguese Order of the Tower and Sword.

Sir James Leith returned to the 5th Division on 30 August 1814, to find it engaged in the siege of **San Sebastian (29 June–8 September 1813)**. The failure of the first assault, on 25 July 1814 had left the division demoralised, with its commander, Oswald **[29]**, and his senior staff (all of whom had supported his objections to the plan of attack) openly talking of the impossibility of success. Wellington had decided to shame them by making the division continue to labour in the trenches, but calling on the 1st, 4th and Light Divisions to provide forty volunteers from each battalion 'to show the 5th Division how to mount a breach'. Leith, on resuming command, refused to allow these volunteers to lead the assault, and instead deployed them to give covering fire to his own men. When the fortress was stormed on 31 August 1813, Leith was hit by a musket ball but refused to leave the field until loss of blood left him too weak to stand. He remained in Spain for another two months and then went home to recuperate.

With the Peninsular War over, Leith was appointed C-in-C, West Indies, and governor of the Leeward Islands, where he landed at Barbados on 13 June 1814. In accordance with the treaty of Paris (30 May 1814), all the French West Indian islands under British occupation, except for St Lucia and Tobago, were handed back to France, under the newly-restored Louis XVIII. Scarcely had Leith's troops been withdrawn when news came that Napoleon had escaped from Elba and returned to Paris in triumph. In the West Indies, most French islands declared for Napoleon. In co-operation with the local naval C-in-C, Rear Admiral Sir Philip Durham (one of Nelson's Trafalgar captains), Leith mounted an expedition from Barbados in June 1814, capturing Martinique in the same month without bloodshed and Guadeloupe on 8 August 1815, at a cost of about seventy casualties. This was the last engagement of the Napoleonic Wars, as Waterloo had been fought two months previously and Napoleon had once more abdicated. Leith was awarded the French Order of Military Merit for this campaign and his

KB had become a GCB on the re-organisation of the Order of the Bath in January 1815. He remained at Barbados until his death from yellow fever, after a week's illness, on 16 October 1816. He was buried the following day at Pilgrim, Barbados. He never married and his properties were inherited by his nephew and former aide-de-camp, Sir Andrew Leith Hay.

LONDONDERRY, Marquess of *see* VANE, CHARLES WILLIAM STEWART [40]

McGRIGOR, Director General Sir JAMES, baronet, KCB, MD (1771–1858) [27]

James McGrigor, the eldest of three sons of a merchant of Aberdeen, was born at Cromdale, Inverness-shire, on 9 April 1771. After attending Aberdeen Grammar School and Marischal College, Aberdeen, he graduated as an MA in 1788 and studied medicine for a year there and at Edinburgh. In 1789 he was an apprentice at the Aberdeen County Infirmary where, with other students of modest means, he was a founder member of the Aberdeen Medical Society and, allegedly, became involved in body-snatching. He then moved to London to study anatomy with a view to becoming a military surgeon. McGrigor became regimental surgeon in the newly-raised De Burgh's Regiment (soon to be the 88th Foot, the Connaught Rangers) on 25 September 1793 after being told by his army agents that if he joined a Scottish regiment he would find too many other young Scottish doctors standing in his way. With the French Revolutionary War in progress since February 1793, he served in the **Low Countries (March 1793–April 1795)**, where his hospital was hit by enemy artillery while he was treating the wounded, and was himself laid low with typhus.

After the Connaught Rangers returned to England, a new commanding officer, Beresford [3], blamed him for the regiment's high number of sick and declared that most of them were malingerers. McGrigor replied that they were not, and that as fast as he cured his patients they became sick again, and would continue to do so unless something was done to improve the poor state of their barracks. After an inspection, Beresford was obliged to admit that the regimental hospital was the only place where men were accommodated in any comfort, but he then criticised McGrigor for failing to appear on morning parades. McGrigor's answer, that he was busy with more important duties, attending the sick in barracks, including the women and children and officers, and that he had sent an assistant surgeon to represent his department, was not satisfactory and he was told to attend in accordance with regimental orders. McGrigor sought a transfer and told his army agent that he would pay a moderate sum to any officer willing to exchange. Beresford, learning of this intention, was much shocked, and said that the only element of the regiment he had reported as satisfactory was the medical one.

McGrigor decided to remain and the two men thereafter became good friends. In November 1795 the Connaught Rangers were ordered to the West Indies with large-scale reinforcements under Sir Ralph Abercromby, but due to a mistaken signal the transport carrying McGrigor sailed ahead of the main convoy, which was dispersed by a severe storm in the Channel. McGrigor's ship reached Barbados, but was thought to have sunk in the storm and another surgeon was appointed to the Connaught Rangers in his place. Surviving a shipwreck after he reached the West Indies, McGrigor joined three companies of his regiment who had arrived there and once more came under fire as he treated the wounded during a slave insurgency in Grenada. He contracted dysentery, but recovered and returned home with other survivors to rejoin the rest of their regiment late in 1796.

Still under Beresford, the Connaught Rangers arrived in Bombay in May 1799 and subsequently served in **Egypt (March–October 1801)**, where they crossed the desert from the Red Sea to the Nile in temperatures soaring to over 100° Fahrenheit (38° C). McGrigor was granted a temporary commission in the East India Company's service to enable him to act as superintendent surgeon over the Company's as well as the British medical officers. He contracted a remittent fever (malaria) which he at first feared might be the plague, a disease that afterwards occurred among the troops, but was contained by strict quarantines. When the British prepared to leave Egypt, many local women who had been the mistresses of French or British officers were murdered by Muslim fundamentalists. McGrigor intervened to save the lives of three of them, but was much relieved when he found some officers returning to India who were willing to become their protectors.

He reached England some months ahead of the Connaught Rangers, but after having held a medical command, was reluctant to revert to the rank of regimental surgeon in an infantry regiment. He accordingly transferred on 9 February 1804 to the more prestigious Royal Horse Guards and served at Canterbury (where his small and ill-ventilated hospital was much troubled by cases of gangrene in even slight wounds) and Windsor (where he was part of the Royal Household). On 20 February 1804 he became an MD of Marischal College. His fellow Scot, Henry Dundas, President of the Board of Control for India in Pitt's Cabinet, nominated him head of the Medical Board in a proposed new East Indian Presidency, to be based at Penang, but the East India Company's Court of Directors objected that this would be at the expense of the aspirations of their existing medical staff, and public opinion condemned the idea as yet another example of Dundas giving lucrative jobs to Scotsmen.

McGrigor was noticed by Francis Knight, the Inspector of Hospitals, one of the three members of the Army Medical Board (and the only one to have served overseas), through whose patronage he was advanced three grades in his service to become deputy inspector of hospitals for the Northern District, based at Beverley, Yorkshire, on 27 June 1805. George III asked him how he could wish to leave so distinguished a regiment as the Royal Horse Guards, and when McGrigor answered that every officer naturally desired to rise in the King's service, said 'Aye, aye, all you Scotsmen are ambitious.'

McGrigor's success in this new post led to his appointment as deputy inspector of hospitals for the South-West District, with responsibility for Portsmouth, the Isle of Wight and West Sussex being added later. He was praised for his care of the sick and wounded returning from overseas campaigns, and coped with a serious outbreak of typhus that spread from Portsmouth to the surrounding area. Beresford offered McGrigor a post as chief medical officer in the Portuguese Army, at that time being re-organised under his command with British officers, but the offer was pre-empted by McGrigor's promotion to inspector in the medical department on 25 August 1809 and deployment to **Walcheren (August–December 1809)**. There, the British were defeated not by enemy action but by disease and McGrigor again contracted malaria. His services received favourable notice, and he told the subsequent parliamentary enquiry that treatment had not been affected by lack of medicines and that, even at times of shortages, 'Peruvian bark' (quinine), had been obtainable from American entrepreneurs.

With the benefit of his promotion, McGrigor married on 23 June 1810 Miss Mary Grant, the sister of an old medical friend, and later had with her a family of three sons and a daughter. Her two other brothers were both senior military officers, one of whom, Colonel Colquhoun Grant, became Wellington's most famous intelligence officer. On 13 June 1811 McGrigor was appointed physician to the Portsmouth garrison, bringing additional pay but only nominal duties. He was soon afterwards appointed principal medical officer of Wellington's army in the Peninsula. His wife, with a new baby, wished to accompany him, but McGrigor said he had seen quite enough of ladies in the field, and reached Lisbon alone on 10 January 1812. He found himself in charge of some 320 medical officers, either on the staff or with regiments, many of whom were themselves sick, and an army sick list of

18,000 men in various stations. He at once joined Wellington's headquarters in the field, where he remained during most of its subsequent engagements, including the sieges of **Ciudad Rodrigo (7–19 January 1812)** and **Badajoz (17 March–6 April 1812)**. Wellington, in the darkness of the final storming at Badajoz, mistook him for a staff officer and gave him a message for Picton [33] only realising the error when McGrigor explained that, without a horse, he would have to carry it on foot. After Badajoz was stormed, he went inside to investigate the number of wounded, specially among the officers, but was caught up in the general sack, and encountered the French commandant, General Phillipon, with his two daughters, being escorted through a mob of drunken soldiers by two British officers. He himself went to help when he saw some of the Connaught Rangers trying to drag the girls away and told them he was a former member of their regiment and they should not disgrace it.

Afterwards, McGrigor asked Wellington to mention the medical as well as the military officers in his despatches. Wellington said he had already finished writing them, but would add 'something about the doctors' and did so, for the first time in the history of the British Army. McGrigor noted at this time that after an action, medical officers were held in great esteem as they went about their work, but afterwards were considered to have done no more than their duty. The financiers long resisted his pleas for pensions for wounded medical officers, on the grounds that their duty did not require them to be within range of the enemy. After **Salamanca (22 July 1812)**, with no time to obtain Wellington's approval if lives were to be saved, he moved his medical purveyors and commissaries to places where large numbers of wounded had been collected. Wellington, who was having his portrait painted at Madrid when McGrigor came in to report, demanded to know who was commanding the army, and told him never again to act without orders. He then mellowed and, when forced to begin the **retreat from Burgos (21 October–19 November 1812)**, warned McGrigor in time for him to collect ambulances and evacuate his patients.

McGrigor himself took the view that he was the only officer who would stand up to Wellington during the latter's periodic bouts of ill temper. He persuaded Wellington to send home for every medical officer then on leave and gained permission to employ as many Spanish doctors as could be found and any French medical officers held as prisoners of war. The base hospital at Belem, Lisbon, was generally regarded as full of malingerers, and the town commandant told McGrigor that the most insubordinate and troublesome part of his charge was the officers' wives.

Wellington approved McGrigor's proposal for a new system of casualty evacuation, with the sick and wounded being taken to regimental field hospitals established close behind the combat zone rather than, as previously, to general hospitals at the base. Men judged likely to make a quick recovery were thus able to be treated by their own regimental surgeons and to remain in touch with their units, instead of returning, if at all, in undisciplined drafts. The most serious cases were sent back to England. McGrigor also proposed hiring carts from local contractors to use as field ambulances, so that minor casualties could move with their regiments. At first this was rejected by Wellington as likely to increase demand on road space, but later he accepted it, as he realised that this, like McGrigor's other reforms, greatly increased his effective strength (McGrigor thought by the equivalent of a full division). McGrigor served at **Vitoria (21 June 1813)**, the battles of the **Pyrenees (25 July–1 August 1813)** and **Toulouse (10 April 1814)**, where on entering the city he was cheered by a crowd under the impression that he was Wellington. At the end of the Peninsular War McGrigor returned home, where he was granted a pension and a knighthood. He would have preferred a baronetcy but Wellington (who by this time had come to address him as 'Mac') advised him to take what was offered.

When Wellington's army was broken up, McGrigor's appointment as its medical chief was abolished and he went on to the half-pay list on 25 October 1814 with a special additional grant of £3 per day. Determined to keep up to date with his professional knowledge, Sir James McGrigor attended lectures at the Hunterian School of Anatomy in Great Windmill Street, Soho, and thought of setting up as a physician in London, anticipating that his links with the officers he had known in the Peninsula would bring him many wealthy patients. He was, however, pre-empted by the resignation of the most senior member of the Army Medical Board, creating a vacancy at its head to which McGrigor, restored to the full-pay list, was appointed as director-general of the Army Medical Department, equivalent in rank to a major general, on 13 June 1815.

McGrigor had to struggle with the usual problems of the British Army in peace-time, including continual demands for what a later age would call 'efficiency savings' and neglect of all things military. He determined that, in a small and shrinking service, only the best should be retained or recruited and personally interviewed all applicants. Thereafter he monitored their further professional studies and encouraged them to obtain the medical qualifications he laid down for promotion to each rank. He supported the chairs of military medicine at Edinburgh and Dublin Universities and introduced the use of the stethoscope into military practice. McGrigor instituted a system of regular returns from medical officers, based on the one he had used in the Peninsula, with details of casualties, illnesses,

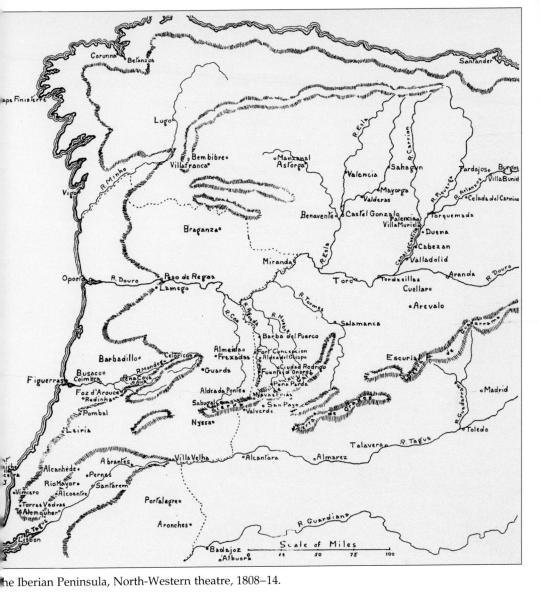

The Iberian Peninsula, North-Western theatre, 1808–14.

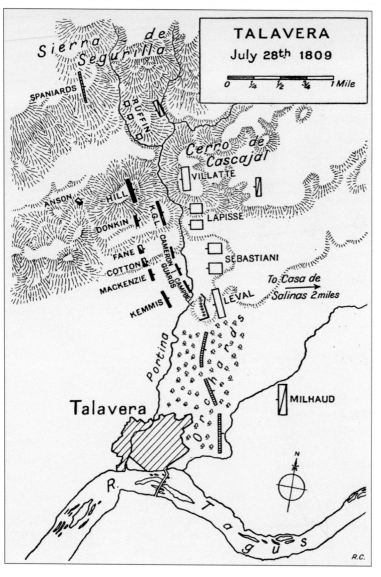

Battle of Talavera,
27–28 July 1809.

The Campaign in
Walcheren, August–
September 1809.

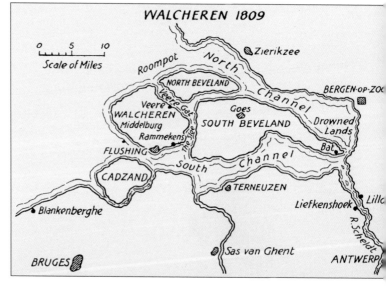

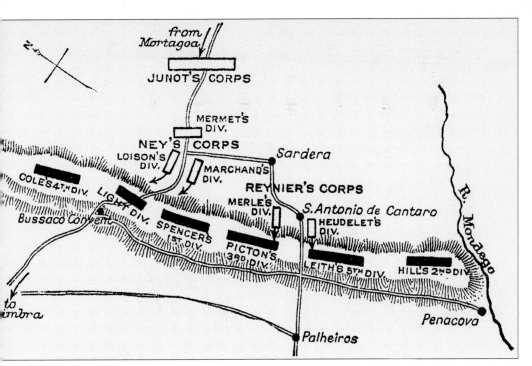

Battle of Busaco, 27 September 1810.

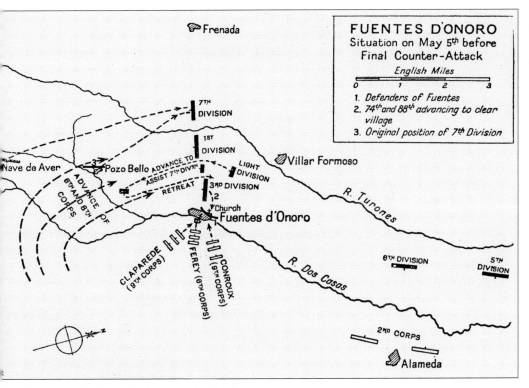

Battle of Fuentes d'Onoro, 2nd day, 5 May 1811.

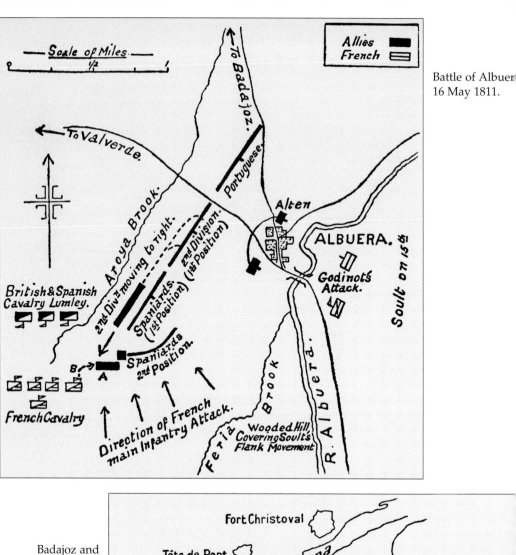

Battle of Albuera
16 May 1811.

Badajoz and
its defences,
March–April
1812.

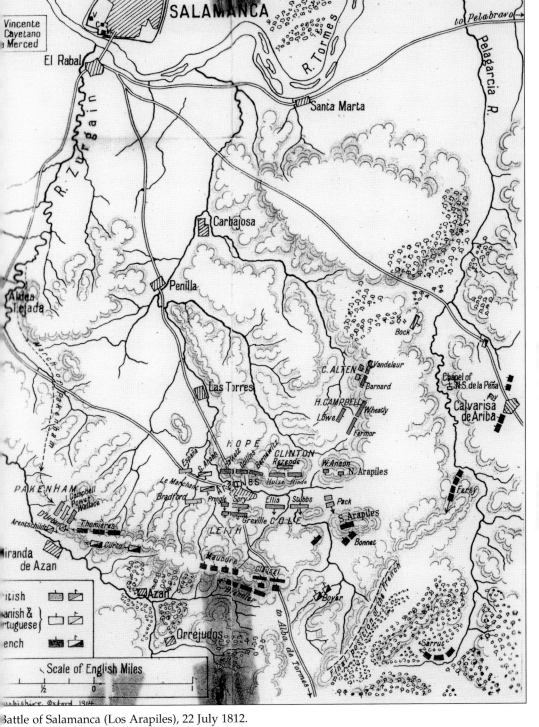

Battle of Salamanca (Los Arapiles), 22 July 1812.

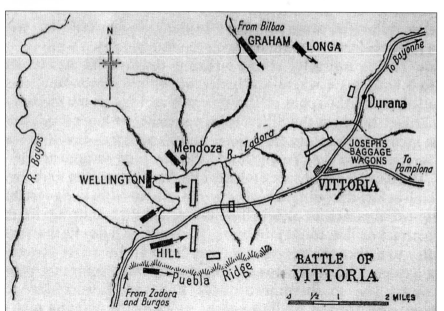

Battle of Vitori
23 June 1813.

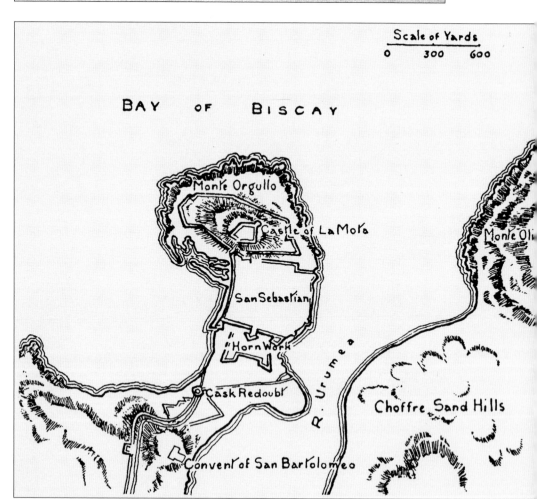

San Sebastian and its defences, June–September 1813.

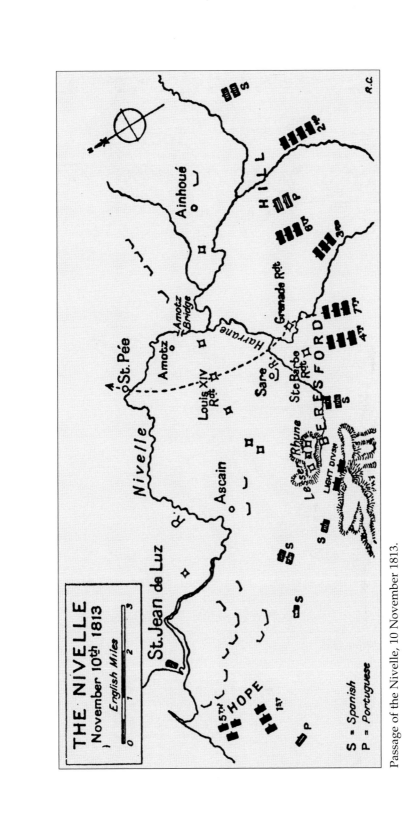

Passage of the Nivelle, 10 November 1813.

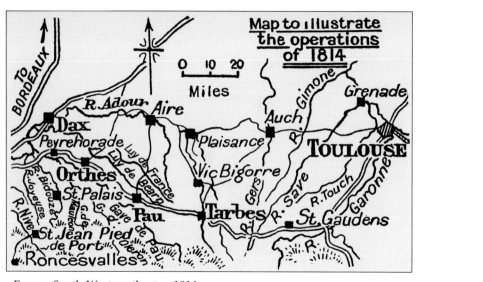

France, South-Western theatre, 1814.

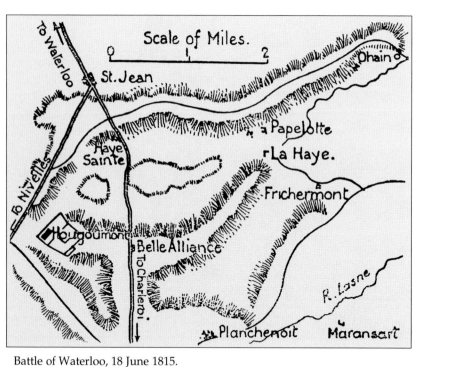

Battle of Waterloo, 18 June 1815.

treatments, and any new hygiene or sanitary measures, thus producing an impressive set of medical statistics that eventually covered the entire period from 1816 to 1850. He established a permanent centre for his service at Fort Pitt, Chatham, (at that time the only large military hospital in England), where he formed a Museum of Anatomy and Natural History to which his officers brought thousands of specimens, and created a large medical library, with the best of both institutions later transferred to the Natural History Museum or other learned bodies. At Fort Pitt he provided lessons in mess etiquette so that men of modest social origins (as many Scottish or Irish medical students then were) would fit in easily with the officers of the regiments to which they were appointed. At a time of post-war hardship, he set up the Medical Friendly Society, for the widows of medical officers, and the Army Medical Benevolent Society, for their orphans or other family members in need.

McGrigor was awarded his baronetcy in 1831, despite objections from the Prime Minister, Lord Liverpool, that this honour should be reserved for landowners. In 1848 he sought permission to retire, but Wellington, three years his senior and still C-in-C of the Army at the age of 79, told him 'No, no, Mac; there is plenty of work in you yet.' In 1849, after years of argument, he secured the eligibility of medical officers for the Order of the Bath and was awarded the KCB himself on 17 August 1850. His other decorations included the Portuguese Order of the Tower and Sword, the Ottoman Order of the Crescent, the Royal Guelphic Order of Hanover, and the Army Gold Medal with five clasps. His academic distinctions included membership of the Council of the University of London when that learned body was founded in 1836. McGrigor finally retired early in 1851, at the age of 80, and died at his home in Harley Street, Belgravia, London, on 2 April 1858. A statue of him was erected outside the Royal Army Medical College, Millbank, London (moved to the former Staff College, Camberley, in 2001) and a memorial column, 70 feet high, was placed in the quadrangle of the Marischal College, Aberdeen (later moved to the nearby Duthie Park). A tablet in his memory was put up in the Royal Garrison Church, Portsmouth. The medical failures of the Crimean War that occurred a few years after his retirement were mostly the consequence of years of underfunding and false economies imposed from above. Through his insistence on maintaining the highest professional standards despite limited resources, he is deservedly remembered as the father of British military medicine.

MURRAY, General the Right Honourable Sir GEORGE, GCB, GCH (1772–1846) **[28]**

George Murray, born at Ochtertyre House, Crieff, Perthshire on 6 February 1772, was the second son of a Scottish baronet, Sir William Murray, and his wife, Lady Augusta, *nee* Mackenzie, seventh daughter of the 3rd Earl of Cromarty. After attending Edinburgh High School and Edinburgh University, he became an ensign in the 71st Foot on 12 March 1789, from which he transferred to the 34th Foot prior to becoming ensign in the 3rd Foot Guards (the Scots Guards) on 7 June 1790. After the outbreak of the French Revolutionary War in February 1793 he served in the **Low Countries (March 1793–April 1795)**, where he was present at most of the engagements in the campaign and was promoted to lieutenant in his regiment and captain in the Army on 16 January 1794.

In July 1795 Murray was appointed aide-de-camp in a force under the Earl of Moira, intended to support the French Royalists in Brittany. This was later reduced to a single brigade landed in the Isle de Yeu, Quiberon, and Murray instead went to the West Indies with the large-scale reinforcements sent under Sir Ralph Abercromby in November 1795. The fleet was scattered by storms in the Channel and Murray was invalided home in February 1796 without reaching his intended destination. During 1797 and 1798 he served as an aide-de-camp at various stations in England and Ireland, and was promoted to captain in his regiment and lieutenant colonel in the Army on 5 August 1799.

Murray served in the quartermaster-general's staff at **the Helder (August–October 1799)**, where he was wounded. After returning to Ireland, he served at Cork until late in 1800, when he joined the quartermaster-general's staff at Gibraltar. From there he served on the staff in **Egypt (March–October 1801)** including the rehearsals in Marmaris Bay, the opposed landing at Aboukir (Abu Qir) on 8 March 1801, the battle of Alexandria (21 March 1801) and the successful sieges of Rosetta (16–19 April 1801), Cairo (21–27 June 1801) and Alexandria (17 August–2 September 1801).

Hostilities with France were ended by a general armistice on 1 October 1801 and the treaty of Amiens (25 March 1802), after which Murray served as adjutant-general in the West Indies. In 1803, when the war with France was renewed, he became assistant quartermaster-general on the staff of the C-in-C of the British Army at the Horse Guards, from where in 1804 he was appointed deputy quartermaster-general of the forces in Ireland. He served in **Hanover (8 November 1805–15 February 1806)** and then returned to his staff appointment in Ireland.

In March 1807 a new Tory government, led by the Duke of Portland, came into office. It decided to continue the war by sending troops to the Baltic, to co-operate with Sweden and threaten Napoleon's lines of communications in his campaign against Russia and Prussia. Murray was appointed quartermaster-general of this expedition, which sailed from England on 16 June 1807 and landed at Rugen in Swedish Pomerania on 16 July, but in the meanwhile the Russians had sustained a major defeat at Friedland (14 June 1807). Tsar Alexander I, exasperated by British delays, had changed sides and made an alliance with Napoleon at the treaty of Tilsit (7 July 1807). Cathcart's expedition was then redeployed to join the British forces gathering off Copenhagen, where it was feared that the Danish fleet was about to fall into French hands. Murray served at **Copenhagen (8 August–7 September 1807)**, and was subsequently quartermaster-general under Sir John Moore in the **Baltic (May–June 1808)**, where he went to Stockholm to make arrangements with the Swedish staff for the disembarkation of the British expedition. He took part in Moore's audiences with the King of Sweden and, when the King threatened to arrest Moore, helped him escape to the British fleet anchored at Gothenburg (Goteborg). Moore, disguised as a peasant, arrived on the quarterdeck of the British flagship *Victory* in the middle of a ball being given for the Gothenburg ladies.

After this expedition was recalled, its troops became available to reinforce Sir Arthur Wellesley's army supporting the Spanish and Portuguese patriots who had risen against French occupation. Murray joined him as quartermaster-general and, after serving at **Vimiero (21 August 1808)**, was one of the principal staff officers who supported the terms of the Convention of Cintra (Sintra) by which the defeated French Army of Portugal was allowed to sail home in British troopships. Murray served under Sir John Moore in the subsequent Peninsular campaign, including the **retreat to Corunna (25 December 1808 –11 January 1809)** and the battle of **Corunna (16 January 1809)**. After being evacuated to England, he was promoted to colonel in the Army on 9 March 1809, and returned to the Peninsula in April 1809 as quartermaster-general under Sir Arthur Wellesley (from September 1809, Lord Wellington) in the new army formed from the British troops still in Portugal. As a principal staff officer, Murray was involved in most of Wellington's operations, including the **passage of the Douro (12 May 1809)**, **Talavera (27–28 July 1809)**, **Busaco (27 September 1810)** and **Fuentes d'Onoro (3–5 May 1811)**. In December 1811 he became a local major general, shortly before breaking his collar-bone in a hunting accident. He went home to recuperate and was promoted to substantive major general on 1 January 1812. At the end of May 1812, Murray was appointed quartermaster-general in Ireland, a move that Wellington believed was arranged by the Duke of York (newly reinstated as C-in-C of the British Army) to create a vacancy in the Peninsula for Colonel James Willoughby Gordon [18], a favourite of the Prince of Wales.

When Gordon returned home in January 1813, Murray rejoined Wellington as quartermaster-general and, by his capable staff work and efficient planning, played an important role in the Allied advance through Spain to **Vitoria (21 June 1813)** and the **Pyrenees (25 July–1 August 1813)**. He was appointed colonel commandant of the 7th Battalion, 60th Foot (Royal American Regiment) on 9 August 1813 and was awarded the KB in September 1813. In the following year, Sir George Murray served at the **passage of the Nivelle (10 November 1813)**, the **passage of the Nive (10–13 December 1813)**, **Orthez (27 February 1814)** and **Toulouse (10 April 1814)**. With the war ended by Napoleon's abdication, he returned to Ireland as quartermaster-general. At the end of 1814, in the closing months of the American War of 1812, he was sent to Canada, with promotion on 19 December 1814 to the rank of local lieutenant general (North America), to report on the frontier defences. In January 1815 he became a GCB in the restructured Order of the Bath and arrived at Quebec in March 1815 after a hazardous sled journey from Halifax, Nova Scotia. On 25 April 1815 he was appointed temporary lieutenant-governor of Upper Canada, on the recall of Sir George Prevost, C-in-C and governor of British North America, following the latter's defeat by United States forces at the battle of Plattsburgh, Lake Champlain (11 September 1814).

Learning of Napoleon's return to France, Murray resigned office on 1 July 1815, in order to join Wellington in the Allied army being formed in Belgium. He arrived too late to take part in the Hundred Days' campaign, which was over before he even sailed, but was made a local lieutenant general (Continent of Europe) and served as quartermaster-general with the Army of Occupation in northern France until this was withdrawn in November 1818. In 1820, the 39-year-old Lady Louisa Erskine (*nee* Lady Louisa Paget), sister of the Marquess of Anglesey (Wellington's cavalry commander at Waterloo) and sister-in-law of the late Major General Sir William Erskine [16], ran away from her husband, Lieutenant General Sir James Erskine and, to the scandal of polite society, went to live with Murray. They married in 1825, as soon as Sir James Erskine died, and had a daughter, who later married Murray's aide-de-camp, an officer of the 2nd Life Guards.

Murray was colonel of the 72nd Foot from 24 February 1817 to 6 September 1823, when he became colonel of the 42nd Royal Highlanders. Between 1819 and 1824 he was governor of the Royal Military College,

Sandhurst. He was elected a Tory Member of Parliament for Perthshire in 1823 and served as lieutenant general of the Ordnance from March 1823 to March 1824, when he was appointed C-in-C, Ireland with substantive promotion to lieutenant general on 27 May 1828. In May 1828 Murray entered Wellington's Tory Cabinet as Secretary of State for War and the Colonies. While Wellington lived, no minister or senior military officer was in a position to make any changes to the Army with which he had defeated Napoleon, though even he was forced, under Treasury pressure, to make savings in the logistic services.

Several of the colonial governors with whom Murray worked had served with him in the Peninsula. Dalhousie [34], in British North America, complained that Murray would not support him in disputes with Canadian politicians over control of the revenues, and the issue of extensive areas of undeveloped land allotted to the Anglican Church. Colville [10], governor of Mauritius, faced difficulties when Murray insisted on the return of a noted abolitionist as advocate general of a colony dominated by French slave-owners. The colony of Western Australia was established during his time in office, with many members of his family and friends going there as settlers or officials through his patronage. Perth, the seat of Western Australia's colonial government, was named after his native county, and his name was given to the Murray River in south-eastern Australia.

Murray retained office until Wellington's administration was replaced by the Whigs under Earl Grey in November 1830. He lost his seat at Perth in the general election of 1832, but regained it in a by-election in 1834 before losing it again at the end of the year. He re-entered the Cabinet in December 1834, as Master-General of the Ordnance in the Tory government under Sir Robert Peel. He left office when Lord Melbourne and the Whigs replaced Peel in April 1835 and stood unsuccessfully for re-election at Westminster in 1837 and Manchester in 1838 and 1841. When Peel formed his second administration in September 1841, Murray was re-appointed Master-General of the Ordnance, though not in the Cabinet, and retained this post until the Whigs returned to power under Lord John Russell early in July 1846. He was promoted to general on 23 November 1841 and became colonel of the 1st Foot (the Royal Scots). Murray died at his London house in Belgrave Square on 28 July 1846, and was buried at Kensal Green cemetery beside his wife, who predeceased him in January 1842.

Though Murray never commanded a formation in battle, he took part in many actions as a principal staff officer and his planning and logistics played a vital role in Wellington's successful operations. After Wellington, he was the most highly decorated officer in the Army, with five Peninsular clasps to his Army Gold Medal, as well as Portuguese, Austrian, Russian and Ottoman awards. A marble tablet in his memory was placed in the chapel of the Royal Military College (later the Royal Memorial Chapel of the Royal Military Academy Sandhurst).

OSWALD, General Sir JOHN, GCB, GCMG (1771–1840) **[29]**

John Oswald was born at Dunnikier, Kirkaldy, Fife, on 2 October 1771, the second son of James Townsend Oswald, a Scottish parliamentarian and landowner. Destined for a military career, John Oswald studied for several years at a military school in Brienne-le-Château, north-central France, beginning in 1785, the year after Napoleon Bonaparte completed his studies there. He made friends with Louis-Antoine Fauvelet de Bourienne (one of Bonaparte's fellow students and later his private secretary) and maintained their friendship until the latter's death in 1834. Like Wellington, who also studied at a French military school, he acquired a command of the French language that would later prove of great value. Oswald entered the British Army on 1 February 1788 as a second lieutenant in the 23rd Foot (Royal Welsh Fusiliers) and became a lieutenant in the 7th Foot (Royal Fusiliers) on 29 January 1789. He was promoted to captain of an independent company of Foot on 24 January 1791 and transferred to the 35th Foot on 23 March 1791. After serving for a time as a brigade-major, he went to the West Indies as captain of the 35th's grenadier company following the outbreak of the French Revolutionary War in February 1793.

Oswald was in a composite grenadier battalion at the capture of Martinique (February–March 1794), Guadeloupe and **St Lucia (April 1794)**, and formed part of the British occupation force in French San Domingo (Haiti) until he was sent home with the officers and sergeants of his regiment to recruit replacements for the many men killed by tropical disease. He was promoted in the regiment to major on 1 September 1795 and to lieutenant colonel on 30 March 1797. At **the Helder (August–October 1799)** the 35th Foot, composed mostly of recruits from the militia, suffered heavy casualties covering the withdrawal of their Russian allies at Bergen (19 September 1799) and Oswald himself was badly wounded. During 1800 he was with the 35th in Minorca (captured from the Spanish in November 1798) and moved from there to Malta and the siege of Valletta, where the French garrison left behind by Bonaparte on his way to Egypt surrendered on 5 September 1800. Hostilities ended in October 1801 with a general armistice followed by the treaty of Amiens (25 March 1802) and Oswald returned home. The war was renewed in May 1803, largely over the British retention of Malta, and he at once rejoined his regiment there. He was promoted to colonel in the Army on 30 October 1805.

Oswald landed in Naples late in 1805 with an Anglo-Russian force supporting King Ferdinand of Naples and Sicily. A French invasion drove the King from the mainland to his Sicilian kingdom, where in March 1806 Oswald was appointed commandant of the fortress of Melazzo. During June 1806 Neapolitan patriots in Calabria, the 'toe' of Italy, rose against French occupation and British troops from Sicily were sent to their aid. Oswald commanded one of the three brigades in this expedition and led a successful attack on French Polish troops who arrived to oppose the British landing at St Euphemia (1 July 1806). He served at Maida (4 July 1806), where a hasty attack by over-confident French troops resulted in a British victory, and was then sent against the French-held fortress of Scilla. A powerful and well-built man, over 6 feet tall, who customarily used his sword in hand-to-hand combat, Oswald led an assault that forced Scilla to surrender on 24 July 1806. The arrival of French reinforcements then forced the British to evacuate Calabria and return to Sicily, where Oswald was given command of a brigade of two battalions of the 35th.

In the British expedition to Egypt (17 March–19 September 1807), one of several measures intended to force the Ottoman government to break diplomatic relations with France, Oswald's brigade was the first to land. It took part in the capture of Alexandria (20 March 1807) and the advance to the nearby port of Rosetta where the British found themselves fighting in urban areas and were driven out with heavy losses. William Stewart [39], with Oswald in support, was sent to recover the place, but after a two-week's siege, they decided that their 2,500 men were inadequate for the task and made a hard-fought retreat to Alexandria. Oswald remained there until the British evacuated Egypt in September 1807, after an agreement with the local Ottoman commander, Mehemet Ali Pasha, an Albanian general who would later become ruler of Egypt and almost gain the Ottoman throne for himself.

Oswald returned with his brigade to Sicily, where he was appointed commandant of Augusta and his local rank as brigadier was extended from Sicily to the whole Mediterranean. In June 1809 he commanded the reserve brigade in the British descent on the islands of Ischia and Procida in the Bay of Naples, a move intended to show support for the Austrians who had re-entered the war against Napoleon in April 1809. The British arrival off Procida (24 June 1809) caused a panic among its low-quality garrison troops and Oswald, without waiting for a formal capitulation, landed a battalion of grenadiers to prevent a breakdown of order in the island. Napoleon's victory at Wagram (6 July 1809) was followed by Austria's withdrawal from the war by the humiliating treaty of the Schonbrunn (14 October 1809). The two Neapolitan islands proved untenable and the British returned to Sicily.

The Ionian islands of south-western Greece, long under Venetian control, had fallen to France when Bonaparte's army took Venice in 1797. Two years later they were occupied by a joint Russian-Ottoman force and reconstituted as the Septinsular Republic, a Russian protectorate under Ottoman jurisdiction. At the treaty of Tilsit (7 June 1807) Russia became a French ally and returned the islands to French rule. Two years later, concerned at French expansion in the area, Vice-Admiral Lord Collingwood, the British naval C-in-C, Mediterranean, urged that they should be captured, in order to give him an anchorage at the entrance to the Adriatic. Accordingly, in October 1809 a small expedition under Oswald seized the islands of Zante (Zakynthos), Cephalonia (Kefalonia), Ithaca (Ithaki) and Cerigo (Kythira), with no resistance from their French garrisons and a cordial welcome from the Greek inhabitants. At the treaty of the Schonbrunn, Austria ceded all her Adriatic provinces to France, to be combined with those Ionian islands still under French occupation and formed into the French province of Illyria. To strengthen the British position in the Ionian Sea, Oswald landed on Santa Maura (Levkada) on 22 March 1810 and took its French-occupied fortress after a week's siege, where he personally led a successful assault on one of the outworks. He was appointed military governor of the British Ionian islands and retained this office when he returned home in 1811, leaving the noted philhellene Colonel (later Sir) Richard Church to act on his behalf until the post was replaced by a High Commissioner in 1815.

In 1810 Oswald's 20–year-old sister Elizabeth married another keen philhellene, the 44-year-old 7th Earl of Elgin (divorced from his first countess), who was later responsible for bringing to England the Elgin Marbles from the Parthenon at Athens. On 11 February 1811 Oswald became colonel of the Greek Light Infantry Corps, a British Army unit raised from Greek mercenaries for local service. As governor, he maintained good relations with the neighbouring Ottoman authorities while at the same time conciliating the Ionians, who sympathised with the demands of Greek nationalists for freedom from Ottoman rule. After returning home, Oswald was promoted to major general on 4 June 1811 and given command of the Western District. On 28 January 1812 he married Charlotte, eldest daughter of the Very Reverend Lord Charles Murray-Aynsley, a younger son of the 3rd Duke of Atholl.

Oswald joined Wellington in the Peninsula on 22 October 1812 and three days later was given command of the 5th Division during the **retreat from**

Burgos (21 October–19 November 1812). He handed over to Hay [20] in January 1813, but resumed command in April 1813 and, under Graham [19] as corps commander, led the 5th Division in the advance through Spain to **Vitoria (21 June 1813)** and the opening stage of the siege of **San Sebastian (29 June–8 September 1813)**. There, the failure of the first attempt to storm the city on 25 July 1813 left the division demoralised, with Oswald and his senior staff making it clear that they had opposed Graham's plan of attack. When Leith [26], a previous divisional commander, returned from convalescence on 30 August 1813, Oswald reverted to command of a brigade and was wounded when San Sebastian was stormed on 31 August 1813. Leith was badly wounded in the same action and command of the 5th Division briefly reverted to Oswald until he went home later in the month.

Oswald's return was caused by domestic reasons as, through the death of his elder brother, he had become heir to the estates of their 65-year-old father, who had lavished vast sums on a new Regency-style mansion but was seriously ill with only months to live. Oswald was awarded the Army Gold Medal for Maida, with clasps for Vitoria and San Sebastian, and became a KCB on 4 June 1815. After the disbandment of the Greek Light Infantry in 1818, Sir John Oswald was for a short time colonel commandant of a battalion in the Rifle Brigade, followed by promotion to lieutenant general on 12 August 1819 and appointment as colonel of the 35th Foot on 9 October 1819. He was awarded the GCB in 1824 and stood unsuccessfully for Parliament as Tory candidate for Fife. Charlotte, Lady Oswald, died in 1827, and Oswald married her 29-year-old cousin, Amelia (Emily) Jane, the daughter of Lord Henry Murray, in October 1829. He was promoted to general on 10 January 1837 and maintained his connections with the Ionian Islands, for which he was awarded the GCMG in 1838. With a keen taste for literature and a readiness to speak at social occasions, he remained a popular figure until his death at his family seat, Dunnikier, on 8 June 1840.

PAGET, General the Honourable Sir EDWARD, GCB (1775–1849) [30]

The Honourable Edward Paget, fourth son of the 1st Earl of Uxbridge, was born on 3 November 1775. He joined the military as a cornet in the 1st Life Guards and lieutenant in the Army on 23 March 1792 and became a captain in the 54th Foot on 1 December 1792. After the outbreak of the French Revolutionary War in February 1793, he was promoted to major on 14 November 1793 and lieutenant colonel in the 28th Foot on 30 April 1794, at the age of 18. He served in the **Low Countries (March 1793–April 1795)** and in the unsuccessful expedition undertaken in support of French Royalists in the Ile de Yeu, Quiberon, in the autumn of 1795. In November 1795 his regiment sailed with the large-scale reinforcements sent to the West Indies under Sir Ralph Abercromby, but the convoy was dispersed by a violent storm in the Channel, so that the 28th landed at Portsmouth in January 1796 and was sent to Gibraltar in July 1796.

Embarked as marines in the Mediterranean Fleet, Paget and his men took part in the battle of St Vincent (14 February 1797). He was promoted to colonel in the Army on 1 January 1798 and served at the British capture of Minorca later that year. In **Egypt (March–October 1801)** he was badly wounded at Alexandria (21 March 1801), where the 28th, already engaged with French infantry in front, was attacked by cavalry from behind. Paget ordered the rear rank to turn about and continue fighting in line, an episode that was later commemorated by the custom of the regiment and its several successors (at the time of writing, The Rifles) wearing a badge on the back as well as the front of its headdress. The war with France, formally ended by the treaty of Amiens (25 March 1802), began again in May 1803, and Paget became a brigadier at Fermoy, County Cork, in October 1803. He moved to England in July 1804 and was promoted to major general on 1 January 1805. He married Frances Bagot, sixth daughter of the 1st Baron Bagot, on 1 May 1805 and subsequently served in **Hanover (8 November 1805–15 February 1806)**. Frances Paget died on 30 June 1806, a week after the birth of her first child. Paget then served with the British army in Sicily until January 1807 when, with most of the troops there, he was recalled to England. He was appointed colonel of the 80th Foot on 23 February 1807 and served in the **Baltic (May–June 1808)** after which, following Wellesley's victories in the Peninsula at **Rolica (17 August 1808)** and **Vimiero (21 August 1808)**, he led the advanced guard in the unopposed British advance to Lisbon. Sir John Moore, under whom Paget had served in Egypt, Sicily and the Baltic, took over command in the Peninsula late in September 1807 and appointed him to lead the Reserve division in the British advance into Spain.

Paget played an important part in covering the **retreat to Corunna (25 December 1808–11 January 1809)**, during which, on 3 January 1809, after retiring from Bembibre, he gathered his men to tell them how stragglers left behind there had been cut down by the French dragoons. Soon after he finished, a group of three men were brought before him after being caught plundering local villages, a capital offence. As ropes were being put round their necks, a hussar galloped in to report that the enemy were approaching. With his battalions drawn up to witness punishment, Paget at first said he would hang plunderers even if the whole French Army was coming. Then, to the sound of distant musketry, he asked his troops if they would conduct themselves well if he let the three malefactors go. They all shouted 'Yes', after which he cancelled the punishment parade and turned to meet the French. In the retreat, the Reserve Division suffered fewer desertions than any other formation, a reflection in part of the fact that it was the one most frequently engaged, but also of Paget's firm discipline. At **Corunna (16 January 1809)** it held the British right flank, and Paget was one of the officers spoken of by the dying Moore, who asked 'Is Paget in the room? Remember me to him – he is a fine fellow'.

In May 1809 Paget returned to Portugal to command a division of two brigades in Sir Arthur Wellesley's army. He took part in the advance from Quimbra (Coimbra) to Oporto and the **passage of the Douro (12 May 1809)**, where he crossed the river in the third boat and took command of the bridgehead inside the city. In this action, he was badly wounded by a musket ball, with the subsequent loss of his right arm, and went back to England to recover. Paget was promoted to lieutenant general on 4 June 1811, followed by the award of the Portuguese Order of the Tower and Sword on 29 April 1812 and the KB on 12 June 1812. Sir Edward Paget rejoined Wellington on 11 October 1812, when he took command of the 1st Division in the siege of **Burgos (16 September–21 October 1812)**. In the **retreat from Burgos (21 October–19 November 1812)** he saw signs of the drunkenness and disintegration he had witnessed in the **retreat to Corunna** and warned his men that he would show no leniency to offenders. As the British retreated towards the Huelva, French cavalry attacked on 17 November 1812 and a wide gap opened between the 5th and 7th Divisions. Paget, acting effectively as Wellington's second-in-command, rode out to the threatened point accompanied only by a Spanish orderly. He was captured by three troopers of the French 10th Chasseurs and remained a prisoner of war until the end of hostilities in 1814.

When the Order of the Bath was re-organised in January 1815, Paget became a KCB. In February 1815 he married the 24-year-old Lady Harriet Legge, fourth daughter of the 3rd Earl of Dartmouth, and later had with her a family of eight children, of whom five survived to adulthood. During the Hundred Days, after Napoleon escaped from Elba, Paget was considered as a possible corps commander, but active operations ended before he agreed to serve, and he declined to join the Army of Occupation. On 26 December 1815 he became colonel of the 28th Foot. He expected to become C-in-C, Ireland, but the post was awarded to the veteran General Sir David Baird, and Paget was made governor of Ceylon (Sri Lanka) in August 1821. The colony was still unsettled following a recent rebellion to restore the independent kingdom of Kandy, but Paget's time there passed off without incident and he moved to Calcutta to become C-in-C, India, in March 1823.

In the war with Burma (Myanmar) that began in 1824, the British at first made little headway. They decided to open a second front, in the Arakan, but sepoys of the Bengal Army were disheartened by reports of Burmese skill in jungle warfare and of the superhuman powers of their general, Maha Bandula. Men of the 47th Bengal Native Infantry at Barrackpur, near Calcutta, refused orders to embark, claiming that travel by sea was contrary to their religion. They were told they could march overland, but protested that there was no transport. Eventually the authorities provided some animals and offered an advance of pay so that the men could hire their own, but the transport contractors promptly raised their charges to take account of war risks and scarcity of supply to meet this new demand.

When the 47th refused to march, Paget, who as C-in-C, India, was in direct command of the Bengal Army, went to Barrackpur with two British battalions, the Governor General's Bodyguard (an Indian cavalry squadron) and a troop of horse artillery. He assembled the sepoys on 2 November 1824 and, through an interpreter, assured them that they would not be sent by sea. The men said that they asked only to be allowed to take their discharge. Paget replied that he would not negotiate until they returned to duty and, in response to further protests, ordered them to ground arms. When only one man obeyed, the horse artillery (previously concealed behind other troops) opened fire. The sepoys fled without resistance, some were killed and others arrested, and the 47th's name was subsequently deleted from the Bengal Army List.

Bengal Army officers blamed Paget for enforcing British Army concepts of discipline into a force that had its own local ways of resolving such problems. The sepoys, they said, had not loaded their muskets, even though each man had the regulation sixty rounds in his pouches, nor had they attempted to return fire. Paget's answer was that this did not make them any less guilty of mutiny, and he had had no intention of allowing them to load. 'There is a great spirit of insubordination in the army' he wrote '…..totally inconsistent with our ideas of military discipline.' The subsequent court of enquiry (dominated by Bengal officers) found that the refusal to obey orders was an act of despair at being compelled to march without the means of doing so and that if transport had been provided at the right time, none of the subsequent complaints would have arisen.

The Court of Directors of the East India Company pressed for Paget's recall, but Wellington, who had firm views on any kind of disorder, and knew that the Company's troops, officers and men alike, had a record of mutiny, publicly supported him. Paget was promoted to general on 27 May 1825 and returned to England after completing the normal period in office and handing over to Cotton [11] on 7 October 1825. He was governor of the Royal Military College, Sandhurst, from 1826 to 1837, and of the Royal Hospital, Chelsea, from 1837. He died on 13 May 1849, at Cowes Castle, of which he had been captain since 1818, and was buried in the cemetery of the Royal Hospital, with a tablet in his memory placed in the chapel of the Royal Military College (later the Royal Memorial Chapel of the Royal Military Academy Sandhurst).

PAKENHAM, Lieutenant General the Honourable Sir EDWARD MICHAEL, GCB (1778–1815) [31]

Edward (Ned) Pakenham, was born at Pakenham Hall (Tullynally Castle), County Westmeath, on 19 April 1778, the second son of an Irish peer, the 2nd Baron Longford. He became the Honourable Edward Pakenham on 27 January 1794 when his father succeeded to another Irish peerage as Earl of Longford. With the French Revolutionary War having begun the previous year, he joined the Army on 28 May 1794 as a lieutenant in the 92nd Foot and became a captain in the regiment three days later. Still only 16, he became on 6 December 1794 a major in the 33rd Light Dragoons, raised in Ulster the previous October. When this was reduced in February 1796, Pakenham remained on its full-pay list until he transferred to the 23rd Light Dragoons on 1 January 1798 and served in the **Irish Rising (May–September 1798)** before joining the 64th Foot on promotion to lieutenant colonel on 17 October 1799.

Early in 1800, Denmark and Sweden joined the Armed Neutrality of the North, an alliance formed, with French encouragement, to counter the British policy of searching neutral ships for contraband. British reprisals included the capture in 1801 of the Danish West Indian islands of St Thomas, St John and St Croix and the Swedish West Indian island of St Bartholomew. Pakenham embarked with his regiment for the West Indies in January 1801, and commanded the British occupation forces in St Bartholomew. When peace was restored by the treaty of Amiens (25 March 1802), all colonial possessions captured during the war were restored to their original owners but, after hostilities with France were resumed in February 1803, French colonies again came under British attack and Pakenham took part in the recapture of St Lucia (22 June 1803), where he was wounded. He returned home after transferring to the 7th Royal Fusiliers on 5 May 1805 in which he assumed command of the 1st Battalion on 19 September 1805. He became Wellington's brother-in-law when Wellington married Pakenham's sister, the Honourable Catherine 'Kitty' Pakenham, on 10 September 1806. Pakenham served at **Copenhagen (18 August–7 September 1807)** and in Canada in 1808, from where he took part in the British recapture of the French West Indian island of Martinique (30 January–24 February 1809) and was again wounded.

His battalion then returned to Nova Scotia, from where Pakenham joined Wellington in the Peninsula in July 1809 as assistant adjutant-general. Promoted to colonel in the Army on 25 October 1809, he was advanced, on Wellington's recommendation, to the previously unfilled post of deputy adjutant-general on 7 March 1810. Late in September 1810, Pakenham was given command of a newly-formed brigade, including his old battalion (just arrived from Nova Scotia), with which he served at **Busaco (27 September 1810)**. On 6 October 1810 this formation was transferred from the 1st to the 4th Division, and reconstituted as a fusilier brigade, composed of the 1st and 2nd Battalions, 7th Royal Fusiliers, and the 1st Battalion, 23rd Royal Welsh Fusiliers. Pakenham returned to the adjutant-general's staff in January 1811 and served at **Fuentes d'Onoro (3–5 May 1811)**. After his successor in command of the fusilier brigade was killed at **Albuera (16 May 1811)**, Pakenham returned to the brigade in July 1811, but rejoined Wellington's staff after promotion to local major general on 26 October 1811. At the final siege of **Badajoz (17 March–6 April 1812)**, he took part in the storm and was among the first to enter the Castle with the 3rd Division.

During the following year, while on leave at home, Pakenham proposed to an heiress, Anne Isabella (Annabella) Milbanke, who refused him on the grounds that there was a tendency to insanity in his family. At about the same time she also refused the romantic poet Lord Byron, though she eventually married him in 1815 only to regret her decision and leave him a year later. Pakenham became a substantive major general on 4 June 1812. In July 1812 Picton was invalided home and suggested Pakenham as his successor in command of the 3rd Division. Pakenham commanded the division at **Salamanca (22 July 1812)**, and was praised by Wellington for his speed in leading the British attack when a gap opened in the French line. 'Pakenham may not be the brightest genius' he wrote, 'but....he is one of the best we have.'

Pakenham remained in command of the 3rd Division until October 1812 and took over the 6th Division on 26 January 1813 when Clinton **[8]** went home on sick leave. He was appointed Wellington's adjutant-general in succession to Charles Stewart **[40]** on 10 May 1813 and again commanded the 6th Division at Sorauren (28–30 July 1813) in the **Pyrenees (25 July–1 August 1813)**. He was made colonel of the 5th West India Regiment on 21 May 1813 and was awarded the KB on 11 September 1813. Sir Edward Pakenham remained with Wellington as adjutant-general until the end of the Peninsular War and was present at the **passage of the Nivelle (10 November 1813)**, the **passage of the Nive (10–13 December 1813)**, **Orthez (27 February 1814)** and **Toulouse (10 April 1814)**.

Many of Wellington's infantry were then sent to join the American War of 1812, in which Pakenham was given command of an expedition against New Orleans. Delayed by adverse winds, he did not arrive until 25 December 1815, after most of the troops had already disembarked. He found that his army was short of provisions and boats, with some units suffering from poor morale, and the whole deployed in a narrow position with the Mississippi on one flank, a swamp on the other, and a strong enemy-held breastwork to his front. He expressed himself in strong language at the state of the expedition but decided to continue with the campaign. At New Orleans (8 January 1815), despite being told that part of his force was not yet in position, Pakenham refused to call off a planned assault, saying that he had already cancelled it three times. When an ill-executed frontal attack resulted in a panic among some of his troops, he rode forward under heavy fire in an attempt to rally them, but was first hit in the knee, then had his horse shot under him, and was finally killed by a shot in the spine as he was mounting another charger. His body was taken back to Ireland preserved in a cask of rum and wits said that he returned in better spirits than he left, in allusion either to his allegedly surly temperament or his lack of enthusiasm for command of this expedition. War with the United States had been ended by the treaty of Ghent (24 December 1814) but news of this did not reach America until the following February. Pakenham was buried in his family vault at Kinucan, Westmeath, and a memorial statue was placed in St Paul's Cathedral. His victorious opponent at New Orleans, General Andrew Jackson ('Old Hickory'), later became the seventh president of the United States.

PAYNE, General Sir WILLIAM, baronet (1759–1831) **[32]**

William Payne was born in St Kitts (St Christopher Island), in the Leeward Islands, in 1759, the youngest son of Ralph Payne, a sugar plantation owner, and his second wife Margaret, *nee* Gallwey, also of St Kitts. Both families had lived on the island for generations and played an important part in the life and government of the colony, as leaders of the elected assembly and local society in general. William Payne's eldest half-brother, Sir Ralph Payne, was twice governor, the first time between 1771 and 1776 and the second, after being created Baron Lavington, from 1799 to his death in August 1807. The wealth from his family's plantations (heavily dependent on slave labour) allowed William Payne to join the Army as a cornet in the 1st (The Royal) Dragoons on 25 January 1776, at the age of 16. He was promoted to lieutenant on 14 July 1777 and captain on 15 April 1782. The regiment did not see active service during the American War of Independence, but remained in the United Kingdom (where it was called out to suppress riots by Birmingham workmen in 1791) until the outbreak of the French Revolutionary War in February 1793.

Payne was promoted in the regiment to major in February 1794 and lieutenant colonel on 1 March 1794. In 1796 he transferred to the 3rd (the Prince of Wales's) Dragoon Guards, followed by promotion to colonel in the Army on 1 January 1798. On 19 November 1804 he married Lady Harriet Quin, only daughter of an Irish peer, Lord Adare, later 1st Earl of Dunraven and Mount Earl. They later had a family of two sons and a daughter and Lady Harriet Payne was painted by Sir Joshua Reynolds carrying a small son on her back. Payne became a major general on 1 January 1805 and transferred to the 10th (the Prince of Wales's Own Royal) Light Dragoons on 15 September 1805 as lieutenant colonel in the regiment. He spent the next four years on the staff in Ireland, and was appointed colonel of the 23rd Light Dragoons on 18 November 1807. Despite his family's long tradition of public service in St Kitts, and his ownership of property there, he was not selected to succeed Lord Lavington as governor of the Leeward Islands when the latter died in 1807.

At the beginning of the Peninsular War, he joined the British army in Portugal as the third senior ranking officer after Sir Arthur Wellesley and Sherbrooke [36] and was given command of the cavalry with promotion to local lieutenant general on 12 April 1809. He became the first commander of the Cavalry Division when this was formed on 18 June 1809 and led it at **Talavera (27–28 July 1809)**. During the subsequent campaign, in which lack of the food and forage promised by their Spanish allies reduced the men and horses of Wellington's army to bundles of rags and bone, many British generals blamed their logisticians for failing to produce supplies from the barren hills through which they passed. Payne, frustrated and angry, shouted at Commissary Schaumann that a commissary who did his duty in such terrain could not possibly remain alive, and as all his commissaries were still living, they were clearly not doing their duty. Schaumann noted in his journal that most Englishmen of high rank, especially in a hot climate, were always a little mad. Payne was also reported to have called Assistant Commissary Moore 'a d——d scoundrel', but when the aggrieved commissaries complained to Wellington, they received no sympathy.

Payne returned home in May 1810. He was promoted to substantive lieutenant general on 4 June 1811 and was created a baronet on 8 December 1812. On 7 March 1814 Sir William Payne changed his name to Payne-Gallwey, as a condition of inheriting the estate of his maternal uncle, Tobias Wall Gallwey, of St Kitts. Payne-Gallwey was appointed colonel of the 19th Light Dragoons on 13 July 1814 and moved to become colonel of the 12th (the Prince of Wales's) Light Dragoons on 12 January 1815. He was promoted to general on 27 May 1825 and was appointed colonel of the 3rd (Prince of Wales's) Dragoon Guards on 2 June 1825, a post he retained until his death on 16 April 1831.

PAYNE-GALLWEY *see* **PAYNE**, Sir WILLIAM [32]

PICTON, Lieutenant General Sir THOMAS, GCB (1758–1815) [33]

Thomas Picton, seventh of the twelve children of a wealthy Welsh country squire, was born at Poyston, Haverfordwest, Pembrokeshire, Dyfed, on 24 August 1758. Determined from an early age on a military career, and with his long-term independence secured by his position as heir to his mother's fortune, he attended the local grammar school and a private military academy in Chelsea and on 14 November 1771 became an ensign in the 12th Foot under his uncle, Lieutenant Colonel William Picton. He joined his regiment in 1773, in the garrison of Gibraltar where he learned Spanish, an accomplishment that would prove valuable later in his career, and was promoted to lieutenant in March 1777, during the American War of Independence. He became a captain in the newly-raised 75th Foot in the United Kingdom on 26 January 1778, thus missing the great siege of Gibraltar and seeing no more dangerous duty than quelling a mutiny when his regiment was disbanded in 1783 in the usual post-war reductions. Picton went onto the half-pay list and returned to Haverfordwest, where he came into his inheritance and lived as a country gentleman while vainly trying to find another military appointment. At the end of this period he fought a duel in which he was hit in the throat by a pistol ball and left permanently hoarse.

Despite the outbreak of the French Revolutionary War in February 1793, he remained unable to find active military employment. In 1794 he sailed at his own expense to the West Indies, hoping that the new C-in-C there, Lieutenant General Sir John Vaughan, a fellow-Welshman with whom he was slightly acquainted, would find something for him. An impressive figure, over six feet tall, he was appointed by Vaughan as an aide-de-camp, and became a captain in the 17th Foot on 13 January 1795. He became a major in the regiment on 22 June 1795 and lieutenant colonel in the Army, later back-dated to 19 November 1794, with appointment as Vaughan's deputy quartermaster-general. Vaughan's death from fever in July 1795 left Picton without a patron and he lost his staff appointment. He transferred to the 68th Foot on 1 September 1795 and decided to return home, but was advised to remain until the expected arrival of Lieutenant General Sir Ralph Abercromby (a friend of Picton's uncle William) at the head of large-scale reinforcements. Abercromby reached the West Indies in March 1796 and gave him a place on his staff, where Picton served in Abercromby's suppression of a major slave revolt in the British colonies and recapture of the French colony of St Lucia (26 April–25 May 1796).

Picton became a lieutenant colonel in the 56th Foot on 1 May 1796 and returned with Abercromby to the United Kingdom. They both re-embarked for the West Indies in November 1796 in an expedition to capture the Spanish colony of Trinidad, achieved with only token resistance on 17 February 1797 after which Abercromby moved to Martinique, leaving Picton to occupy Trinidad with 1,000 men. Tropical fevers soon halved Picton's effective strength but, by establishing a police system and rigorously enforcing the existing laws, he succeeded in establishing order throughout the island, and published his own Slave Code. His early measures included the expulsion of almost every Spanish and English lawyer from the island on the grounds that 'they were like carrion crows, who flocked around carcasses and corruption'. Concerned at the proximity of French and Spanish-held territory, and the constant prospect of a slave insurrection, he expelled anyone suspected of contact with the enemy or of holding revolutionary ideas. French slave-owners who had fled from their plantations were allowed entry, with their possessions, as men likely to support good government.

Picton was formally appointed governor and C-in-C of Trinidad, and moved into Government House, Port of Spain, where he lived openly with his mistress, Rosetta Smith, a lively Spanish-speaking lady of mixed race, and had four children with her during the next four years. He established good relations with the plantation owners (making significant investments himself) and encouraged settlers in the neighbouring Spanish colonies to fight for their independence from Madrid. Local Spanish governors responded by putting a price on his head, but the British government, with its supporters in the City hungry for rich South American markets, made Trinidad the only British conquest to be retained when the war with France and Spain was ended by the treaty of Amiens (25 March 1802). Picton was promoted to colonel on 1 January 1801 and became a brigadier on 22 October 1801.

With Trinidad having become a British, rather than an occupied Spanish, colony, Picton's personal style of government came under criticism. English artisans whom he had encouraged to settle in Trinidad, with a view to establishing a population that could hold the island against Spain, called for the introduction of trial by jury rather than by the magistrates appointed under the old Spanish system. There were demands for an elected Assembly, on the lines of those that existed in the long-established British West Indian colonies. Picton's resistance to this was supported by the London government, where the Anti-Slavery movement was gaining influence and it was thought that an assembly dominated by plantation owners would do little to improve the lot of the slaves who composed over half of Trinidad's population.

Nevertheless, to placate various pressure groups, the Prime Minister, Henry Addington, without informing Picton, decided to make Trinidad the model for a new kind of government. It was to be ruled by three commissioners whose combined expertise would be wider than that of a single governor. The senior of these, Colonel William Fullarton, arrived to take up office in January 1803. Fullarton, a Scottish politician of evangelical and humanitarian views, had served in the East Indies and might well have become President of the Board of Control for India but for the failure of his Whig friends to gain office. After attacking Warren Hastings, the first governor-general of Bengal, for alleged corruption and cruelty, he had switched his support to the Tories and was rewarded with the new post in Trinidad. Soon after his arrival he questioned Picton's previous conduct and laid thirty-six charges of misgovernment against him. Picton, who had been appointed the junior member of the commission, resigned on 6 February 1803. Commodore (later Admiral Viscount) Hood, the second member of the Commission, arrived on 10 February 1803, but soon afterwards, sympathising with Picton against Fullarton, also resigned. The rich Spanish and French planters petitioned in Picton's support to no avail. On 24 June 1803 his old friend Brigadier Frederick Maitland arrived with orders to take over the military command and Picton, leaving his Trinidadian family behind, sailed for home.

En route, with the war against France just renewed, he took part in the British recapture of St Lucia (21 June 1803) and Tobago (30 June 1803). Appointed military commandant of Tobago, he learnt that Fullarton, claiming to be in fear of his life from Picton's sympathisers, had gone home to lay charges against him before the Privy Council. Picton subsequently returned to the United Kingdom himself, where he was arrested in December 1803 and widely depicted in the Press as a brutal tyrant whose hands were stained with the blood of his victims and whose reign of terror had been sustained by unimaginable cruelty. Bailed for £40,000 (his uncle William standing surety), Picton eventually stood trial in February 1806 for allegedly approving judicial torture to obtain a confession from a mixed-race teenager, Luisa Calderon, accused of stealing her employer's life savings. Amid a flurry of sensational pictures and pamphlets from both sides, the prosecution claimed that Castilian Spanish law (the code by which Picton had been instructed to govern Trinidad under British occupation) forbade torture for anyone under 14, and that torture in any case was not applicable in the Spanish colonies. Picton was found guilty, but appealed against the decision and collected testimony from various Trinidadian worthies to the effect that his rule had restored law and order to the island and brought a time of peace and prosperity from which every respectable inhabitant had benefited. Fullarton died of pneumonia in February 1808, and opinion moved behind Picton, who continued to enjoy the support of Hood (by this time a popular naval hero).

A second trial, held in June 1808, heard that judicial torture of suspects was indeed legal in Spanish colonies and that had English law been in force those found guilty of theft would have faced the gallows. Luisa, whom the prosecution had presented as a child of 11 or 12 at the time of the incident (December 1801), was portrayed as a cigar-smoking 15-year-old of questionable morals, with her black lover as the thief. Several witnesses (allegedly under pressure from Picton's supporters) changed their stories, and Picton was acquitted. He was obliged to bear his own costs, though these were mostly shouldered by his uncle William, so that when sympathisers (including the 83-year-old wealthy eccentric 4th Duke of Queensberry) offered to subscribe to his fighting fund he was able to decline, and when a fire devastated Port of Spain he returned a large contribution from the Trinidad planters to be used for local relief.

Picton was promoted to major general on 25 August 1808 and served as a brigade commander in **Walcheren (August–December 1809)**. He was appointed governor of Flushing (Vlissingen) when this was occupied by the British on 16 August 1809 but contracted malaria and was sent home with eye problems that continued to affect him for the rest of his life. At the end of 1809, with nine of his fifteen divisional or brigade commanders having been killed or disabled during the previous year, Wellington asked for generals to replace them, naming Picton and several others junior in the British Army to Beresford [3], whose promotion to local lieutenant general and Portuguese marshal had caused problems of precedence. Picton was given command of the 3rd Division and at his first parade maintained his reputation as an irascible disciplinarian by immediately ordering two Connaught Rangers, who arrived with a stolen goat, to be flogged.

In the summer of 1810, when the French took Ciudad Rodrigo and advanced towards Almeida, Picton refused to move to the aid of the Light Division under Craufurd [12], as Wellington (who supported this decision) had ordered his generals to avoid an engagement against superior numbers on an open plain. He subsequently served at **Busaco (27 September 1810)**, Sabugal (3 April 1811), **Fuentes d'Onoro (3–5 May 1811)**, **Badajoz (19 May–10 June 1811)** and El Bodon (25 September 1811) where, attacked by 3,000 French cavalry in an open plain, he conducted a skilful retreat, moving from battalion to battalion with his cane at his shoulder and ordering each in turn to form square and act as the rearguard. With his usual bad language, he warned the men to keep their dressing and told them that the credit of the army and their own safety depended upon it. When a final charge seemed likely, he took off his cocked hat and used it to shade his eyes from the Spanish noonday sun, before declaring, after a long stare 'No, it is but a *ruse* to frighten us, but it won't do.' Picton was appointed colonel of the 77th Foot on 15 October 1811.

In the siege of **Ciudad Rodrigo (7–19 January 1812)** the 3rd Division, (the Fighting Division, as it had become known) vied with its rival, the Light Division, for the honours of the final assault. Picton told the Connaught Rangers that it was not his intention to expend powder that evening and that 'We'll do this business with the cold iron'. He was given a loud cheer, and the next day, after the city was stormed, was called on by some of the Rangers to cheer them in return. Raising his hat, he gave them a rare smile and called 'Here then, you drunken set of brave rascals' (this term, as elsewhere in anecdotes of Picton, was possibly stronger in the original) 'hurrah! We'll soon be at Badajoz.'

In the final siege of **Badajoz (17 March–6 April 1812)** the 3rd Division was left out of the attempt on the breaches and instead, when Picton asked for a role, was allowed to make a diversion by escalading the castle wall. After the first storming parties were thrown back, Picton formed his division under cover of the cliffs on which the castle stood and led another assault in person. He was wounded in the thigh and the attack was completed under his second-in-command, but its unexpected success, just when Wellington was about to abandon his main attack at the breaches, dislodged the French garrison and allowed the British to reach the city streets. Arriving at the breaches, from which the defenders had fled, Picton found Wellington in tears as he stood amid the bodies of the fallen and, surprised at the distress of his normally unemotional chief, could only say 'Good God, what is the matter?' Afterwards, having inherited £5,000 from the Duke of Queensberry in December 1810, he gave a guinea to every man of his stormers who survived the night. Riding his cob, he went with his troops to Salamanca, but his wound kept him out of battle and he was invalided home with a recurrence of malaria later in July 1812. He recuperated at Cheltenham, bought a large estate and house at Towy (Tywi) near Carmarthen (Caerfyrddin), Dyfed, and entered Parliament as Tory Member of Parliament for Pembroke following the election of November 1812.

Awarded the KB, Sir Thomas Picton returned to the Peninsula and resumed command of the 3rd Division in May 1813. At **Vitoria (21 June 1813)** Picton, whose division was the only one to reach its position at the correct time, asked one of Wellington's staff for orders. On being told that the 7th Division, arriving late under Dalhousie [**34**], was to capture the bridge over the Zadora at Mendoza, he called back that the 3rd Division, under his command, would do so in less than ten minutes, which, urged on by his usual oaths, his men promptly did. He took part in the battles of the **Pyrenees (25 July–1 August 1813)** where he was stationed with the 3rd Division in support of Cole [**9**] and the 4th Division at the pass of Roncesvalles. As the senior ranking officer in this sector, he concurred with Cole in the decision to retreat towards Sorauren, rather than risk Marshal Soult turning their flanks.

Promoted to lieutenant general on 4 July 1813, Picton was again in the United Kingdom between October and December 1813, where he took his seat in Parliament and spoke in praise of his division. Picton resumed command of the 3rd Division at **Orthez (27 February 1814)** and **Toulouse (10 April 1814)** where, remembering his achievements at Badajoz, he tried to convert a diversionary attack into a real one, but was repulsed with 400 needless casualties. He seems to have been suffering from combat stress, or 'nervousness' as he put it, about this time, as he consulted Dr McGrigor [**27**], complaining of difficulty in sleeping before any major operation, and spoke of having to give up and retire.

When the Peninsular army was broken up at the end of the war, Picton was not one of the five generals whose services were rewarded with a peerage.

The Ministers claimed, implausibly, that this was because he had never commanded a separate corps. His own comment was that, if a coronet were to be found at the top of a breach, he would have had as good a chance as any of them. He received (for the seventh time) the thanks of Parliament and his KB was converted to a KGB when the Order of the Bath was reconstituted in January 1814. He then retired to his Carmarthen estate and returned to his previous life as a country gentleman.

At the beginning of the Hundred Days, after Napoleon's escape from Elba, Picton's services were asked for by Wellington, who did not much care for Picton personally, but was anxious to re-assemble as many of his Peninsular veterans as he could. Picton, mindful that the young Prince of Orange, of whose abilities he had formed an unfavourable view in the Peninsula, was then the senior ranking officer in the Allied army in the Netherlands, accepted on the condition that he should serve under no-one but Wellington. He therefore did not join until after Wellington had arrived from Vienna to take command on the night of 4 April 1815. He was given command of the 5th British Division in the Third or Reserve Corps, under Wellington's direct control, and reached Brussels on the evening of 13 June, amid reports that Napoleon had crossed the Belgian frontier.

Summoned to report to Wellington the next morning, he encountered him walking with the British Ambassador, the Duke of Richmond, and greeted him with his usual lack of formality. 'I am glad you are come, Sir Thomas,' was the brusque response, 'The sooner you get on horseback the better. No time is to be lost. You will take the command of the troops in the advance. The Prince of Orange knows by this time that you will go to his assistance.' Thus dismissed, despite Richmond's attempt at a more courteous exchange, he went angrily off. In the dawn of 15 June, after the Duchess of Richmond's Ball, he was in better spirits, exchanging cheerful greetings with his friends as he rode through Brussels in top hat and frockcoat (the trunks with his uniforms had not yet arrived), with his spyglass slung over his shoulder, on the way to join his troops. He reached Quatre Bras (16 June 1815) in time to turn back the French cavalry attack on the Prince of Orange's corps, but was wounded by a musket ball that broke his ribs. He concealed this from everyone but his aide-de-camp, who helped him bandage the wound and, after a painful night, joined Wellington's main force at **Waterloo (18 June 1815)**.

There, when a Dutch-Belgian brigade in front of his line fled, Picton moved his own reserves to fill the gap and, conspicuous on his horse and still wearing his top hat, was killed by a shot through the forehead while rallying the 92nd Highlanders. The senior ranking officer on either side to fall at Waterloo, he was brought back to London and buried in his family vault at

St George's, Hanover Square, from where he was re-interred in St Paul's Cathedral in June 1859. A memorial bust of him was placed there, near to Wellington's tomb. Another monument in his memory was erected in the town centre at Carmarthen, and a statue was put up with those of other Welsh heroes in the City Hall, Cardiff. Later, in the British Empire's expanding colonies, his name was given to new settlements in New South Wales, New Zealand and Ontario.

RAMSAY, General GEORGE, 9th Earl of Dalhousie, GCB (1770–1838) **[34]**

The Honourable George Ramsay was born at Dalhousie Castle, Edinburgh, on 22 October 1770, the eldest son of a Scottish peer, George, 8th Earl of Dalhousie, whom he succeeded in 1787. He was educated at the Royal High School, Edinburgh and at Edinburgh University before joining the Army as a cornet in the 3rd (Prince of Wales's) Dragoon Guards on 2 July 1788. Dalhousie transferred to the 2nd Battalion, 1st Foot, on 4 May 1791 with promotion to captain on 24 January 1791 and became a major in the 2nd Foot on 27 June 1792, when most of the regiment was at sea serving as marines. After the outbreak of the French Revolutionary War on 1 February 1793, the regiment was concentrated ashore and in the following year was ordered to the West Indies, with Dalhousie promoted to lieutenant colonel in the regiment on 22 August 1794.

Dalhousie was serving with this regiment in the British occupation of Martinique when a French expedition from St Lucia landed on the island at Vauclin in December 1795. St Lucia had been captured from the French along with Martinique in April 1794, but a slave insurrection, inspired by the French Revolutionary government's Declaration of the Rights of Man and aided by endemic yellow fever, forced the British out in June 1795. The invaders aimed to raise the slaves in Martinique to fight for their freedom just as those in St Lucia had done. Dalhousie, commanding a detachment of the 2nd Foot and local militia in the landing area, moved to oppose them, but was driven back with heavy losses and was wounded himself. British retention of Martinique was ensured by the arrival of troops from St Vincent. Dalhousie, popular with his own men and the local planters, remained in Martinique until sent home with despatches in May 1797.

Dalhousie was elected a representative Scottish peer, but remained with his regiment and formed a second battalion, stationed in various towns throughout south-west England. In the **Irish Rising (May–September 1798)** they reached Wexford in time to drive off an insurgent force and rescue the Earl of Kingston and other Protestant landlords who had been taken hostage. Dalhousie served at **the Helder (August–October 1799)**, was promoted to colonel in the Army on 1 January 1800 and was in **Egypt (March–October 1801)** until hostilities were ended by a general armistice. With peace confirmed by the treaty of Amiens (25 March 1802), Dalhousie returned to Scotland, where he became a brigadier. After the renewal of the war with France in May 1803, he remained in Scotland, where on 14 May 1805 he married the 19-year-old Christian Broun, the daughter of Charles Broun of Colstoun. They later had three sons, of whom the third became governor-general of India. Dalhousie was promoted to major general on 25 April 1808 and commanded an infantry brigade at **Walcheren (August–December 1809)**. On 31 August 1809 he was appointed colonel of the 6th Garrison Battalion, formed in Dublin for full-time home defence in much the same way as the Militia.

In February 1811, when Wellington asked for general officers to replace those who had gone home on leave, he was told that Dalhousie's private affairs were in such a state as to prevent him going abroad without financial ruin. Dalhousie joined Wellington in the Peninsula with promotion to local lieutenant general (Spain and Portugal) on 3 September 1812 and, during the **retreat from Burgos (21 October–19 November 1812)**, was given command of the 7th Division on 25 October 1812. During the retreat, together with William Stewart [39] and Clinton [8], commanding the 1st and 6th Divisions respectively, he incurred Wellington's anger by departing from the route they had been ordered to take to Ciudad Rodrigo. He was appointed colonel of the 26th Foot on 21 May 1813, followed by promotion to substantive lieutenant general on 4 June 1813 and the award of the KB later that year. At **Vitoria (21 June 1813)** his division was late arriving and Picton [33] captured the vital bridge at Mendoza without him. Thereafter, under Hill [21], he was in charge of the blockade of Pamplona until Spanish troops arrived to take over. In the battles of the **Pyrenees (25 July–1 August 1813)** Dalhousie served at Sorauren (28–30 July 1813) and the Dona Maria Pass (31 July 1813). He took part in the **passage of the Bidasoa (7 October 1813)** and then, Wellington's army having entered France, returned home. In the post-war honours following Napoleon's abdication, he was created Baron Dalhousie in the United Kingdom peerage, giving him membership of the House of Lords in his own right.

In 1816 Dalhousie became lieutenant-governor of Nova Scotia, where he encouraged improvements in education, agriculture and communications, but resisted attempts by the colonial assembly to control public finances. In November 1819, in succession to Sherbrooke [36], he was appointed as governor of British North America, where the various separate colonies had a number of issues between themselves, agreeing only on the issue of local self-government. Canadian politicians claimed that all government income should be under local control, on the grounds that if the governor had a separate source of revenue, he could override local opinion and the concept of responsible government would be meaningless. Dalhousie, following instructions from London, countered that this would allow local politicians to prevent expenditure on any policy with which they disagreed, and saw himself as the champion of royal authority against an encroaching legislature. By demanding the personal deference he considered due to him both as a Scottish earl and the King's representative, in a manner contrary to North American ways, he alienated many local oligarchs who otherwise might have supported him. In 1827 he dissolved the Canadian Assembly but his unsuccessful attempt to rig the subsequent election only made things worse, and in 1828 his projected appointment as C–in–C, India, was brought forward.

At the same time a parliamentary select committee, convened to examine the administration of Lower Canada, received a petition from 87,000 Canadians complaining of Dalhousie's dismissal of magistrates and militia officers whom he regarded as politically unsound. The committee's report strongly criticised him and he received no support from his old comrade Murray [28], the Secretary of State for War and the Colonies. His resentment at what he saw as an injustice turned to depression and his tenure of the lucrative Indian command (January 1830–January 1832), where he was promoted to general on 22 July 1830, ended with him resigning on medical grounds. Between 1832 and 1834 he travelled on the Continent in search of a cure before returning to Dalhousie Castle. He died there on 21 March 1838 and was buried at Cockpen, Edinburgh.

ROBE, Colonel Sir WILLIAM, KCB, KCH (1765–1820) [35]

William Robe was born in 1765 at Woolwich, Kent, the son of Lieutenant William Robe of the Royal Artillery's Invalid Battalion, then serving as proof-master in the Royal Arsenal, Woolwich. On 20 October 1780, he joined the Royal Military Academy, Woolwich, listed as an extra cadet, the RMA having exceeded its normal establishment to cope with the increased demand for officers during the American War of Independence. He was promoted to second lieutenant in the Royal Artillery on 24 May 1781 and served in Jamaica from June 1782 to July 1784 as adjutant and storekeeper. He then returned to the United Kingdom, before going in 1786 to British North America, where he was promoted to 1st lieutenant on 22 November 1787 and married Sarah, daughter of Captain Thomas Watt of Quebec, in 1788. Robe went home in 1790 with his wife and their Canadian-born twins, the first members of a family that would include five sons, all of whom followed him into the Army, and four daughters.

In February 1793, when the French Revolutionary War began, Robe was stationed at the Royal Artillery Depot, Woolwich, from where he joined the campaign in the **Low Countries (March 1793–April 1795)**, arriving just in time to take part in the defence of the Dutch fortress of Willemstadt in March 1793, and serving later as the army's inspector of ammunition. He was present at Famars (23 May 1793), the siege of Valenciennes (24 May–28 July 1793), Cambrai (9 August 1793), the siege of Dunkirk (abandoned 7 September 1793), several engagements around Tournai during May 1794 and, as the army retreated into the Netherlands in the autumn of 1794, at Waarlem and Nijmegen. He did duty as an artillery staff officer and was promoted to captain-lieutenant on 9 September 1794.

After returning to Woolwich, Robe was appointed quartermaster of the 1st Battalion, Royal Artillery, on 25 November 1794 and set up the first regimental school for soldiers' children, an establishment subsequently adopted by the Board of Ordnance. He served as brigade-major, Royal Artillery, at **the Helder (August–October 1799)** and was promoted to captain on 2 October 1799, with command of a company in the 2nd Battalion, Royal Artillery, at Woolwich. The following year he was transferred to command a company of the 4th Battalion, Royal Artillery, in Canada.

Robe, like all former cadets at the Royal Military Academy, had been trained in draughtsmanship, engineering and surveying and had additionally developed an interest in architectural construction. During 1803 he applied these skills to planning and building the new Anglican cathedral church of the Holy Trinity, Quebec, with his neo-Palladian design based on James Gibbs's well-known 1721 London church of St Martin's-in-the-Fields. He was promoted to major in the Army on 1 June 1806, and then returned to Woolwich. Robe became a lieutenant colonel in the Royal Artillery on 13 January 1807 and served at **Copenhagen (8 August–7 September 1807)**, where he commanded the left flank batteries in the British bombardment of the city and was mentioned in despatches.

Robe landed in Portugal in August 1808, commanding the artillery in the British army sent to support the Portuguese and Spanish patriots who had risen against French occupation. He served under Sir Arthur Wellesley at

Rolica (17 August 1808) and **Vimiero (21 August 1808)** where he was so impressed by the effects of the relatively new 'spherical case' shot, invented by Lieutenant Colonel Henry Shrapnel, Royal Artillery, that he asked to be sent as many rounds as possible. The arrival of reinforcements brought a more senior artillery officer, Colonel John Harding, who took charge of the artillery in the field, leaving Robe to command the depot at Lisbon.

One of Robe's major problems in supporting the field artillery was the supply of horses, for which he had to compete with the demands of the cavalry and the commissariat. He managed to find enough animals, though of very bad quality, to mobilise a few units, but reported that he urgently needed 270 horses or mules for the remainder. Cavalry mounts were eventually obtained from North Africa, but artillery horses had to be sent from England. Robe joined Wellesley's field army in command of the reserve artillery and supported the **passage of the Douro (12 May 1809)** and **Talavera (27–28 July 1809)**. In 1810 he was appointed commander of the four troops of Royal Artillery Drivers in the Peninsula, distributed among the troops and companies of horse and field artillery which had no drivers or grooms on their own establishment. Robe was at **Busaco (27 September 1810)** and in the retreat to the Lines of Torres Vedras during October 1810. In 1811 he took part in Wellington's advance through Portugal to Spain, though he was left behind sick at Coimbra and did not reach the main army until the evening after **Fuentes d'Onoro (3–5 May 1811)**. He went on with it to reach the plain of Ciudad Rodrigo in August 1811, but then returned home on sick leave.

Robe rejoined Wellington on 2 April 1812, in time to begin the operations of the main breaching battery at **Badajoz (17 March–6 April 1812)**, where he was mentioned in despatches. He served at the reduction of the Arapile forts on the outskirts of Salamanca (27 June 1812) and at **Salamanca (22 July 1812)**, and was the senior Royal Artillery officer in the entry into Madrid (12 August 1812), two days after its hasty evacuation by King Joseph Bonaparte and his chief of staff, Marshal Jourdain. The last French troops left in the capital, holding a strongpoint constructed in the grounds of the Retiro palace, were bombarded into surrender by Robe's guns on 14 August 1812. At the siege of **Burgos (16 September–21 October 1812)** Robe, with only three 18-pdr guns and five 24-pdr howitzers, could make little impression on the defences, though he was mentioned in despatches for his efforts. In the subsequent **retreat from Burgos (21 October–19 November 1812)** he was with Sir Edward Paget [30] and the 1st Division at the defence of the bridge over the Pisuerga at Cabezon, near Valladolid, on 27 October 1812. When a French general rode up to reconnoitre the bridge, Robe fired a few rounds of shrapnel to discourage him. The French then unlimbered a field battery and answered the shrapnel with grape-shot. Robe, declining to follow the example of Paget and his staff, who lay down to avoid being hit, was badly wounded. He was carried back some 400 miles to Lisbon in a litter, and was then evacuated home.

Robe was promoted to colonel in the Army on 4 June 1814 and became a KCB on 3 January 1815. His other decorations included the Hanoverian KH, the Portuguese Order of the Tower and Sword, and the Army Gold Cross for Vimiero, Talavera and Badajoz, with a clasp for Busaco. Sir William Robe was promoted to colonel in the Royal Artillery on 16 May 1815. He died on 5 November 1820 at Shooter's Hill, Woolwich, and was buried in his family vault at the nearby parish church of St Nicholas, Plumstead.

SHERBROOKE, General Sir JOHN COAPE, GCB (1764–1830) [36]

John Sherbrooke, the third son of a wealthy country squire, was born at Oxton, near Newark, Nottinghamshire, on 29 April 1764. He entered the Army during the American War of Independence as an ensign in the 4th Foot on 7 December 1780 and was promoted to lieutenant on 22 December 1781. He became a captain in the 85th Foot on 6 March 1783 and, when this was about to be disbanded in the usual post-war reductions, transferred on 23 June 1784 to the 33rd Foot, then stationed in Halifax, Nova Scotia. Following the outbreak of the French Revolutionary War in February 1793, Sherbrooke was promoted in the regiment to major on 30 September 1793 and lieutenant colonel on 24 May 1794. With the Honourable Arthur Wesley (the future Duke of Wellington) as his battalion commander, he served in the **Low Countries (March 1793–April 1795)**, where he landed at Ostend in June 1794 in a force under the Earl of Moira and served at Bokstel (13 September 1794) and in the retreat to north-west Germany during the winter of 1794–95.

In October 1795 Sherbrooke embarked with the 33rd as part of large-scale reinforcements despatched to the West Indies under Sir Ralph Abercromby, but their convoy was dispersed by storms in the Channel and at the end of the year they were re-assigned for service in India and reached Calcutta in February 1797. With Colonels Arthur Wesley and Alexander Campbell [7], they joined an expedition against the Spanish Philippines, only for it to be recalled on reaching Penang. Sherbrooke was promoted to colonel in the Army on 1 January 1798 and, with Sir Arthur Wellesley (as Wesley had become), took part in the Fourth Mysore War in southern India and was at the storming of Seringapatam (Srirangapattana), where Tipu Sultan, ruler of Mysore, fell fighting on 4 May 1799.

Sherbrooke, affected by what was probably malaria, returned home early in 1800 and went on half-pay in 1802, after the treaty of Amiens (25 March 1802) brought a general peace. When hostilities with France were renewed in May 1803, he was given command of the 4th Battalion of the Army of Reserve, a force raised for full-time home defence in much the same way as the Militia, and was stationed in eastern England, one of the areas where invasion was feared. He became a major general on 1 January 1805 and, once more alongside Wellesley, served in **Hanover (8 November 1805–15 February 1806)**. Between June 1806 and June 1808 he served under Sir John Moore in the British army in Sicily, where King Ferdinand of Naples and Sicily had taken refuge after being driven from his mainland kingdom by a French invasion. In October 1807, when Moore and most of his troops were withdrawn, command of the remaining British forces in the island devolved on Sherbrooke. Turning a deaf ear to proposals from the Neapolitan court for a descent on the mainland, he devoted his energies to completing the defence works begun by Moore, and to improving the efficiency of the garrison in anticipation of a French landing. On 5 February 1805 he was appointed colonel of the Sicilian Regiment, a corps on the establishment of the British Army, under British officers, and paid from British funds, but with Sicilians and Neapolitans in the ranks.

In February 1808 the command in Sicily was resumed by Lieutenant General Sir John Stuart. Sherbrooke went back to the United Kingdom in June 1808 and was appointed colonel of the 3rd West India Regiment on 25 January 1809. In February 1809 he was given command of 4,000 men intended to support the Spanish patriots at Cadiz. As the Spaniards were reluctant to accept a British presence there, the troops were diverted to Lisbon, where Sherbrooke once more found himself serving with Wellesley. He was promoted to a local lieutenant general on 12 April 1809 and, in terms of seniority, was second-in-command of the army, though Wellesley (after September 1809, Wellington) never assigned any duties to such a position, either then or later. Sherbrooke became colonel of the 68th Foot on 27 May 1809. In the subsequent advance to Oporto and **passage of the Douro (12 May 1809)**, he commanded a formation that on 18 June 1809 became the 1st Division when Wellington established a formal divisional organisation. Sherbrooke led the 1st Division at **Talavera (27–28 July 1809)** where it threw back the advancing French infantry, but an uncontrolled pursuit by three of its four brigades left them open to French counter-attack and created an almost fatal gap in Wellington's line.

Sherbrooke was noted for his short temper and violent language, to which he gave full vent during the subsequent British retreat to Portugal and threatened to hang his divisional commissary if the necessary food and forage was not produced. When that officer complained to Wellington, he was told that he had better comply with the requisition, as General Sherbrooke was a man of his word and if he had said he would hang him, would certainly do so (though Wellington afterwards wrote to Sherbrooke urging him to make allowances for the harassed logisticians). Despite this, when the army went short of food and forage as it passed through the barren hills south of the Tagus, Sherbrooke called Commissary Melville an impertinent scoundrel and threatened to knock him down. Sherbrooke remained in the field for the rest of the year, and was awarded the KB in September 1809, but a recurrence of the fever he had contracted in India obliged him to give up his command on 26 April 1810 and return home. A fellow officer described him at this time as a short, square, hardy little man, of determined fortitude in character, without genius, without education, hot as pepper and rough in his language but with a warm heart and generous feelings, straightforward, scorning finesse and meanness, full of energy, rousing others to exertion and equal to it himself. Wellington thought him the most passionate man he ever met, but regarded him as a good officer and regretted his departure.

Sir John Sherbrooke was promoted substantive lieutenant general on 4 June 1811, followed by appointment as lieutenant-governor of Nova Scotia on 19 August 1811. He married on 24 August 1811 the 28-year-old Katherina Pyndar, daughter of the rector of Madresfield, near Stourport-on-Severn, Worcestershire. They landed at Halifax on 16 October 1811, where Sherbrooke was soon involved in the tension with the United States that preceded the American War of 1812. He complained that the colony's fortifications were in a neglected condition, while reinforcements from Europe were hurried through to Ontario, and protested at the Royal Navy's practice of withdrawing its ships to the West Indies for the winter. When hostilities broke out, he at first waged a phoney war, allowing trade to continue with the fishermen and farmers of Maine. As in Europe, licences were issued for commercial activities from which British subjects benefited, and large-scale smuggling, profitable for all parties, was winked at.

After the end of hostilities in Europe in April 1814, the British took the offensive in North America, and Sherbrooke landed with 2,000 regular troops at Castine, Maine, on 3 September 1814. Dispersing the local militia, he advanced up the River Penobscot to Hampden, which was then sacked by drunken British soldiers and seamen, though Sherbrooke intervened to prevent the Navy from burning the town. The neighbouring town of Bangor then capitulated, with its militia undertaking not to bear arms against the British for the remainder of the war. Sherbrooke withdrew his troops to Castine and announced the formal annexation of Eastern Maine (a long-standing aim of Nova Scotians), under its British name of New Ireland. New Ireland remained under British administration until April 1815, when it was restored to the US by the peace treaty of Ghent (24 December 1814). The surplus customs revenues collected by the British at Castine were eventually used for the foundation of Dalhousie College (later University) set up in 1819 by Sherbrooke's successor, Lord Dalhousie [34].

Government defence expenditure gave a war-time boost to the economy of Nova Scotia, where Sherbrooke, in addition to encouraging the resumption of trade between New Brunswick and New England, displayed an unexpected talent for civil administration. Much of his attention was taken up by the question of providing for the established Church of England in a colony where most of the population were dissenters. The colonial assembly resolutely declined to vote the necessary supplies, and he could do no more than grant small sums from a tax on spirits, and allot undeveloped land for the endowment of a dean and chapter, church schools and glebes. Appreciating the need to conciliate the Nonconformist majority, he stressed that when a new Anglican bishop was being appointed, the see should go to a moderate rather than a zealot who would disturb the peace of the colony.

Sherbrooke's policy of keeping clear of local religious and factional disputes made him a good choice for appointment on 16 April 1816 as governor of British North America. He inherited a bitter political division between, on the one hand, the French-speaking 'Canadian' party, led mostly by Roman Catholic clergy, which had given its support to the British cause in the recent war, and on the other, the 'English' party, including many Scots, which had forced the recall of the previous governor, Sir George Prevost, following his defeat by United States forces at the battle of Plattsburgh, Lake Champlain (11 September 1814). The Francophone majority in the colonial assembly of Lower Canada had impeached the Chief Justice, James Sewell, but he, acquitted by the Privy Council, had just returned in triumph. By skilful diplomacy, Sherbrooke managed to avoid a constitutional crisis. While showing support for Sewell, he also established cordial relations with Bishop Plessis, leader of the French-Canadians, and appointed him to the colony's Legislative Council, thus gaining a valuable ally and conciliating the French-Canadian population. The ambitious speaker of the Lower House of the colonial assembly, Louis-Joseph Papineau, was given a permanent salary, while the English party was mollified by similar arrangements for Sewell, whom Sherbrooke appointed speaker of the Upper House.

Sherbrooke then turned his attention to Lower Canada's complicated public finances, and secured an agreement whereby supplies for the colony's ordinary expenditure were voted by the Assembly, while the governor used any remaining revenue to balance the budget. Development of this into a formal system, which would have avoided many of the subsequent disputes between governors and local politicians, was pre-empted by a breakdown in Sherbrooke's health. During 1817 he warned that the cold Canadian winters brought on a recurrence of his Indian fever and that, though he deplored another change of governorship, and regretted the loss to his own income, he would have to retire during the following year. On 6 February 1818 he suffered a stroke, and at once submitted his resignation, suggesting Dalhousie as his replacement.

Sherbrooke returned home in September 1818, recovering something of his health by visits to the spas at Bath and Cheltenham and living in retirement at Calverton, Nottinghamshire, near his family estates, with promotion to general on 27 May 1825. He died at Calverton on 14 February 1830 and was buried in his family church at Oxton.

SLADE, General Sir JOHN, baronet, GCH (1762–1859) [37]

John 'Black Jack' Slade, son of John Slade of Maunsell House, Somerset, a member of the Navy Victualling Board, was born on 31 December 1762. He joined the Army on 11 May 1780 as a cornet in the 10th Dragoons (later Light Dragoons) in which he was promoted to lieutenant on 28 April 1783 and captain on 24 October 1787. He married, on 20 September 1792, Anna Eliza Dawson, the daughter of an Irish landowner, and later had a large family with her. Slade was promoted in his regiment to major on 1 March 1794 and lieutenant colonel on 29 April 1795, before exchanging to the 1st (Royal) Dragoons on 18 October 1798 and becoming equerry to Lieutenant General Prince Ernest Augustus, fifth son of George III, newly created Duke of Cumberland and a future King of Hanover. One of Slade's sons, born in 1805, would be named Ernest Augustus in honour of his royal patron. Slade was promoted to colonel in the Army on 29 April 1802 and became a brigadier in June 1804.

After the British Cabinet decided to support the rising of Spanish and Portuguese patriots against French occupation, Slade was given command of a brigade of light dragoons and landed at Corunna with Sir David Baird on 14 October 1808. After a difficult march Baird joined forces with Sir John Moore at Mayorga, Leon, on 20 December 1808. Moore's cavalry commander, Lieutenant General Lord Paget, had reservations about the inexperienced Slade, and reduced his brigade to two regiments by transferring the 7th Light Dragoons to the brigade under Charles Stewart [40]. Slade served in the **retreat to Corunna (25 December 1808–11 January 1809)** and took part in the successful British cavalry charge at Sahagun (21 December 1808). After his cavalrymen were safely embarked, he remained ashore and fought in the battle of **Corunna (16 January 1809)** as a volunteer.

Slade returned to the Peninsula in August 1809 to take over command of a cavalry brigade from Cotton [11] when the latter became second-in-command of the Cavalry Division. Promoted to major general on 25 October 1809, he served at **Busaco (27 September 1810)** and Wellington's subsequent retreat to the Lines of Torres Vedras. When Cotton (who had succeeded Payne [32] at the head of the Cavalry Division in June 1810) went home in January 1811, Slade took his place and commanded the cavalry in the pursuit of the retreating French in the spring of 1811. Then as later, he seemed to lack good judgement, being over-cautious when boldness was needed and *vice versa*, so that Wellington was glad to see Cotton return in March 1811.

Slade's brigade performed creditably at **Fuentes d'Onoro (3–5 May 1811)** but far less so at Maguilla, Llera (11 June 1812). It routed a regiment of French dragoons but fell into disorder during the pursuit and made a headlong retreat when it found a second enemy dragoon regiment drawn up on its flank. Slade had ridden in the charge, leaving only one squadron in reserve, and was unable to rally his brigade, which was pursued for several miles with heavy losses in men and horses. Wellington blamed this disaster on his cavalry officers' habit of 'galloping at everything and then galloping back as fast as they gallop on the enemy' and deplored their lack of any attempt to manoeuvre. Slade's reports of the action were greeted with derision by the rest of the army, and at the end of 1812 Wellington asked the Duke of York, as C-in-C, to find Slade another post. York, struggling to accommodate other generals whom Wellington wished to send home, replied that he could not re-appoint inefficient officers merely to spare their feelings. At the same time, it was generally agreed that Slade should be re-assigned, as otherwise, if Cotton were to become a casualty, command of the cavalry would devolve upon Slade, who had become a local lieutenant general on the staff on 3 September 1812.

The problem was eventually solved by the promotion of Clinton [8] to local lieutenant general on the staff on 8 April 1813. As Army regulations did not allow two local lieutenant generals to serve on the staff at the same time, Slade, as the senior (by five months as a lieutenant colonel) had to leave. He was ordered home on 23 April 1813 and given a command in Ireland, which he retained until promoted to substantive lieutenant general on 4 June 1814. He was not mentioned in the victory honours of 1815, but was awarded the Army Gold Medal for Corunna with one clasp for Fuentes d'Onoro, and the Portuguese Order of the Tower and Sword. His wife died in 1819, but in 1822 he married her kinswoman, Matilda Ellen Dawson, of Forkhill, County Armagh, with whom he had later a second family, becoming father in all to eleven sons and four daughters. Slade was appointed colonel of the 5th (Princess Charlotte of Wales's) Dragoon Guards on 20 July 1831, became a baronet on 30 September 1831 in William IV's coronation honours and was made GCH in 1835. Sir John Slade was promoted to general on 10 January 1837. He died at his home, Montys Court, Norton Fitzwarren, near Taunton, Somerset, on 13 August 1859, at the age of 97, the second-oldest serving officer in the Army.

SPENCER, General Sir BRENT, GCB (1760–1828) [38]

Brent Spencer, the son of an Anglo-Irish Protestant squire, was born in County Antrim, Northern Ireland, in 1760 and joined the Army during the American War of Independence as an ensign in the 15th Foot on 18 January 1778. He took part in the capture of the French West Indian island of St Lucia (14–28 December 1778) and was promoted to lieutenant on 12 November 1779, but became a prisoner of war when the British garrison of Brimstone Hill, St Kitts, was starved into surrender by the French on 12 February 1782. On the conclusion of hostilities, he was released and became a captain in the 99th Foot (Jamaica Regiment) on 29 July 1783, shortly before it was disbanded in the usual post-war reductions. He exchanged back to the 15th Foot on 4 September 1783 and returned with it to the West Indies in 1790, where on 6 March 1791 he became the junior major of the 13th Foot, stationed in Jamaica.

Following the outbreak of the French Revolutionary War in February 1793, Spencer took part in the British attack on French San Domingo (Haiti) where he was mentioned in despatches for his services at Cap Tiburon (2–3 February 1794), L'Acul (18 February 1794) and Port-au-Prince (4 June 1794). He was promoted to lieutenant colonel in the newly-raised 115th Foot on 2 May 1794 and, on its disbandment, transferred on 22 July 1795 to the 40th Foot, a regiment that arrived in the West Indies in September 1795. During 1796 Spencer took part in operations against Carib insurgents in St Vincent and then moved to Jamaica from where, in April 1797, his regiment joined the British occupation forces in Haiti. He became a local brigadier on 9 July 1797, aide-de-camp to the King on 1 January 1798 and colonel in the Army on 28 May 1798.

Commanding La Grande Anse, on Haiti's south-east peninsula, Spencer came under siege by insurgents early in 1798. Lieutenant Colonel Thomas Maitland, who was sent by the British Cabinet to investigate the widespread disturbances in the island, reported that 'Spencer's failure is due to …stuffing all his men into posts without leaving any moving force, so that when one of his posts was attacked, he could not hope to relieve it.' Spencer was reinforced in April 1798 to give him 8,000 men, but most were local colonial levies who had little spirit for offensive operations and suffered some 400 casualties in minor skirmishes before the British evacuated Haiti in October 1798. He returned home with the 40th at the end of 1798 and oversaw the raising of its 2nd Battalion, prior to commanding both battalions of the 40th, brigaded with the 50th Foot, at **the Helder (August–October 1799)**. He led a stout defence of St Maarten (10 September 1799) and was mentioned in despatches at Alkmaar (19 September 1799). In March 1800 Spencer sailed for the Mediterranean, and after serving in Minorca and Malta, commanded the flank companies of the 40th in **Egypt (March–October 1801)**, where he was mentioned in despatches at Aboukir (Abu Qir) and Alexandria (17 August 1801).

Hostilities with France were ended by a general armistice in October 1801, leading to the treaty of Amiens (25 March 1802). Spencer returned home where, after the war with France was renewed in May 1803, he commanded a brigade in Sussex, one of the areas where a French invasion was feared. He was promoted to major general on 1 January 1805 and became an equerry to George III, whose second daughter, Princess Augusta Sophia, he was rumoured to have secretly married. Certainly neither party made any other marriage. On 25 November 1806 Spencer was appointed colonel of the 9th Garrison Battalion, raised for full-time home defence in much the same way as the Militia. He led a brigade at **Copenhagen (8 August–7 September 1807)** and later in the year was given command of an expedition intended to raid Spanish naval installations at Cadiz and the Mediterranean. The convoy was dispersed by bad weather and Spencer arrived at Gibraltar in March 1808 to find that some of his troops had been sent on to reinforce Sherbrooke [36] in Sicily. When Spanish and Portuguese patriots rose against French occupation in the summer of 1808, Spencer's force was available to go to their support, though the Spaniards firmly declined a British offer that he should land in Cadiz. Instead, he sailed to Ayamonte on the Spanish-Portuguese border, where his appearance led to the recall of a French corps on its way to support General Dupont's advance on Seville. On 25 June 1808 he was appointed colonel of the 2nd West India Regiment.

Spencer received orders on 15 July 1808 telling him that Sir Arthur Wellesley was on his way to the Peninsula and that he was to join him at Cadiz as second-in-command as soon as his own operations allowed. After confirming that Dupont had been defeated by the Spanish at Baylen on 19 July 1808, he sailed to the mouth of the Tagus, correctly anticipating fresh orders from Wellesley to join him there. Wellesley (after September 1809, Wellington) never allotted his seconds-in-command any specific duties as such, and usually employed them as corps or divisional commanders, nominated to succeed him if he became a casualty. Spencer was Wellesley's second-in-command at **Rolica (17 August 1808)** and **Vimiero (21 August 1808)**, where he was mentioned in despatches, and then returned to England on medical grounds in October 1808. Giving evidence at the inquiry into the Convention of Cintra (Sintra), by which the French had been taken home from Portugal in British troopships, carrying all their public and private property with them, he expressed his support for the terms agreed, but also for Wellesley's view that the victory at Vimiero could have been more fully exploited. He was awarded the KB on 26 April 1809 and was appointed colonel-commandant of the 2nd Battalion, 95th Foot (Riflemen), on 31 August 1809.

Sir Brent Spencer returned to the Peninsula in May 1810 to succeed Sherbrooke in command of the 1st Division. Promoted to local lieutenant general (Spain and Portugal) on 5 May 1810, he remained as Wellington's second-in-command and served at **Busaco (27 September 1810)**, where he was again mentioned in despatches; the retreat to the Lines of Torres Vedras, during which he wrote letters home forecasting defeat; the subsequent advance into Spain in 1811 and **Fuentes d'Onoro (3–5 May 1811)**. He became a substantive lieutenant general on 4 June 1811 and commanded the army in northern Portugal while Wellington was absent supporting Beresford [3] further south. In early June 1811, to Wellington's displeasure, he retreated before an enemy half his own strength and allowed the French to re-provision Ciudad Rodrigo. Though always cool and courageous in battle, Spencer still believed that the British were more likely to abandon Portugal than use its border fortresses for another advance into Spain and accordingly ordered the destruction of Almeida and its stores, although it was under no serious threat at this time.

Spencer was described by Wellington as unreliable when left on his own and someone who gave an opinion on every subject and, being easily swayed by others, changed it with the wind. 'If any misfortune occurs, or the act recommended by him is disapproved of, there is no effort to be looked for from him.' Wellington had, in fact, asked for Graham [19], not Spencer, as a replacement for the ailing Sherbrooke at the end of 1809, but the needs of the Cadiz command kept Graham from joining him until August 1811. Spencer then returned home, ostensibly on grounds of ill-health, but actually (on his own admission) in chagrin at being superseded as the second senior-ranking officer. He was awarded the Army Gold Medal for Vimiero, and the Portuguese Order of the Tower and Sword, and his KB was replaced by the GCB in January 1815, but he saw no further active service. Spencer became colonel of the 40th Foot on 2 July 1818 and was promoted to general on 27 May 1825. He made his home in the village of The Lee, near Great Missenden, Buckinghamshire, where he died on 29 December 1828.

STAPLETON-COTTON, *see* **COTTON**, Sir STAPLETON [11]

STEWART, CHARLES, *see* **VANE**, CHARLES WILLIAM STEWART, 3rd Marquess of Londonderry [40]

STEWART, Lieutenant General Sir WILLIAM, GCB (1774–1827) [39]

The Honourable William Stewart, the second surviving son of a Scottish peer, the 7th Earl of Galloway, was born on 10 January 1774. He was first commissioned at the age of 12, on 8 March 1786, as an ensign in the 42nd Royal Highlanders, from which he became a lieutenant in the 67th Foot on 14 October 1787 and captain of an independent company of foot on 24 January 1791. At a time of increasing international concern at the development of the French Revolution, and an insurgency in the Austrian Netherlands arising from the centralising reforms of the Austrian Emperor Joseph II, Stewart went to Vienna with the veteran diplomat Lieutenant General Sir Robert Murray Keith. They presented their credentials to the new Emperor, Leopold II, and attended the Congress of Sistova (August 1791) that ended a war between Austria and the Ottoman Empire. Stewart's company was disbanded in December 1791.

Stewart joined the 22nd Foot on 31 October 1792 and, after the outbreak of the French Revolutionary War in February 1793, served in the West Indies, where he commanded the grenadier company of the 22nd at Martinique (February–March 1794) and Guadeloupe (April and July 1794) where, in the second engagement, he was wounded. After returning to the United Kingdom in November 1794 he briefly became a major in the 31st Foot, allowing him promotion to lieutenant colonel in the Army on 14 January 1795. During the autumn of 1795, he was assistant adjutant-general in the expedition sent under the Earl of Moira to the Ile de Yeu, Quiberon, in support of the French Royalists in Brittany. On reaching the age of 21, Stewart became eligible to stand for Parliament and in 1795 was elected Tory member for Saltash, Cornwall, a seat owned by his family. He remained in the Commons for the next twenty-one years, as Member of Parliament for his family stronghold of Wigtownshire, Galloway, from 1796 to 1802, then for the burghs of Wigtown from 1803 to 1805, and finally for Wigtownshire again from 1812 to 1816.

On 1 September 1795 Stewart became a lieutenant colonel in the 67th Foot, which he commanded in the British occupation of French San Domingo (Haiti). With the local rank of colonel, he was commandant of Mole St Nicholas prior to this being handed over to the Haitian patriot Toussaint L'Ouverture in August 1798. After returning to Europe, he was appointed to the British missions with the Austrian and Russian armies in south-west Germany, northern Italy and Switzerland, until their defeat by the French at Zurich (25–26 September 1799). In January 1800, the Duke of York, C-in-C of the British Army, ordered that detachments, each of three officers and thirty-four men, should be sent from fifteen different regiments for training as light infantry and armed with rifles in place of the smooth-bore musket. A royal equerry, Colonel Coote Manningham, who had commanded light infantry in the 1794 West Indies campaign, was appointed colonel of this experimental corps of riflemen, with Stewart (who had served with Manningham in the West Indies and seen Tyrolean foresters using rifles in the Austrian service) as lieutenant colonel. It was originally envisaged that this experimental corps should be a specialist training school, whose members would return to their own battalions and teach the existing light companies the use of the rifle and associated skills of marksmanship and scouting, though initially, as is usual at the beginning of such ventures, commanding officers only sent those they were most willing to spare.

In July 1800, when troops were needed for a planned descent on the Spanish naval installations at Ferrol, Stewart suggested that the experimental rifle corps should be mobilised and go with them. The expedition, including three companies of riflemen, landed on 26 August 1800 but was forced to re-embark after a minor action with Stewart himself wounded in the chest as he led his men up a cliff. In August 1801 the experimental school was re-organised as a combatant unit, the Corps of Riflemen (Manningham's

Sharpshooters), under Manningham as colonel and Stewart as lieutenant colonel. Under Stewart's leadership, the Riflemen, with their distinctive green uniform, soon developed a high level of proficiency and morale. Signals were given by the forester's bugle rather than the drum, men marched at a quicker pace than those in regiments of the Line, carrying their rifles in their hands rather than on the shoulder, and drill was simplified, allowing men to use their common sense instead of waiting for successive words of command.

In December 1800, the Baltic powers formed the Armed Neutrality of the North, in response to the British blockade of their seaborne trade with France. When the Danes placed an embargo on British shipping, the British despatched a powerful fleet under Sir Hyde Parker, with Nelson as second-in-command. Stewart and 800 men were embarked in Nelson's flagship, the 74-gun *Elephant*, with a view to storming the Trekronner Battery at the head of the defences of Copenhagen. In the subsequent naval battle (2 April 1801) Stewart stood beside the sea officers on the exposed quarterdeck and was much praised by Nelson, who described him as 'an excellent and indefatigable young man … the rising hope of our army', and asked that Stewart's next son be named Horatio. Stewart was sent home with the despatches as a mark of honour and was promoted to colonel in the Army with effect from the date of the battle.

The Corps of Riflemen was added to the Army's permanent establishment as the 95th Foot on 25 December 1802, with Stewart remaining as lieutenant colonel in the regiment. War with France, ended by the treaty of Amiens (25 March 1802), was renewed in May 1803. Stewart became a brigadier in February 1804 and served in eastern England, where, until Nelson's victory at Trafalgar, there was a fear of invasion. His command included the local Volunteers, a part-time auxiliary force recruited mostly from men whose position in society gave them an independent spirit very appropriate for light infantry duties. In 1804 he married Frances Douglas, granddaughter of the Earl of Morton, a Scottish peer and later had with her a daughter, Louisa, and a son, born in August 1806 and named Horatio as Nelson had asked. Still making a serious study of his profession, Stewart published in 1805 his *Outlines of a Plan for the General Reform of the British Land Forces*, advocating the extension throughout the Army of the principles he had adopted in his Rifle Corps.

In December 1806 Stewart was given command of a brigade in the British garrison of Sicily, where King Ferdinand of Naples and Sicily had been driven by a French invasion of his mainland kingdom. He then served in an expedition to Egypt (17 March–19 September 1807), part of the British attempt to force the Ottoman government to break off relations with France. Alexandria was captured on 20 March 1807, but an attempt to seize the nearby port of Rosetta was defeated with heavy losses in fighting in urban areas.

Stewart, supported by Oswald [29], was sent to make a second attempt, but decided that their 2,500 men were inadequate for the task and, with enemy reinforcements approaching from Cairo, ordered a retreat. He himself was wounded by a bullet in the arm and narrowly escaped capture by the Ottoman cavalry. Finding that an 800–strong detachment left at El Hamid had been wiped out, he formed his remaining troops into a hollow square, with the wounded carried on camels inside it, and fought his way back to Alexandria. Negotiations with the Ottoman commander, Mehemet Ali Pasha, a brilliant Albanian general who would later become ruler of Egypt and Syria, led to the British evacuation of Egypt in September 1807. Though he was later accused of various atrocities, Mehemet treated his British prisoners of war chivalrously and ransomed those who had been taken to distant parts as slaves. Stewart was exonerated from blame for the disaster at Rosetta and, on returning to Sicily, was appointed commandant of Syracuse. He was promoted to major general on 25 April 1808 before returning home in February 1809, where he was appointed colonel commandant of the 1st Battalion, 95th Foot (Riflemen), on 31 August 1809. At **Walcheren (August–December 1809)** he commanded a light infantry brigade until he was invalided back to Kent in September 1809.

In January 1810 Stewart was given temporary command of the Anglo-Portuguese troops in Cadiz, prior to the arrival a month later of Graham [19]. He left Cadiz in July 1810 and joined Wellington's main army, where on 27 July 1810 he succeeded Leith [26] in command of a brigade in the 2nd Division, with which he served at **Busaco (27 September 1810)**. When Hill [21] went home on sick leave in November 1810, Stewart took his place at the head of the 2nd Division and led it at Badajoz (5–13 May 1811) and **Albuera (16 May 1811)** where he was twice wounded but refused to leave the field. Afterwards he was criticised for incurring needlessly heavy casualties by an over-hasty deployment of his leading brigade in the presence of French cavalry, and Wellington wrote that it was necessary for him to be under somebody's supervision. In July 1811 he returned home on medical grounds and was employed in Eastern District.

Stewart rejoined Wellington with promotion to local lieutenant general (Spain and Portugal) on 2 September 1812. In the **retreat from Burgos (21 October–19 November 1812)** he was given command of the 1st Division when Paget [30] was taken prisoner. As the army neared Ciudad

Rodrigo, he held a Council of War with Clinton [8] and Lord Dalhousie [34], commanding the 6th and 7th Divisions respectively, and decided to depart from the route Wellington had ordered them to take. This had the effect of delaying the march and Wellington expressed his anger to all three generals, though holding Stewart mostly to blame. In March 1813, when the Guards brigade in the 1st Division insisted on the convention that Guards formations could only be commanded by Guards officers, Stewart handed over to Howard [25] and returned to the 2nd Division, where Hill [21] had been commanding the division as well as the corps of which it formed part.

Stewart was promoted to substantive lieutenant general on 4 June 1813. Under Hill's command, he served at **Vitoria (21 June 1813)** and in the battles of the **Pyrenees (25 July–1 August 1813)** where, at the Maya Pass (25 July 1813) he left his position in order to investigate reports of a French attack elsewhere. While he was doing so, the French attacked Maya, taking his second-in-command, who had joined the division only the previous day, by surprise. Stewart returned late in the action and was slightly wounded as he tried to re-deploy his troops, losing four Portuguese guns in the confusion. His absence, in Wellington's report, was caused by 'the fancy which people have to attend to other matters than their own concerns', and he blamed Stewart for losing the guns. When the latter protested, Wellington answered that he considered that the loss was due to an unfortunate accident of war and 'above all, to that most unfortunate accident of your being absent when the attack was made'. A further protest by Stewart received no reply.

Stewart served at Marcalain (30 July 1813) and the Dona Maria Pass (31 July 1813) where he was badly wounded leading an attack on the French rearguard. He was awarded the KB in September 1813. Sir William Stewart remained with his division, where, nicknamed 'Old Grog Willie', he was very popular on account of the extra rum rations he sanctioned (though Wellington later made him pay for them out of his own pocket). He served at the **passage of the Nivelle (10 November 1813)** and the **passage of the Nive (10–13 December 1813)**, where every member of his staff became a casualty and an enemy missile exploded alongside him. 'A shell, Sir, very animating,' he remarked before continuing his conversation.

Stewart served at **Orthez (27 February 1814)**, the passage of the Aire (2 March 1814), and **Toulouse (10 April 1814)** and returned home after Napoleon's abdication brought the war to an end. His KB became a GCB on 2 January 1815 when the Prince Regent restructured the Order of the Bath and he received, with other awards, the Army Gold Cross with two clasps for his Peninsular battles, the Portuguese Order of the Tower and Sword and the Spanish Order of San Fernando. He gave up his seat in Parliament in 1816, possibly through political disagreement with his elder brother George, who had succeeded as 8th Earl of Galloway in 1806. On 23 February 1816 the 95th was remustered as the Rifle Brigade, with Sir William Stewart becoming colonel of its 1st Battalion. In 1817 he settled at Cumloden, near Newton Stewart, in his family's Wigtownshire heartland, where he died at the relatively young age of 52 on 7 January 1827 and was buried at Minigaff.

VANE, General CHARLES WILLIAM STEWART, 3rd Marquess of Londonderry, KG, GCB, GCH (1778–1854) [40]

Charles Stewart, the only son of the second marriage of an Irish peer, the future 1st Marquess of Londonderry, was born in Dublin, on 18 May 1778. After attending Eton College between 1790 and 1794, the Honourable Charles Stewart became an ensign on 11 October 1794 in the 121st Foot, one of the many units raised following the outbreak of the French Revolutionary War in February 1793. He was promoted in the regiment to lieutenant on 30 October 1794 and captain on 12 November 1794 and, still aged only 17 and with less than a year's service, transferred to the recently-raised 106th Foot with promotion to major on 31 July 1795. He served in the **Low Countries (March 1793–April 1795)** with the reinforcements landed at Ostend in June 1794 under the Earl of Moira and afterwards joined the British mission with the Austrian army in south-west Germany, where he was wounded in the face and suffered permanent damage to his sight.

Stewart returned home, where he became an aide-de-camp to his maternal uncle, the 2nd Earl Camden, appointed Lord-Lieutenant of Ireland in 1795. Stewart's regiment was disbanded in 1795 and on 4 August 1796 he joined the 5th Royal Irish Dragoons, followed by promotion to lieutenant colonel in the regiment, at the age of 19 with less than three years' service, on 1 January 1797. Camden's repressive policies led to the **Irish Rising (May–September 1798)**, in which men of the 5th Dragoons sympathised so strongly with the nationalist cause that their regiment was disbanded on 8 April 1799. Stewart was exonerated from blame by Lord Cornwallis, who had succeeded Camden as Lord-Lieutenant, and was appointed to the 18th Light Dragoons on 12 April 1799. He served with this regiment at **the Helder (August–October 1799)** and was slightly wounded at Schagenburg (10 October 1799).

In March 1800 Stewart was elected to the Irish Parliament as MP for Thomastown, County Kilkenny. On the Union of Ireland with the United Kingdom on 1 January 1801, he was returned to Westminster as Member of

Parliament for County Londonderry, a seat owned by his family, which he retained until 1814. He was promoted to colonel in the Army on 25 September 1803 and in August 1804 married the 30-year-old Lady Catherine Bligh, daughter of a Scottish peer, the 3rd Earl of Darnley. Stewart's half-brother, Viscount Castlereagh, succeeded Camden as Secretary of State for War and the Colonies in July 1805 and, when a new Cabinet was formed in 1807, secured Stewart's appointment as his Under-Secretary of State. With the beginning of the Peninsular War, when the British Cabinet decided to support the Spanish and Portuguese patriots who had risen against French occupation, Stewart was given command of a light dragoon brigade, including his own regiment. He joined Sir John Moore's army in Portugal and served under Hope [23] in a long detour with the cavalry and most of the artillery before re-establishing contact with the rest of the army at Salamanca on 5 December 1808.

Castlereagh was among the ministers with whom Moore had been on bad terms. Knowing that Stewart was fully identified with his half-brother, Moore took him into his confidence and explained his decision to retreat when large-scale French reinforcements arrived in Spain under Napoleon in person. Stewart nevertheless wrote to Castlereagh that a retreat would ruin the Allied cause, and that Sir Arthur Wellesley should be reinstated in command. During the **retreat to Corunna (25 December 1808–11 January 1809)** Stewart's brigade, part of the rearguard, fought several successful engagements, including Sahagun (29 December 1808) where Stewart led the charge. Moore paid full tribute to his personal courage and leadership, but thought him 'a very silly fellow' in judgement and common sense. After returning home with the remains of Moore's army, Stewart resumed office as Castlereagh's under-secretary in January 1809.

In April 1809, through Castlereagh's influence, Stewart became adjutant-general in Wellesley's army in the Peninsula. He retained this post until April 1813, during which period he was at Grijo (11 May 1809), the **passage of the Douro (12 May 1809)** and **Talavera (27–28 July 1809)**, where he was grazed by a shell splinter. He was promoted to major general on 25 July 1810 and served at **Fuentes d'Onoro (3–5 May 1811)**, where he captured a French cavalry colonel, and **Ciudad Rodrigo (7–19 January 1812)**, where he was mentioned in despatches.

Wellington acknowledged Stewart's gallantry in combat, but had little confidence in his judgement and refused to appoint him to a command, on the grounds that his impaired vision and poor hearing might cause difficulties in battle. He also felt that Stewart wore out the cavalry by continually demanding (contrary to orders) patrols to gather information.

Writing home to Castlereagh (a practice that irritated Wellington), Stewart complained that the roles of neither adjutant-general nor quartermaster-general were properly understood in the British Army, and that Wellington in practice regarded them as little more than chief clerks and preferred to send orders through his military secretary. He also insisted that the adjutant-general's branch was not responsible for interrogating prisoners of war. When he refused to comply with instructions on this point, he was summoned before Wellington, who threatened to dismiss him and send him home under arrest unless he admitted his error and promised to obey orders. Stewart, reduced to tears, was forced to apologise and beg Wellington's pardon. Lady Catherine Stewart died in February 1812, leaving her husband with a young son. Stewart was awarded the KB on 1 February on 1813, followed by the Portuguese Order of the Tower and Sword on 27 March 1813.

Increasingly discontented with his prospects under Wellington, Sir Charles Stewart sought help from his half-brother in taking up a diplomatic career. Castlereagh had resigned office in September 1809 after fighting a duel with the then Foreign Secretary, George Canning, but had returned to the Cabinet in June 1812 as Foreign Secretary in Lord Liverpool's administration. Following Napoleon's retreat from Moscow, Prussia declared war on France a few days before the Russians entered Berlin on 4 March 1813. In the same month, Crown Prince Charles John of Sweden (formerly the French Marshal Bernadotte) signed a pact of friendship with the United Kingdom and, in return for a British subsidy, agreed to send 30,000 men to co-operate with the Russians in North Germany. On 9 April 1813 Sir Charles Stewart was appointed British Ambassador at Berlin. Napoleon gathered a new army and defeated the Allies at Lutzen (2 May 1813) and Bautzen (20–21 May 1813). Stewart served as British military commissioner with the Prussians at Bautzen and at Haynau (26 May 1813), where twenty squadrons of Prussian cavalry (Stewart riding with them) ambushed eight battalions of French infantry and captured eighteen guns. To maintain the new Coalition, Castlereagh offered £2 million for the maintenance of 150,000 Russian and 80,000 Prussian troops in the field, terms achieved by Stewart at the treaty of Reichenbach (14 June 1813). Austria, at this time a French ally, negotiated a truce lasting from 4 June to 10 August 1813 but, when Napoleon refused the terms of a proposed settlement, turned against him and entered the war on the side of the Allies.

Stewart, whose duties included the supervision of British subsidies to Prussia and Sweden, remained with the armies and fought at Dresden (26–27 August 1813), where he took a French redoubt, and Kulm

(29–30 August 1813), where the Prussians, retreating from Dresden, defeated their French pursuers and Stewart was badly wounded. At Leipzig (16–19 October 1813), riding at the head of the Brandenburg Hussars, he captured an enemy battery. Crown Prince John, with ideas of obtaining Napoleon's throne for himself, was reluctant to shed French blood, and responded to Allied complaints about his slow progress with a series of violent gasconades. Stewart replied in equally undiplomatic language and reminded the Crown Prince of the terms of the British subsidy.

The Allied diplomats assembled at Vienna, where the Earl of Aberdeen was the British Ambassador, and Castlereagh arrived to conduct foreign policy in person in January 1814. Stewart, appointed colonel of the 25th Light Dragoons on 30 November 1813, crossed into France with the Prussians early in 1814, and fought at La Rothiere (1 February 1814), Fere-Champenoise (25 March 1814) and Montmartre (30 March 1814) before entering Paris on 31 March. With the war ended by Napoleon's abdication, Stewart was promoted to lieutenant general on 4 June 1814, and raised to the peerage as a baron on 1 July 1814. Lord Stewart was appointed British ambassador to Austria on 27 August 1814 and (not least by his skill in note-taking) proved a valuable colleague to Castlereagh and Wellington successively at the Congress of Vienna.

In the social whirl of the Congress, frequently appearing in uniform ('peacocking', in the opinion of his critics), Stewart proved a great lady-killer and conducted affairs with Lady Priscilla Burghersh (one of Wellington's nieces and the wife of a British diplomat, the future Earl of Westmoreland); Katarina, Princess Bagration (widow of a Russian war hero killed at Borodino, and known variously as the 'white cat' from her blue eyes and pale complexion or 'the naked angel' from her transparent ballgowns) and the divorced Wilhemina, Duchess of Sagan (who had nursed him after he was wounded at Kulm and was the mistress of Prince von Metternich, the Austrian Chancellor). In January 1815, when the Prince Regent restructured the Order of the Bath, Stewart became GCB, followed by the award of the GCH in March 1816.

On 3 April 1819, despite the opposition of her family, Stewart married the 19-year-old Frances Vane, who had inherited great estates in County Durham and northern Ireland (where her mother was Countess of Antrim in her own right). He adopted his new wife's surname and later had with her a family of three sons and four daughters. On the disbandment of the 25th Light Dragoons in 1820, he was appointed colonel of the 10th Hussars. He continued his diplomatic career and represented the United Kingdom at the international conference at Laibach (January 1821) where he maintained

Castlereagh's policy of resisting Austrian, Prussian and Russian plans for a permanent European Union to prevent the recurrence of revolution. Castlereagh, who succeeded as 2nd Marquess of Londonderry in April 1821, committed suicide on 12 August 1822 after allegations of gross indecency. When George Canning, Castlereagh's great political rival, was appointed Foreign Secretary in his place, Stewart (who succeeded as 3rd Marquess of Londonderry) felt unable to work with him and resigned from the embassy at Vienna. He was persuaded, nevertheless, to accompany Wellington to the Congress of Verona (October–December 1822) where the British refused to support international intervention in the civil war then in progress in Spain, or in the internal affairs of any other state, thus bringing to an end the international alliance that had lasted since the fall of Napoleon. Londonderry returned from Vienna in 1823, and was rewarded with an advance in the peerage as Earl Vane and Viscount Seaham. His applications for other military and financial awards were rejected, leading to accusations, then and later, that he asked for too much.

Londonderry made his first visit to his new regiment at Dublin in 1824, accompanied by his wife, who wore a fetching hussar jacket and busby of her own design for the occasion. As colonel, he was asked to decide a disciplinary matter involving a junior subaltern, Cornet William Battier. When the decision went against him, Battier challenged Londonderry to a duel. Despite duelling being a criminal offence, and the Army regulations specifically forbidding colonels from accepting such challenges, Londonderry met Battier, stood to receive his fire, and then fired his own pistol into the air. His second (who four years later performed the same office for Wellington in his duel with Lord Winchilsea) was Sir Henry Hardinge, who was not only a fellow veteran of the Peninsular War, but the second husband of Londonderry's sister Emily. Londonderry was reprimanded and Battier was removed from the Army.

Londonderry developed his wife's coal mines in the north-east of England and built a new town and harbour at Seaham, County Durham, to take sea-going colliers. In 1831, despite opposition from his fellow coal-owners, he used his diplomatic experience to settle a coal-miners' strike. He broke with Wellington over the 1832 Reform Bill (which he strongly opposed), but continued to support the Tories with money and influence. Despite his wife's money, the unreliable nature of income from coal and his own extravagant life-style frequently left Londonderry in financial difficulties and in 1834 he was so depressed that there were fears he would take his own life. In March 1835, as a reward for his political support, he was nominated by the Conservative Prime Minister, Sir Robert Peel (with the agreement of Wellington, then Foreign

Secretary) as ambassador to Russia. Protests from those who recalled Londonderry's sympathy for the Russians during the Polish revolt of 1833 (when British public opinion had supported the Poles) obliged him to withdraw just before Peel's administration fell the following month. Londonderry fought his second duel in 1839, with the Irish MP Henry Grattan the Younger, over the 'bedchamber crisis' of May 1839, when the young Queen Victoria refused to replace the Whig ladies of her household with Tories. As previously, he accepted his opponent's fire and fired his own pistol into the air. In 1841 Peel returned to office and offered him the Vienna embassy, though Queen Victoria, aware of his previous reputation there, was opposed to the idea. Londonderry declined this post, feeling that he deserved either the more prestigious Paris embassy, or appointment as Lord-Lieutenant of Ireland, but received neither. He was promoted to general on 10 January 1837 and became colonel of the 2nd Life Guards on 21 June 1843.

Public opinion at this period was increasingly concerned at the conditions of employment in coal mines. Peel's Mines Act, prohibiting the employment of women and young children underground, was passed in 1842 in the teeth of opposition in the Lords, where Londonderry championed the employers. During the 1844 Coal Strike he refused requests from the miners to act as arbitrator, and passed into the folk-lore of the Labour movement as the archetypal callous coal-owner, with even his public benefactions dismissed as paternalism. When the Conservatives returned to office in the brief Derby-Disraeli administration of 1852, Londonderry, who included Disraeli among his younger admirers, hoped to become Master-General of the Ordnance. The post was given instead to Lord Raglan (formerly, as Lord Fitzroy Somerset, Wellington's military secretary) and on January 1853 Londonderry was compensated with the Garter, filling the vacancy created by Wellington's death. He died at his London home, Holderness House, Park Lane, on 6 March 1854, and was buried in a mausoleum at Wynyard Park in the parish church of St Mary, Long Newton, largely rebuilt by his marchioness (who also took over the management of their collieries), with a white marble figure of Londonderry placed in the transept. An equestrian statue of him was erected in the market place at Durham.

WALKER, General Sir GEORGE TOWNSEND, baronet, GCB (1764–1842) **[41]**

George Walker was born on 25 May 1764, the eldest of five children of Nathaniel Walker, an Army officer, and his wife, the only daughter and heiress of a captain in the Royal Navy. During the American War of Independence, Nathaniel Walker served as a major in a regiment of loyalist American Rangers and obtained a nomination for his son as ensign in the 95th Foot on 4 March 1782. George Walker was promoted to lieutenant on 13 March 1783, just before his regiment was disbanded in the usual post-war reductions, and joined the 71st Foot on 22 June 1783, shortly before this was disbanded at Stirling in October 1783. On 15 March 1784 he transferred to the 36th Foot, stationed in southern India, where during February 1786 he served on the quartermaster-general's staff in operations against the polygars (military tax farmers) of Tinnevelli, where the Nawab of Arcot had ceded control of the revenue to the East India Company.

Walker was invalided home, where he exchanged into the 35th Foot on 25 July 1787 and served as an aide-de-camp in Ireland during 1788. He was promoted to captain-lieutenant in the 14th Foot on 13 March 1789, though he did not join it in Jamaica, but instead went on study leave in Germany. In July 1789 he married Anna Allen, the only daughter of Richard Allen of Bury, Lancashire, and later had with her a family of two daughters. Walker became a captain in the 60th Foot (Royal American Regiment) on 4 May 1791 and remained at its depot in the UK until the outbreak of the French Revolutionary War in February 1793. He then served in the **Low Countries (March 1793–April 1795)** where he was at Tournai (10 May 1794) and on the quartermaster-general's staff during the British retreat into north-west Germany during the winter of 1794–95.

Walker was then appointed inspector of foreign corps and sent to south-west Germany and Switzerland, where Baron de Roll, a former officer of the Swiss Guards in the Royal French Army, was raising a regiment of mercenaries for the British service. During 1795, with the Coalition against France collapsing, Walker took over the regiment and arranged its march through Italy to embark at Civitavecchia, the port of Rome. After making peace with the French Republic in July 1795, Spain declared war on the United Kingdom in October 1796 and threatened to invade Portugal unless the Portuguese closed their ports to British trade. The Portuguese appealed to the British for aid and a force of 2,000 British regulars and 6,000 foreign mercenaries, Baron de Roll's Regiment among them, landed at Lisbon during June 1797. Walker, who had returned home with promotion to major in the 60th Foot on 27 August 1796, was in the advanced party, and reached Portugal in March 1797.

The British commander, Lieutenant General Charles Stuart, was ordered to place his troops under the Portuguese C-in-C, the aged Prince of Waldeck, a former lieutenant general in the Austrian Army. Walker served as an aide-de-camp first to Stuart's second-in-command, Major General Simon Fraser (a veteran of the Seven Years War), and then to Waldeck until June 1797. After returning home on medical grounds, he was employed from February 1798 to March 1799 as an inspecting field officer of recruiting at Manchester, with promotion to lieutenant colonel in the 50th Foot on 6 September 1798. He then served briefly with his regiment in Portugal before being sent in October 1799 to **the Helder (August–October 1799)** in the British military mission with the Russian contingent, with which he remained when it was evacuated to the Channel Islands.

During the general armistice preceding the treaty of Amiens (25 March 1802) and the end of the war with France and Spain, Walker joined his regiment at Malta in October 1801. He subsequently commanded it in Ireland and at **Copenhagen (16 August–5 September 1807)**, in a brigade under Spencer [38]. In December 1807 they sailed with Spencer to raid Spanish naval installations at Cadiz and the Mediterranean, but the transports were dispersed by bad weather and by the time that they reached Gibraltar in March 1808 any chance of a surprise attack had gone.

The rising of the Spanish patriots against French occupation in May 1808 turned Spain from an enemy into an ally. Walker landed with his regiment at Mondego Bay early in August 1808, in the army sent to Portugal under Sir Arthur Wellesley. At **Rolica (17 August 1808)**, the 50th formed part of the reserve, but it was engaged at **Vimiero (21 August 1808)**, where Walker displayed great tactical skill by wheeling his right wing to take an advancing French brigade in the flank. He briefly returned home, with promotion to colonel in the Army on 25 September 1808 and was then sent back to the Peninsula with despatches for Sir John Moore, but arrived two days after Moore's death at **Corunna (16 January 1809)**. Walker returned to the 50th Foot and served at **Walcheren (August–December 1809)**, where he commanded a brigade.

Walker returned to Corunna as a brigadier in August 1810, to act as a special agent liaising with the patriots in Galicia and the Asturias. He spent the next year there, but found that the general conscription ordered by a new Spanish government had alienated most of those subject to it and produced a rabble of under-equipped recruits under incompetent officers. The Army of Galicia had achieved little, but the better-led Army of the Asturias seemed, in Walker's view, worth encouragement. In April 1811 he persuaded the Earl of Liverpool, Secretary of State for War and the Colonies, to support a descent by 3,000 British troops on the fortified port of Santona, with the aim of establishing a base for the Royal Navy and a supply point for the Army of the Asturias. Wellington was prepared to see Santona occupied, but not by British troops whom he needed for his army in Portugal. They were re-assigned accordingly, leaving the armies of Galicia and the Asturias to undertake a diversionary campaign while Wellington threatened Ciudad Rodrigo.

Walker was promoted to major general on 4 June 1811. His Spanish allies occupied large numbers of French troops by both conventional and guerrilla attacks and stormed Santander on 14 August 1811. Nevertheless, their mutually-conflicting demands for such arms and funds as he could supply exhausted his patience and he applied to Wellington for a command in the field army. On 2 October 1811 he was given a brigade in succession to Dunlop [14], which he led in Wellington's advance into Spain in January 1812 and at **Badajoz (17 March–6 April 1812)**. In the storming of Badajoz, Walker's brigade headed the assault by the 5th Division, under Leith [26], in what was planned as a feint attack against the San Vincente bastion. Leith had persuaded Wellington to give him a few scaling ladders, which Walker's men used to climb the ramparts and capture three bastions. They then retreated in confusion when it seemed that the defenders were about to spring a mine. Walker himself, trying to rally his soldiers, was hit by a musket ball that, fired from a range of about 2 yards, hit the edge of his breast pocket watch, splintered one of his ribs and then passed out through his body. Subsequently bayoneted four times, he was found and cared for by a French soldier until fighting ended the next morning. Walker was mentioned in despatches, but lost so much blood that his life was for a time in danger, and he was unable to be evacuated from Badajoz for the next three months. He was able to locate his saviour among the French prisoners of war, and rewarded him for his chivalrous conduct.

After returning home, Walker was appointed on 24 October 1812 colonel of De Meuron's Regiment, a Swiss mercenary corps that had become part of the British Army in 1795. He went back to the Peninsula early in the following year, and was given command of a brigade in the 2nd Division on 25 May 1813, though he did not actually join until 4 August 1813, during the battles of the **Pyrenees (25 July–1 August 1813)**. The divisional commander, William Stewart [39] had been wounded on 31 July 1813 and Walker briefly succeeded him before serving as a brigade commander at the **passage of the Nivelle (10 November 1813)**. On 18 November 1813, in the absence of Dalhousie [34], Walker was given command of the 7th Division, which he led at the **passage of the Nive (10–13 December 1813)**, and **Orthez (27 February 1814)**, where he was wounded and mentioned in despatches. Dalhousie returned soon afterwards and Walker reverted to command of a brigade but then, suffering from the effects of his wounds and learning that his wife had died on 15 February, decided to go home. He was awarded the Army Gold Medal with two clasps, was made a knight commander of the Portuguese Order of the Tower and Sword and in January 1815 became a KCB.

Sir George Walker saw no further active service. On 21 May 1816, following the disbandment of De Meuron's Regiment in the usual post-war reductions, he was appointed colonel commandant of a battalion of the 95th Rifles, and served between April 1815 and February 1817 as governor of Grenada. On his return home, he was awarded the GCB on 21 April 1817 and became groom of the bedchamber to Augustus, Duke of Sussex, fourth son of George III. Walker was appointed colonel of the 84th Foot on 13 May 1820. In August 1820 he married again, to Helen Caldcleugh, youngest daughter of Alexander Caldcleugh of Croydon, a Fellow of the Royal Society and a correspondent of Charles Darwin, and later had with her a second family of four sons and two daughters.

Walker was promoted to lieutenant general on 19 July 1821 and became colonel of the 52nd Foot on 19 September 1822. Between March 1826 and May 1831 he was C-in-C of the East India Company's Madras Army. He was created a baronet on 28 March 1835, appointed lieutenant-governor of the Royal Hospital, Chelsea, on 24 May 1837, promoted to general on 28 June 1838 and made colonel of the 50th Foot on 23 December 1839. He died at the Royal Hospital, Chelsea, on 14 November 1842.

The Battles

Major engagements, Expeditions and Campaigns in which five or more of Wellington's Peninsular War generals took part.

Low Countries (March 1793–April 1795)

For the British, the French Revolutionary War began on 1 February 1793, when the French Republic, already at war with Austria and Prussia, declared war on the United Kingdom and the United Provinces (the Dutch Netherlands). As part of an international coalition against revolutionary terror, a British expeditionary force under the Duke of York was sent to the defence of the Austrian Netherlands (Belgium). After initial successes, York was forced to abandon the siege of Dunkirk and, following a defeat at Hoondschoote (8 September 1793), retreated to Ostend.

In April 1794 Coalition forces prepared to advance along a line stretching from the sea to the Sambre but were pre-empted by a French offensive driving a salient deep into their positions. This was countered at Beaumont (Le Cateau, 26 April 1794), where a French army advancing to relieve Landrecies was routed. The Allies then launched a counter-offensive, in which York gained a victory at Willems, near Tournai (10 May 1794). He suffered heavy losses at Tourcoing (18 May 1794), where Austrian generals left him unsupported, but fought a more successful battle at Tournai (22 May 1794). Prussian inactivity on the Rhine front allowed the French to embark on a new offensive in the Low Countries and besiege Charleroi. The Austrians moved to its relief but withdrew from the battle of Fleurus (26 June 1794) on learning that the city had fallen. Their retreat towards the Rhine uncovered the British flank and forced York to make for the sea at Antwerp. Reinforcements under the Earl of Moira landed at Ostend in June 1794, found the place about to be abandoned, and joined York after marching through enemy-held territory.

After another Austrian retreat, the British fell back into the Dutch Netherlands late in July 1794. Further French offensives led to the fall of the major Austrian fortress of Valenciennes (29 August 1794) and a British outpost at Bokstel (13 September 1794). While their Austrian and Prussian allies concentrated on the partition of Poland, the British retreated behind the flooded Waal for the winter. This proved one of the coldest on record and, together with inadequate logistics, caused intense hardships among the British troops. The Waal froze over and changed from a barrier into a highway, over which the French, defying all the rules of contemporary warfare, launched a winter offensive. The Dutch-held sector gave way and the British retreated, in freezing weather, to north-west Germany. The Prince of Orange fled to England and on 20 January 1795 the French entered Amsterdam and set up the Batavian Republic. Hostilities in Germany were ended by the treaty of Basle (5 April 1795). The surviving British infantry were evacuated through Bremen, leaving the cavalry to protect Hanover. Wellington afterwards said this campaign taught him 'what not to do, which is always something'.

Wellington; Alten [1]; Clinton [8]; Cotton [11]; Craufurd [12]; Erskine [16]; J Hope [22]; Houston [24]; Howard [25]; McGrigor [27]; Murray [28]; Paget [30]; Robe [35]; C Stewart [40]; W Stewart [39]; Walker [41]

Toulon (August–December 1793)

On 27 August 1793 leading citizens of Toulon, the major French naval base in the Mediterranean, horrified by Republican atrocities at Marseilles, invited the British admiral blockading their city to take possession of it in the name of their King. There were initially only 1,500 British marines and seamen, together with some Spanish troops, to hold a 15-mile-long perimeter. With the British Army stretched by campaigns elsewhere, only two regiments could be spared for Toulon, where they arrived on 27 October 1793. The defence of the city rested on a 20,000-strong multinational force (financed by the British) of Spaniards, Neapolitans, Piedmontese and French royalists. Against these, the French government assembled 35,000 troops, including the young Napoleon Bonaparte commanding a siege battery. While the polyglot defenders were weakened by disease and dissension, the besiegers, inspired by revolutionary zeal and patriotic fervour, made steady progress. An assault on 17 December 1793 brought French artillery within range of the harbour, causing the Coalition commanders to evacuate their troops and abandon the city to its fate. The following night, amid scenes of chaos, some 15,000 panic-stricken refugees were packed into every available craft and taken out to the fleet, leaving thousands more to be murdered by criminals or executed by the Republican authorities.

Beresford [3]; Gordon [18]; Graham [19]; Hill [21]; Leith [26]

St Lucia (April 1794)

After capturing the French West Indian island of Martinique on 23 March 1794, the British moved to St Lucia on 1 April 1794. As at Martinique, the troops made a series of landings under the protection of the fleet, and took the coastal defences from the landward side. The 150-strong garrison of French regulars surrendered on 4 April 1794 and were given passage home, but the British soon faced an insurrection by the local population, to whom the French Revolution had brought human rights and the abolition of slavery. Counter-insurgency operations in the thickly-wooded mountains of the interior failed, and after suffering heavy casualties, mostly from tropical diseases, the surviving British troops were evacuated by the Navy on 18 June 1795.

Clinton [8]; Cole [9]; Fletcher [17]; Oswald [29]; W Stewart [39]

Irish Rising (May–September 1798)

The French Revolution, with its promises of liberty, equality and fraternity, was initially welcomed by many members of the Protestant community in Ireland. To divert them from republican ideals, the local government encouraged Ulster Protestants to attack their Roman Catholic neighbours, whose priests had originally condemned the Revolution as the work of godless regicides. Many Catholics were driven as refugees to southern counties of Ireland, where their arrival rekindled the hatred of the majority population for a regime that occupied its land and persecuted its religion. Terrorism by dissidents and counter-terrorism by indisciplined troops led to organised rebellion. On 26 May 1798, 30,000 insurgents, after routing local militia at New Ross, County Wexford, entrenched themselves at Vinegar Hill and called on all Irish patriots to rally to them. Poorly-armed and ill-led, they were defeated with heavy losses by a British army under Lieutenant General Gerard Lake on 21 June 1798.

The long-expected French invasion to support the Irish patriots consisted of only 1,000 men under General Jean-Joseph Humbert and landed, too late, in Killala Bay, County Mayo, on 22 August 1798. After Vinegar Hill, few joined him, but at Castlebar (24 August 1798) Lake's army, despite outnumbering Humbert by four to one, fled with the loss of its guns and stores. Humbert was then pursued by British regulars until he surrendered at Ballinamuck, County Longford, on 8 September 1798. Resistance continued in some areas, but was suppressed with great severity.

Clinton [8]; Colville [10]; Craufurd [12]; Dalhousie [34]; Howard [25]; Pakenham [31]; C Stewart [40]

The Helder (August–October 1799)

Coalition strategy in the summer of 1799 included the landing of a combined British and Russian army on the coast of the French-controlled Batavian Republic, while the Russians and Austrians operated in Switzerland, Italy and south-western Germany. After landing with 10,000 men south of the Helder (Den Helder) on 27 August 1799 Lieutenant General Sir Ralph Abercromby defeated a French-Batavian force at Krabbendam (Zijpedijk) on 10 September, but lacked the resources to advance further. The Duke of York, with 30,000 Anglo-Russian reinforcements, assumed command on 12 September and attacked at Bergen (19 September 1799) but Abercromby's caution, Russian indiscipline and British inexperience cost him heavy losses and the French-Batavians held their positions. At the second battle of Bergen (2 October 1799) Abercromby captured Alkmaar and Egmont. York was initially successful at Kastrikum (6 October 1799), but the outnumbered French-Batavians made a counter-attack that won the day. York's generals, mistakenly believing that enemy reinforcements had arrived, persuaded him to withdraw to the Zype. On 15 October the British Cabinet decided to abandon the expedition. On 17 October York, having only three days' rations left, accepted an armistice that allowed him a retreat to his ships before the continuing bad weather drove them off station.

Barnard [2]; Craufurd [12]; Dalhousie [34]; Hon J Hope [23]; Howard [25]; Murray [28]; Oswald [29]; Robe [35]; Spencer [38]; C Stewart [40]; Walker [41]

Egypt (March–October 1801)

In October 1800 the British decided to attack the French army in Egypt, a formidable force occupying the richest province of the Ottoman Empire and posing a continual threat to either Constantinople (Istanbul) or British India. Lieutenant General Sir Ralph Abercromby, commanding the expedition, was even less sanguine than he had been at **the Helder (August–October 1799)**, as he was expected to land an army of 15,000 men, without adequate logistical resources, in the presence of a numerically superior enemy well-prepared for his arrival. After leaving Malta on 24 November 1800, he spent six weeks at Marmoris Bay in Asia Minor practising his army in beach landings. They reached the Egyptian coast at Aboukir (Abu Qir) on 2 March 1800, in a convoy of 200 transports escorted by the Mediterranean Fleet and, after waiting for the weather to moderate, landed from boats on 8 March. The French were driven off and Abercromby marched for Alexandria on 12 March. At Mandora (13 March 1801) he took the first French line, but incurred severe losses in a failed attempt on the second. Aboukir Castle surrendered on 18 March just before the main French army reached Alexandria from Cairo.

With complete superiority in cavalry and a slight numerical advantage overall, the French decided to strike before Ottoman troops from Syria could join the British. They attacked at dawn on 21 March but, after desperate fighting, retreated with heavy casualties. British casualties, almost as heavy, included Abercromby, who was mortally wounded. Command of the British expedition was assumed by Lieutenant General Sir John Hely-Hutchinson, while the French retired into Alexandria and the Ottomans began to arrive on 25 March. Allied troops under Brent Spencer [38] took Rosetta, at the mouth of the Nile, on 19 April, thus opening the way into Egypt.

While Abercromby landed from the Mediterranean, another British expedition, including sepoys of the East India Company's Army, sailed for Egypt from Bombay. Led by Major General Sir David Baird, they landed on the Red Sea coast at Kosseir (Quseir) and, after marching across 100 miles of desert, reached the Nile north of Luxor (El Uqsur) on 8 July 1801. They then moved down the river to reach Rosetta on 31 August 1801, two days before the French surrendered Alexandria in return for an undertaking that they would be taken home in British troopships.

Beresford [3]; Cole [9]; Colville [10]; Dalhousie [34]; Elphinstone [15]; Fletcher [17]; Graham [19]; Hill [21]; Hon J Hope [23]; Houston [24]; McGrigor [27]; Murray [28]; Paget [30]; Spencer [38]

Hanover (8 November 1805–15 February 1806)

When war between France and the United Kingdom was renewed in May 1803, the French invaded Hanover, whose Elector was also King of England. After a brief resistance, the Hanoverians capitulated at the Convention of the Elbe or Arlenburg-Lauenburg (5 July 1803) and accepted French occupation of their fortresses, the imposition of a French governor and the disbandment of their Army. At the end of 1805, after Napoleon had withdrawn most of his troops for a coming war against Austria and Russia, the British landed an expedition in Hanover to encourage the Prussians to enter the war against France. The expedition, first under Lieutenant General Sir George Don and later under Lieutenant General Sir William Cathcart, was welcomed by the population, but saw no actual fighting and, when Napoleon responded by handing over Hanover to Prussia, re-embarked in February 1806. After Prussia's defeat at Jena (13 October 1806), Hanover became part of the newly-created Kingdom of Westphalia, under Napoleon's brother Jérôme.

Wellington; Alten [1]; Bock [5]; Burne [6]; Hill [21]; J Hope [22]; Hon J Hope [23]; Murray [28]; Paget [30]; Sherbrooke [36]

River Plate (June 1806–July 1807)

In April 1806, Commodore Sir Home Popham, after escorting a convoy of British troops to recapture the Cape of Good Hope, persuaded their commander, Sir David Baird, to give him the 71st Highlanders under Beresford [3] for a descent on the Spanish colonies of the River Plate. These offered immense opportunities for British trade and many local patriots hoped for British help in achieving independence from Spain. Popham's original plan was to capture Montevideo but, on reaching the Plate, he made for the richer prize of Buenos Aires. The city was taken on 27 June 1806 so easily that, when the news reached London, three more expeditions against Spanish America were projected, including one, under Sir Samuel Auchmuty, to reinforce Beresford on the Plate. There, when Popham shipped off all the gold in the public treasury to London, the Argentinians came to regard the British not as liberators but as pirates. In August 1806 the people of Buenos Aires rose against British occupation and, after hard fighting in the urban areas of the city, forced Beresford to surrender.

Auchmuty reached the Plate in January 1807 and decided that Buenos Aires was too strong to attack before the arrival of reinforcements, some already sent by Baird from the Cape, and others, under Craufurd [12], diverted from an intended descent on Valparaiso, Chile. Instead, he laid siege to Montevideo, which he took by assault on 3 February 1807. Lieutenant General John Whitelocke arrived to take command of the enlarged force on 10 May 1807, with Craufurd finally reaching Montevideo on 14 June 1807. They started for Buenos Aires three days later and disembarked on the Argentinian side of the Plate estuary on 28 June. Much hampered by swamps in which supplies had to be abandoned for lack of transport, Whitelocke concentrated his starving troops outside Buenos Aires on 2 July 1807 and re-established contact with the fleet. On 4 July 1807 he attacked the city but soon discovered that the street map on which he based his plan was inaccurate. After several hours of desperate street-fighting, almost 2,000 officers and men (Craufurd among them) had been surrounded and captured, with another 400 killed and 600 wounded. Appalled by these losses and the unexpected ferocity of Argentinian resistance, on 5 July 1807 Whitelocke accepted terms offered by the Spanish commander. In return for an unimpeded embarkation and exchange of prisoners, he agreed to evacuate all the River Plate colonies and return to Europe. Violently condemned by British public opinion, he was subsequently cashiered.

Beresford [3]; Bisset [4]; Burne [6]; Craufurd [12]; Dickson [13], Elphinstone [15]

Copenhagen (16 August–5 September 1807)

Following Napoleon's victory at Eylau (14 June 1806), the Russian Tsar Alexander I, despairing of British promises to open a second front in north Germany, made peace with Napoleon at the treaty of Tilsit (25 June 1807) and agreed to revive the Armed Neutrality of the North, aimed at closing the Baltic to British shipping. A British expeditionary force under Lord Carthcart, sent to support the Russians, landed, too late, at Rugen, Swedish Pomerania, on 16 July 1807. Fearing that, under French pressure, Denmark would join the Armed Neutrality and prevent British access to grain and vital shipbuilding materials from the Baltic, the British Cabinet sent a naval squadron to Copenhagen with an ultimatum requiring the surrender of the Danish fleet in return for financial compensation and a British alliance. This pre-empted a French ultimatum offering the Danes a choice between a French alliance or invasion. After a week's negotiation, the Danish Crown Prince refused the British terms, saying that he knew too well what happened to those who allied themselves with England.

By 16 August 1807, 18,000 troops from England, joined by Cathcart's force from Rugen, were ready to invade. The first element, under Sir Arthur Wellesley, landed on Zealand and pushed on rapidly to the outskirts of Copenhagen. Nevertheless, the Danes refused to treat, and on 2 September Cathcart reluctantly opened fire on the city. Under a rain of rockets and red-hot shot, it rapidly caught fire, but the defenders maintained a stout resistance before seeking an armistice on 5 September. The Danish fleet and naval stores were surrendered to the British, who in return agreed to evacuate Zealand. Although followed by a Danish declaration of war on the United Kingdom, the campaign removed fifteen battleships and thirty smaller combatants from a potential enemy and had a moral effect comparable with the British bombardment of the French fleet at Mers-el-Kebir in 1940.

Wellington; Alten [1]; Fletcher [17]; J Hope [22]; Murray [28]; Pakenham [31]; Robe [35]; Spencer [38]; Walker [41]

Baltic (May–June 1808)

In March 1808, threatened by Russia in the east and France and Denmark from the west, King Gustavus Adolphus IV of Sweden appealed to his British allies for aid. They responded by sending a naval squadron, 35,000 stands of muskets and 12,000 men under Lieutenant General Sir John Moore, with Hope [23] as second-in-command and Murray [28] as quartermaster-general. When the troops arrived on 21 May 1808, the King refused to allow them to disembark in Sweden and insisted on their being used either in Swedish Pomerania and Finland, both of which had just been lost to the Russians, or else against Norway, at that time a Danish possession. When Moore refused, the mentally unstable King threatened to arrest him. Moore left Stockholm on 29 June 1808, after which the expedition was recalled.

Clinton [8]; Graham [19]; Hon J Hope [23]; Murray [28]; Paget [30]

Rolica (17 August 1808)

Following the decision of the British Cabinet to support the rising of Spanish and Portuguese patriots against French occupation, Sir Arthur Wellesley disembarked his 14,000-strong army at Mondego Bay (1–8 August 1808) and, together with 2,000 Portuguese troops, advanced on Lisbon. The first shots fired by the British Army in the Peninsular War were at Obidos (14 August

1808) where British riflemen encountered the outposts of a 4,350-strong French force sent to delay the Anglo-Portuguese advance. The French made a stand on 17 August 1808 at Rolica, where they launched several counter-attacks against successive Allied assaults, before being outflanked late in the day and retreating with the loss of three guns and several hundred prisoners.

Wellington; Burne [6]; Elphinstone [15]; Hill [21]; Robe [35]; Spencer [38]

Vimiero (21 August 1808)

After driving the French back from **Rolica (17 August 1808)**, Sir Arthur Wellesley moved to Vimiero, from where he could cover the disembarkation of reinforcements that increased his strength to 17,000 British infantry, 2,000 Portuguese and eighteen guns. After leaving 7,000 men to hold Lisbon and oppose any further landing, General Junot, commanding the French Army of Portugal, marched to meet him with 13,000 men, including a strong force of cavalry and twenty-four guns. He planned to attack at dawn on 21 August 1808, hoping to take the British by surprise, but in the difficult country his troops did not come into action until broad daylight. Nevertheless, confident that the British would once again be driven back to their ships, Junot's veterans advanced bravely, 'seeming', as Wellesley later said, 'to feel their way less than I always found them to do afterwards'. With the British line concealed behind a ridge, in Wellesley's standard defensive tactic, the French skirmishers were unable to screen the columns following them and were outflanked by British riflemen. Junot's attack failed and by midday he was retreating with the loss of fifteen guns. Wellesley was prevented from pursuing by his newly-arrived superior officer, Lieutenant General Sir Harry Burrard, who came ashore during the battle. Lieutenant General Sir Hew Dalrymple, who arrived to supersede Burrard the following day, confirmed the decision to make no move until the disembarkation of further reinforcements arriving under Sir John Moore.

Wellington; Burne [6]; Hill [21]; Murray [28]; Robe [35]; Spencer [38]; Walker [41]

Retreat to Corunna (25 December 1808–11 January 1809)

Early in October 1808 Sir John Moore, who had succeeded to the command of the British army in Portugal, was ordered to leave 10,000 men for the defence of that country and march with the remaining 20,000 to support the patriots in northern Spain. There he would be reinforced by another 17,000 British troops landed at Corunna under Sir David Baird. Moore reached Salamanca on 14 November 1808 to learn that Napoleon had entered Spain and routed the Spanish armies of the North and Centre. On 9 December one of his senior aides, Graham [19], returned from Madrid to report that the city had been occupied by Napoleon. Moore marched north on 11 December, intending to join forces with Baird at Valladolid. En route, he discovered that the French forces in Spain totalled 300,000 men, with Marshal Soult moving westwards from Burgos, followed by Junot's Army of Portugal. Moore then met Baird at Mayorga on 20 December. A success by the British cavalry at Sahagun (21 December 1808) obliged Soult to halt on the Carrion, where Moore hoped to defeat him before Junot could arrive. Abandoning plans to invade Portugal, Napoleon concentrated his forces to deal with Moore and hurried north from Madrid, marching in person through a blizzard with the leading files of his army as they crossed the Guadarramas. Moore, advancing against Soult, found himself in danger of being surrounded by vastly superior numbers. The only course open to him, on 24 December 1808, was to begin an immediate retreat to his nearest seaport, Corunna.

The route lay through 300 miles of harsh terrain with few major settlements and no spare food or firewood. The troops, exhausted by weeks of fast marching to meet the French, were demoralised by being ordered to retreat even faster when they had been confident of victory. The bitterly cold weather, for which the army was quite unprepared, combined with the lack of logistic resources to bring about a collapse of order and outbreaks of plundering, especially of local wineries. Only those troops in contact with the pursuing French, the Reserve Division under Paget [30] and the two light infantry brigades under Craufurd [12] and Alten [1] respectively, remained under discipline.

On 26 December 1808 most of Moore's army, trudging along roads that heavy rain had turned into quagmires, crossed the flooded Esla at Benavente. On 29 December a French cavalry brigade forded the river, but was driven back by a charge of British light dragoons. Moore, moving fast not only to avoid the threat of encirclement but also to reach his depots along the Corunna road before his army starved, arrived at Astorga, at the entrance to the Galician mountains, on 30 December. Beyond the pass, at Bembibre, British and Spanish soldiers alike broke into the wine vaults and drank themselves insensible. When the army moved on, many were left behind, to be cut down by French dragoons who entered the town on 1 January 1809. The same day Napoleon received news that Austria was mobilising against him. With the British having passed beyond easy reach, he handed over the pursuit to Soult, and set out for Paris.

Moore's army reached Villafranca on 1 January 1809, only to sack its own magazines, wasting much of the contents in the rush, so that supplies for two weeks disappeared in two hours. Men broke into houses in search of more wine and not until Moore himself arrived on 2 January was some kind of order restored, with mangled survivors of Bembibre exhibited as a warning. To ease the supply problem, and to guard the line of the Minho, the two light brigades were detached to embark at Vigo, which they reached ten days later. Moore halted at Lugo on 6 January, but when Soult refused to attack, resumed his retreat on 9 January. Morale, which had miraculously soared at the prospect of a battle, even while men held their positions for two days in the bitter cold without shelter or proper food, collapsed. The army struggled out of the icy mountains the next day and saw the sea on 11 January 1809. This, plus an issue of rations and a rise in the ambient temperature, had a magical effect on the troops and they reached Corunna the same day. The casualties in the retreat, however, had been formidable, with at least 5,000 men and many camp followers dying from exposure or exhaustion, or captured when unable to keep up, but, despite the breakdown in discipline, not a gun nor a colour had been lost.

Alten [1]; Beresford [3]; Burne [6]; Clinton [8]; Craufurd [12]; Erskine [16]; Graham [19]; Hay [20]; Hill [21]; Hon J Hope [23]; Leith [26]; Murray [28]; Paget [30]; Slade [37]; C Stewart [40]

Corunna (16 January 1809)

The British under Sir John Moore reached Corunna two days ahead of the French under Marshal Soult, but their transports, delayed at Vigo by contrary winds, did not arrive until 14 January, just as Soult drove in the British outposts. Moore, aware that a battle was unavoidable, embarked his sick, most of his guns and all his cavalrymen, re-armed his men with new muskets from the Corunna depots and established a line outside the city. When Soult did not attack, Moore withdrew his Reserve Division under Paget [30], ready to embark in the early afternoon of 16 January. Soult, with 16,000 men to Moore's 15,000, then rapidly advanced, making full use of his superiority in artillery. The British left flank, held by Hope [23], was driven back and the centre, under Sir David Baird, came under pressure. Believing they had turned the British right flank, the French surged forward, only to be outflanked by Paget. As they retreated, it seemed that a British counter-attack would take the French Grand Battery that had inflicted such terrible casualties but, at the critical moment, Moore was mortally wounded by a cannon shot. With Baird also disabled, command passed to Hope, who decided to disengage and embarked the army under cover of night.

Beresford [3]; Burne [6]; Graham [19]; Hay [20]; Hill [21]; Hon J Hope [23]; Leith [26]; Murray [28]; Paget [30]; Slade [37]

Passage of the Douro (12 May 1809)

After re-entering northern Portugal, Marshal Soult's army sacked Oporto on 29 March 1809. The British Cabinet decided to reinforce the troops left at Lisbon and concluded an agreement with the Portuguese, placing their Army under British control. Sir Arthur Wellesley returned to Portugal on 22 April 1809 and advanced from Lisbon to reach Villa Nova, on the opposite bank of the Douro from Oporto, on the night of 11 May. Soult, expecting the British to take advantage of their maritime resources by landing in the estuary below Oporto, deployed most of his forces to that area and secured the city by dismantling his pontoon bridge and moving all boats to his side of the river. At dawn on 12 May, a local patriot showed Wellesley's scouts a skiff he had kept hidden and told them of four barcas (distinctively-shaped local vessels used for bringing wine barrels down the fast-flowing Douro) lying unguarded on the French bank. These were brought quietly across and loaded with British infantry, thirty men to each boat. After their third return journey, with a British lodgement established in a well-built but unoccupied seminary, the alarm was given. French attempts to take the seminary were countered by British artillery firing across the river from the grounds of a convent, while the barcas continued to deliver another company every twenty minutes. Paget [30], commanding the lodgement, was wounded and his place taken by Hill [21]. About midday, Soult called in his troops from the quayside, at which large numbers of Portuguese emerged from their houses and rowed their boats over to Villa Nova. More British infantry crowded into these and were taken across to Oporto, where the townsmen joined them fighting the French in the streets. Upstream of the city, after the discovery of an abandoned ferry, a British brigade crossed the river at Barca d'Avintas. Soult abandoned Oporto with the loss of 1,600 casualties (mostly taken prisoner) and sixty guns, and began a retreat towards Spain.

Wellington; Cotton [11]; Dickson [13]; Hill [21]; Murray [28]; Paget [30]; Sherbrooke [36]

Talavera (27–28 July 1809)

After driving Marshal Soult from Portugal, Sir Arthur Wellesley crossed into
Spain and joined forces on 10 July 1809 with the Spanish under the 68-year-
old General Don Gregorio Garcia de Cuesta. They advanced against
Marshal Victor's First Corps at Talavera, but the chance of a surprise attack
on 23 July came to nothing when Cuesta proved unable to move his troops.
Victor, heavily outnumbered, became aware of his danger and retreated
towards Madrid. Cuesta pursued him for 30 miles only to find on 26 July that
Victor had been joined by General Sebastiani's Fourth Corps and by King
Joseph Bonaparte with his chief of staff, Marshal Jourdain, and the garrison
of Madrid, producing a total of 46,000 French troops.

Wellesley, for lack of the supplies and transport promised by his Spanish
allies, had refused to go with Cuesta and remained at Talavera, but sent two
infantry brigades to the Alberche, 3 miles east of the city, to maintain contact.
After a rapid retreat, Cuesta halted on the Alberche and joined Wellesley's
line on 27 July. Wellesley allotted the strongest position, with their right flank
secured by the Tagus and the medieval walls of Talavera, to the 32,000
Spaniards, judging that, though incapable of moving, they would stand their
ground. His own 20,500 men held the line for a further 2 miles northwards
until a group of low hills ended in a steep ravine protecting the Allied right
flank.

While supervising the withdrawal from the Alberche on the morning of
27 July, Wellesley himself was nearly captured by French light troops. In the
evening, Victor made a cavalry demonstration, at which four Spanish
battalions fired to no effect and fled to the rear, where they plundered the
British baggage train. The main attack was towards the British left flank
where, in the dusk, Victor's troops reached the summit of the Cerro de
Medellin, before Hill [21] rallied his 2nd Division and drove them back.

In the morning of 28 July 1809 a second attempt on the Medellin was
defeated by volleys of British musketry, followed by an unofficial cease-fire
during which soldiers of both sides fraternised as they filled their canteens
from the Portina stream that ran across the front of Wellesley's line. The
French commanders then learnt that a Spanish army was heading for Madrid.
King Joseph and his chief of staff, Marshal Jourdain, knowing that Napoleon
had ordered Marshal Soult to make another invasion of Portugal, argued for
returning to Madrid, as Soult's movements would oblige Wellesley to retreat.
Victor, thirsting for glory and unwilling to share it with his fellow marshals,
argued that Cuesta's army was a mere rabble, and that he had no fear of the
British, who were outnumbered two to one. He insisted that the attack be
renewed and threatened to denounce any faint-hearts to Napoleon.

The French then made a frontal attack along the whole allied line, preceded by an artillery bombardment by eighty guns against Wellesley's thirty and Cuesta's eight. One French division struck the junction between the Spanish and British armies but, counter-attacked by Spanish cavalry and the 4th Division under Campbell [7], retired with the loss of seventeen guns. Campbell halted his men to keep the line intact, but in the British centre the 1st Division under Sherbrooke [36], after repulsing the French attack, pursued too far across the Portina stream and were themselves routed by French reserves. Sherbrooke's own reserve brigade fought desperately while the rest of his division regrouped and Cotton [11] led a charge by the 14th Light Dragoons to halt an advancing French battalion. Wellesley reinforced the threatened position with elements of the 2nd and 3rd Divisions, so building up a firing line of 3,000 muskets against 10,000 French infantry advancing in column. The French divisional commander was killed at the head of his men, who fell back after fierce fighting. On the extreme north of the line the French tried to outflank the Medellin but were ridden down by a cavalry charge, which succeeded despite the 23rd Light Dragoons riding into a concealed ravine.

Joseph, despite Victor's protest that one more attack would dislodge the British, broke off the battle and, leaving Victor to hold the Alberche, withdrew towards Madrid. Both sides had suffered heavy losses, with the British losing 857 killed, including Major General John Mackenzie, commanding the 3rd Division, and over 3,500 wounded, or a quarter of their strength, against 7,000 French casualties, one-sixth of theirs. The French had lost guns and left their enemy in possession of the field, though they later re-occupied it when Wellesley (created Viscount Wellington for his victory) retreated to avoid encirclement by Soult.

Wellington; Campbell [7]; Cotton [11]; Fletcher [17]; Hill [21]; Murray [28]; Payne [32]; Robe [35]; Sherbrooke [36]; C Stewart [40]

Walcheren (August–December 1809)

In June 1809 the British Cabinet decided to support the Austrians in the war against Napoleon by opening a second front in north-west Europe. By mid-July 40,000 men, the largest single expeditionary force in British history thus far, had been assembled in Kent. In the meantime Napoleon defeated the Austrians at Wagram (5–6 July 1809) and dictated armistice terms two days later. Nevertheless, the expedition sailed on 28 July 1809 with orders to capture the island of Walcheren at the mouths of the Scheldt, including the ships, arsenals and dockyards at Flushing (Vlissingen), and then go on to take those at Antwerp, further up the river. Command was given to Lieutenant General the Earl of Chatham, who had commanded a brigade at **the Helder (August–October 1799)** campaign. He had held various ministerial political appointments under his brother, William Pitt the Younger, but was notorious for his lack of urgency. His troops, delayed by bad weather, appeared before Flushing on 1 August 1809, but it was not until 18 August, after two days of continuous bombardment by the Royal Navy, that the French garrison capitulated and all Walcheren was in British hands.

While Chatham delayed, the French had opened the dykes, which flooded the whole low-lying area, turned the water foul from the manure in the farmers' fields and created stagnant pools rapidly colonised by swarms of mosquitoes. Cases of malaria began within days, accompanied by typhus and various gastro-enteric diseases or 'camp fever', the result of poor sanitation among thousands of men and horses, combined with a diet of salt meat and unripe fruit. Chatham moved to the extreme east of South Beverland, within sight of Antwerp, but on the wrong side of the river. There the first reinforcements, 12,000 strong, joined the original garrison of second line troops on 12 August 1809. Marshal Bernadotte arrived to take command on 16 August and, by 25 August, had 26,000 men in Antwerp. Guns from the naval arsenal were mounted on the ramparts and a chain and boom placed across the river to stop British warships. Chatham, with his army almost literally dissolving before his eyes, his hospitals choked with the dying and his logistics system under-resourced, decided he was not strong enough even to attempt a landing. On 27 August he decided that no more could be achieved and began to take his army home. Sir Eyre Coote was left to hold Walcheren with 18,000 men, of whom half were on the sick list within a week. When Austria made a humiliating peace with Napoleon at the treaty of Schonbrunn (14 October 1809), the British decided to abandon Walcheren, already under threat from Bernadotte, and the last troops embarked on 9 December 1809. All told, seven officers and ninety men were killed in action or died of wounds, forty officers and 2,041 men died of disease in Walcheren, and another twenty officers and 1,859 men died after returning home.

Alten [1]; Bisset [4]; Burne [6]; Dalhousie [34]; Erskine [16]; Graham [19]; Hay [20]; Hon J Hope [23]; Houston [24]; Leith [26]; McGrigor [27]; Picton [33]; W Stewart [39]; Walker [41]

Busaco (27 September 1810)

In the summer of 1810 Napoleon determined to complete the conquest of Spain and drive the British from the Peninsula. At the head of the Army of Portugal, he placed Marshal Massena, one of his most capable and cunning generals, who began cautiously by sending Marshal Ney with 30,000 men to take Ciudad Rodrigo, guarding the road from Spain to northern Portugal. An unexpectedly heroic defence by the Spanish garrison of this run-down fortress held out for five weeks, so that it was not until 24 July 1810 that Ney suddenly invaded Portugal and drove Craufurd [12] back across the River Coa. Wellington's strategy was to fall back steadily to Lisbon, while the Portuguese scorched the earth ahead of the invaders and local militia fought a guerrilla war. There he would stand upon the impregnable lines his engineers were secretly building at Torres Vedras, so that eventually Massena, living off the country in the Napoleonic style, would be defeated by starvation. To maintain morale, and especially to put heart into his Portuguese auxiliaries, Wellington made a stand on the heights of Busaco, 12 miles north-east of Coimbra.

With 27,000 British and 25,000 Portuguese troops, Wellington's position stretched along a ridge for 9 miles. His northern (left) flank was held by the 4th Division, under Cole [9], from where the line was continued by the Light Division under Craufurd, the 1st Division under Spencer [38], the 3rd Division under Picton [33], the 5th Division under Leith [26] and the 2nd Division under Hill [21], mostly deployed out of sight on the reverse slope of the ridge. Massena, approaching with 62,000 men, was confident of success, believing that Hill and Leith had been outmanoeuvred and were still far away, and that the Portuguese would break as they had so often before. To a subordinate who drew attention to the strength of Wellington's position, he snapped back that he had seen many stronger.

Massena launched his attack early on 27 September 1810. The first columns clambered up the steep hillside and emerged from the morning mist at a weak point in Picton's thinly-held line. As the Frenchmen recovered their breath, British and Portuguese reinforcements counter-attacked and drove most of them back down the slope, though one division held on to a position it gained near the top of the ridge. Under intense fire from British artillery and sharpshooters, the attack was renewed under General Foy. It reached the summit behind Picton, only to be taken in the flank by Leith's 5th Division and again driven back. About 4 miles further north, 6,000 men under Marshal Ney advanced up even steeper slopes, hearing the firing and assuming that their comrades had been successful. Exhausted, they reached the summit as Craufurd's riflemen fell back before them, but were unable to stand against the well-drilled light infantry waiting to receive them.

Massena, having suffered 4,600 casualties, including 300 officers (five generals among them), then called off his attack. Wellington's casualties amounted to about 1,300, shared almost equally between British and Portuguese, but the new Portuguese Army, after its first major battle since being re-organised by Beresford [3], congratulated itself on proving it could meet the French in conventional warfare. Massena, realising he had underestimated his enemy, decided on a flank march while Wellington resumed his retreat towards the Lines of Torres Vedras.

Wellington; Cole [9]; Cotton [11]; Craufurd [12]; Fletcher [17]; Hay [20]; Hill [21]; Leith [26]; Murray [28]; Pakenham [31]; Picton [33]; Robe [35]; Slade [37]; Spencer [38]; W Stewart [39]

Fuentes d'Onoro (3–5 May 1811)

Early in 1811, lack of provisions forced Marshal Massena to retreat from the Lines of Torres Vedras and fall back to Spain, retaining only the fortress of Almeida (taken during his invasion of Portugal in August 1810). Almeida and Ciudad Rodrigo, its counterpart on the Spanish side of the border (taken by Marshal Ney in July 1810) guarded the only major road to northern Portugal. The road to southern Portugal was guarded by Elvas on the Portuguese side and Badajoz on the Spanish. Wellington had planned to recapture the two northern fortresses while Massena's Army of Portugal was still disorganised after its retreat, but the premature surrender of Badajoz to Marshal Soult on 11 March 1811 left southern Portugal open to a French invasion. Two of Wellington's eight divisions were therefore sent south to reinforce Beresford [3], with orders to re-take Badajoz while Wellington himself starved Almeida into surrender. Massena responded by marching to Almeida's relief with 42,000 infantry, 4,500 cavalry and thirty-eight guns, obliging Wellington either to fight or abandon the siege.

Wellington, with 34,000 infantry, 1,850 cavalry and forty-eight guns, retreated from the exposed line of the Agueda and took up a position some 5 miles south-east of Almeida, on rising ground behind the ravine of the Dos Casas. His right flank was held by the 1st Division, under Spencer [38], with the recently-formed 7th Division under Houston [24] behind it and the 3rd under Picton [33] on its left. The Light Division under Erskine [16], when it arrived after covering the army's retreat, would form the reserve. The left flank, completing a line stretching along 8 miles, was held by the 5th Division under Dunlop [14] and the 6th under Campbell [7]. The key to the position, immediately in front of the 1st Division, was the village of Fuentes d'Onoro, where the road from Ciudad Rodrigo crossed the Dos Casas, and which Wellington occupied with twenty-eight companies of light infantry.

Massena, approaching from Ciudad Rodrigo, attacked Fuentes d'Onoro in the afternoon of 3 May 1811 and forced a way into the village by weight of numbers. A British counter-attack drove the French out and held the village until fighting ended at dusk, with 259 British casualties and 652 French. During 4 May the French cavalry probed Wellington's left flank, causing him to extend it by moving the 7th Division across an open plain to Poco Velho, 2 miles south-west of Fuentes d'Onoro. At dawn on 5 May Massena attacked that flank with 4,000 cavalry and 17,000 infantry, overrunning Poco Velho and threatening to cut off the 7th Division. Disregarding a feint on his right, Wellington pivoted the 3rd Division to form a new line at right angles to his original while the 7th Division retreated to join it. The Light Division (to which Craufurd [12] had just returned) covered the withdrawal of the 7th and was then threatened by the French cavalry, but skilful tactics allowed the light infantrymen to reach the shelter of rocky ground with minimal losses. Two guns of the Royal Horse Artillery were surrounded by French cuirassiers but galloped through them and were rescued by a British cavalry charge, one of many covering the withdrawal on this flank.

Meanwhile Fuentes d'Onoro, which had become the centre of the British position, was attacked and taken by French infantry. Lieutenant Colonel John Wallace of the 88th Connaught Rangers, watching the fight, told Pakenham [31], Wellington's deputy adjutant-general, that his regiment could retake Fuentes d'Onoro and keep it, certainly in preference to having to cover a retreat across the Coa. Pakenham returned with Wellington's permission for the entire reserve brigade of the 3rd Division to make the attempt. After more desperate fighting, in which the crowded streets of Fuentes d'Onoro negated the French advantage in numbers, the British regained the village by early afternoon. Massena, having lost over 2,000 men, made no more attacks. Unable either to reach Almeida or to sustain his army in a barren countryside already denuded of supplies, on 8 May 1811 he began to withdraw to Spain. Wellington's view was that 'if Boney had been there, we should have been beat'.

Wellington; Burne [6]; Campbell [7]; Colville [10]; Cotton [11]; Craufurd [12]; Dunlop [14]; Erskine [16]; Fletcher [17]; Houston [24]; Murray [28]; Pakenham [31]; Picton [33]; Slade [37]; Spencer [38]; C Stewart [40]

Albuera (16 May 1811)

Learning that a French army under Marshal Soult was approaching, Beresford [3] abandoned the siege of Badajoz and on 15 May 1811 took up a position 14 miles to the south-east, on the reverse side of a low ridge at Albuera. His left flank was held by the Portuguese, north of the road along which Soult was advancing. Albuera village, slightly in advance of Beresford's centre, was held by a brigade of the King's German Legion under Alten [1] with the 2nd Division under William Stewart [39] on the ridge behind it. Behind these, Beresford planned to deploy the 4th Division under Cole [9], which had been left behind to complete the destruction of such stores as could not be moved from Badajoz, but was expected to arrive later in the day. His right wing was allotted to 15,000 Spanish troops, whose generals had agreed to serve under Beresford as the commander of the largest contingent (10,000 British and 10,000 Portuguese) in the Allied force. His forty-eight guns were distributed along the line in the standard British practice. The Spaniards, under General Joaquin Blake, arrived during the night of 15–16 May and were still taking up their positions when Soult opened his attack at about 8 a.m. the following morning 16 May.

Beresford had concentrated his strength behind Albuera village in the expectation that Soult, advancing with 20,000 infantry, 6,800 cavalry and forty-eight guns, would continue along the road to Badajoz. Soult, indeed, began by sending a brigade under General Goudinot against Alten's position, thereby confirming Beresford in his appreciation that this would be the critical point. The main attack, however, was on Beresford's right flank, by 8,400 infantry and 3,500 cavalry under General Girard, soon joined by other French troops previously deployed along Blake's front. The Spaniards, untrained in manoeuvring, became disordered as they tried to meet an attack by five-sixths of Soult's whole army. Only four battalions, under General Jose Zaya, succeeded in changing front and stood firm against two French divisions.

Beresford sent Stewart's 2nd Division from the over-strong centre to pass through the Spanish positions and counter the French advance. On reaching the threatened area, Stewart deployed his leading brigade against the approaching enemy columns regardless of the threat from their cavalry. The brigade halted the French infantry but was then ridden down by Polish lancers who approached under cover of a violent rain-squall. Within minutes 1,300 of the 1,600 men in the two forward battalions were casualties while the rear battalion hastily formed square. Stewart's other two brigades then came up, drove off the cavalry and advanced up a low hill to find themselves opposed by Girard's infantry. A prolonged musketry combat ensued, between 3,000 British in line and 8,000 French in column, with both sides obstinately refusing to give way despite increasingly heavy losses. The stalemate was broken only when Cole, on his own initiative, moved the 4th Division to turn the left of the French line. Soult countered with 5,600 men from his reserve. Cole's fusilier brigade, 2,600 strong, advanced to meet them through a storm of artillery and musketry fire and another prolonged musketry fight took place. The French, hampered by their mass formation, finally broke and the remnant of the fusiliers stood triumphant on the top of the hill. Soult rallied his men under the protection of their cavalry and grenadiers, and took up a defensive position that, with forty guns in line, checked any Allied pursuit.

Both commanders were appalled by the casualties incurred by this, the bloodiest battle of the Peninsular War. The French lost over 7,000 men out of their entire 24,260 and the Allies 5,916 out of their 35,284, including 4,407 out of the 6,500 British infantry. Both sides lost generals as well as men and one of Stewart's brigades ended the day under a junior captain. Beresford's despatches dwelt upon his losses to such an extent that Wellington told him they would drive the people at home mad, and ordered him to rewrite them, presenting the outcome as a victory. Soult fell back towards Seville and claimed a moral victory as, he said, the British were completely beaten and 'the day was mine, and they did not know it and would not run'.

Alten [1]; Beresford [3]; Cole [9]; Dickson [13]; W Stewart [39]

Badajoz (19 May–10 June 1811)

After **Albuera (16 May 1811)**, Beresford [3] withdrew to Elvas, where he was joined by Wellington with the 3rd Division under Picton [33] and the 7th Division under Houston [24]. Wellington, highly critical of Beresford's conduct of the battle, sent him back to his administrative functions at Lisbon and, with 14,000 men, took personal command of a second attempt on Badajoz. Hill [21], newly-returned from England, was detached with the remaining 10,000 to observe the south-eastern flank. The second siege was no more successful than the first as, during Beresford's absence, the French commander, General Armand Phillipon, had repaired and improved the defences. Wellington had brought additional engineers and siege guns, but the thin rocky soil made it difficult to dig saps and trenches and those working in them suffered over 200 casualties. On 6 and 9 June 1811 attempts to storm a breach in the walls of Fort San Cristoval, across the Guadiana on the northern side of Badajoz, were repulsed with heavy losses. Meanwhile, the 36-year-old Marshal Marmont had succeeded Marshal Massena in command of the French Army of Portugal and was marching south to join forces with Soult. Aware of this, and with his heavy gun ammunition almost finished, Wellington raised the siege on 10 June and retreated to Elvas to await reinforcements from his northern army.

Wellington; Colville [10]; Dickson [13]; Fletcher [17]; Houston [24]; Picton [33]

Ciudad Rodrigo (7–19 January 1812)

Taking the French unawares, Wellington advanced from the Agueda on 4 January 1812 with 38,000 British and 22,000 Portuguese and reached Ciudad Rodrigo on 8 January 1812. The Light Division under Craufurd [12] captured the San Francisco redoubt dominating the fortress's northern defences. By 14 January all the major buildings outside the city were in British hands and the first siege batteries had opened fire on its walls. Wellington decided to take the city by storm before Marshal Marmont could concentrate his Army of Portugal and come to its relief. By 19 January his siege guns, operating under Dickson [13], had created two practicable breaches. At nightfall, the 3rd Division under Picton [33] moved against the larger breach and the Light Division attacked the lesser. Both formations suffered heavy losses from French artillery and explosive devices but within half an hour the survivors, with reinforcements pouring after them, were in the streets of the city and the French surrendered. With so many officers having become casualties or separated from their men in the darkness, British discipline collapsed as men went in search of drink and plunder. Order was restored the next morning, when British casualties in the storming were reported as 449. French losses totalled some 1,800, mostly prisoners of war, but also included Marmont's entire siege train which had been stored inside the city.

Wellington; Barnard [2]; Colville [10]; Craufurd [12]; Dickson [13]; Fletcher [17]; Graham [19]; McGrigor [27]; Picton [33]; C Stewart [40]

Badajoz (17 March–6 April 1812)

The installation of a Spanish garrison in Ciudad Rodrigo secured the safety of northern Portugal and allowed Wellington to move his 60,000-strong army south against Badajoz. He reached Elvas on 12 March 1812 and after detaching Hill [21] and Graham [19] to guard his flanks, completed the investment of Badajoz on 17 March with 27,000 men, fifty-two field guns and forty siege guns. Beresford [3], having returned from Lisbon, was given command of the attack on the city's southern side with a corps consisting of the Light Division, temporarily under Barnard [2], the 3rd Division, under Picton [33], and the 4th Division, under Colville [10]. The 5th Division, under Leith [26], arrived on 22 March and was deployed on the northern side of city, where the defences rested on the flooded River Guadiana. The garrison of 5,000 men under General Armand Phillipon, was well-prepared, with several weeks' supply of food and adequate ammunition for its hundred fortress guns. All the damage done by the two earlier British sieges had been repaired. Existing outworks had been strengthened and new ones constructed. The Rivillas stream, a tributary of the Guadiana running along the eastern wall, had been dammed to form a deep inundation. Outside the fortifications, open ground had been ploughed to make movement difficult.

Fletcher [17], the chief engineer, decided that the only weak spot was the south-eastern corner, covered by the San Trinidad and Santa Maria bastions, which were themselves covered by the Picurina lunette on the east side of the Rivellas. Entrenchments were begun, under cover of heavy rain and wind, on the night of 17 March. On 19 March, concealed by a morning mist, the French made a sortie that drove the working parties from the trenches, broke up the pioneers' tools and reached the ordnance field park before being forced back to their walls. The 150 casualties among the besiegers included Fletcher, who was seriously wounded. Despite this setback, the lunette was stormed by the 3rd Division on 25 March with only thirty-two of its 250 defenders escaping across the river to Badajoz.

The besiegers then began their attack on the main defences, but made slow progress. An attempt to blow up the dam of the Rivellas failed, a lucky shell from counter-battery fire hit a magazine in the siege-works, and the stone walls of Badajoz, backed by earth ramparts, proved stronger than expected. Nevertheless, by the morning of 5 April 1812, the engineers reported that two breaches would be practicable by sunset. Wellington, aware that Marshal Soult was coming to raise the siege, ordered an assault accordingly, but the wounded Fletcher, directing the siege from his tent, persuaded him to wait until a third breach, between the two existing ones, was formed. After an intense bombardment, this was achieved by the following afternoon, 6 April 1812, and Wellington ordered the city to be stormed the same night.

The main attacks were on the breaches, where the 4th Division was allotted to the breach of the San Trinidad bastion and the new, third, breach to its east. The Light Division was allotted the Santa Maria breach, east of these two. As a diversion, the 3rd Division was to attempt the escalade of the old Moorish castle, in the north-east corner of the defences. The 5th Division was to make other diversionary attacks, the main one, under Walker [41], against the San Vincente bastion on the north-west corner. At the breaches the assaulting columns lost their way in the darkness and became disordered as they made repeated attempts to clamber through, incurring terrible casualties to no avail. Wellington recalled them and, as the last stragglers returned, sent a message to Picton to try to succeed at the castle. There, the 3rd Division, after suffering severe losses, had taken shelter below the rocky cliffs on which the castle stood. Picton rallied his men and launched a new attack on a different section of the castle wall. With most of the castle's garrison having been withdrawn to hold the breaches, the few defenders left were surprised and driven out into the city below. Meanwhile, Walker gained the under-manned San Vincente bastion. He was driven back but the rest of the 5th Division joined him and then marched through empty streets to the rear of the breaches, where the astonished defenders fled into the night. The survivors of the Light and 4th Divisions, returning for a final assault on the breaches, found them deserted. Phillipon and his staff escaped to Fort San Cristoval across the Guadiana and, after sending their few cavalry to join Soult, surrendered the next morning.

Allied casualties in the twenty-one-day siege amounted to about 4,000 British and 1,000 Portuguese, three-quarters of them during the storming. Even before the official surrender, the victors had begun to sack the city, in some instances guided to wine stores by French troops who joined in the plunder. British soldiers treated the citizens of Badajoz as the inhabitants of an enemy city that had failed to surrender after a practicable breach had been declared, and whose property and persons (especially females) were therefore lawful prize for the stormers. Many crimes were committed and two days passed before all the troops returned to discipline.

Wellington; Barnard [2]; Beresford [3]; Colville [10]; Fletcher [17]; Leith [26]; McGrigor [27]; Pakenham [31]; Picton [33]; Robe [35]; Walker [41]

Salamanca (22 July 1812)

After securing Badajoz, Wellington returned to Ciudad Rodrigo and, with 51,000 men, advanced into Spain on 13 June 1812. Before Marshal Marmont could assemble his Army of Portugal from the several locations among which, primarily for logistic reasons, it was dispersed, Wellington liberated Salamanca on 17 June and captured three small forts the French had built outside the city. Marmont withdrew 30 miles to the upper Douro, but when Wellington did not attack, advanced on 16 July. The two armies were roughly equal in number (50,000 French against 48,000 British, Portuguese and Spanish troops), though Marmont was superior in artillery (seventy-eight guns against Wellington's fifty-four) and neither general was prepared to risk an engagement until sure of victory. When Wellington fell back to safeguard his supply lines, Marmont followed, taking a parallel road and hoping to intercept the British before they could reach Ciudad Rodrigo. In the afternoon of 22 July, after six days of marching, Marmont ordered his leading division to increase speed and get ahead of their opponents. In doing so, he extended his own line while Wellington's army remained concentrated about a mile to its north.

Observing the increasing gap between the French vanguard and centre, Wellington ordered Pakenham [31] to advance with the 3rd Division from its position on his extreme right (western) flank. After moving rapidly forward, Pakenham deployed his infantry in line against the leading French division which, caught still in column, suffered heavy casualties and was forced to retreat, with its commander, General Thomières, killed at the head of his men. Wellington attacked the first two divisions of Marmont's centre with his own 5th Division under Leith [26]. One of them awaited the attack in squares but was unable to stand against repeated volleys of British musketry and both divisions were then routed by a charge of the British cavalry under Cotton [11]. Marmont and his second-in-command were both disabled by British shrapnel fire in the early stages of the battle and the French command passed to General Bertrand Clausel. His division, with that of General Jean Bonnet, turned to face Leith and formed the right flank of the new French line. From the position on a steep knoll, the Grand Arapile, they drove back a Portuguese brigade and the 4th Division advancing under Cole [9]. They then advanced to pursue Cole, only to meet the 6th Division under Clinton [8], with the 1st and 7th Divisions, under William Stewart [39] and John Hope [22] respectively, deployed on his flanks. After a twenty-minute struggle, the French retreated and escaped to the south-east under cover of a valiant stand by the two divisions of Marmont's rearguard. These inflicted the heaviest Allied casualties of the day, on the 6th Division as it tried to dislodge them in the gathering summer dusk.

The French had suffered 15,000 casualties, including Marmont and six other generals. Twenty guns (out of sixty in the field) had been lost, and only one division remained fit for action. Allied casualties amounted to 5,220, including Major General Jean Gaspard Le Marchant (founder of the Royal

Military College) killed and six other generals badly wounded. The battle, a major blow to French prestige, ended the perception that Wellington could only fight defensive battles.

Wellington; Alten [1]; Barnard [2]; Beresford [3]; Bock [5]; Clinton [8]; Cole [9]; Cotton [11]; Dickson [13]; Hay [20]; J Hope [22]; Leith [26]; McGrigor [27]; Pakenham [31]; Robe [35]

Burgos (16 September–21 October 1812)

After his victory at Salamanca, Wellington entered Madrid amid scenes of wild rejoicing on 12 August 1812. Shortly afterwards, General Bertrand Clausel, having rallied the French Army of Portugal, occupied Valladolid, 100 miles north of the city. Leaving the 3rd and Light Divisions at Madrid, with Hill [21] holding the Tagus beyond it, Wellington marched to Valladolid, driving Clausel before him and reached Burgos, 80 miles beyond it, intending to pin the French behind the Ebro for the winter.

Clausel abandoned Burgos on 17 September 1812 but left a 2,000-strong garrison in its medieval castle. Wellington, regarding this as no stronger than the hill forts he had taken in his Indian campaigns, began the siege on 19 September with the 1st, 5th, 6th and 7th Divisions and two Portuguese brigades, totalling some 35,000 men. The San Miguel horn-work, on a hill north of the castle, was taken on the night of 19 September but thereafter the defenders, under General Jean Louis Dubreton, resisted valiantly. They had strengthened and modernised the castle's defences and their heavy guns outnumbered the few Wellington had brought with him.

On the night of 22–23 September, Wellington attempted an escalade. Learning from his experience at Badajoz, he ordered that each ladder party should consist only of twenty men with an officer, and that those in the second wave should go forward only when the first wave was on the walls. The storming parties, made up of officers and men unfamiliar with each other, fell into confusion in the darkness and were thrown back with heavy casualties. Sapping and mining continued until a small breach was blown in the north wall on the night of 29 September but, for lack of engineers, the subsequent assault failed. Hampered by heavy rain that flooded their workings, the besiegers dug another mine and created a new breach west of the first. The mine was sprung on 4 October 1812, and a simultaneous attack on both breaches gave the British possession of the outer wall, only to be faced with a second wall 30 yards behind it. Despite repeated French sorties that filled in trenches and captured essential pioneer tools, one more assault was tried on 18 October. The mine went off in the wrong place and the stormers were met by French counter-mines. By this time, Wellington was aware that Marshal Soult had left Andalusia, joined King Joseph and his chief of staff, Marshal Jourdain, and was marching on Madrid with 60,000 men while the Army of Portugal, under General Joseph Souham, had been reinforced to 41,000 and was approaching Burgos. After suffering over 2,000 casualties against Dubreton's 700, Wellington raised the siege on the night of 21 October and began a retreat.

Wellington; Clinton [8]; Dalhousie [34]; Dickson [13]; McGrigor [27]; Paget [30]; Robe [35]

Retreat from Burgos (21 October–19 November 1812)

The rains that impeded the siege of **Burgos (16 September–21 October 1812)** were late in reaching New Castile, so that the River Tagus, on which Hill [21] had depended to protect his southern flank, was low and fordable. On 31 October 1812 he abandoned Madrid to Marshal Soult and King Joseph and, a few days later, joined Wellington's retreating army at Alba de Tormes. The retreat went badly, with Wellington declaring that the medical department, under McGrigor [27], was the only one he could rely on to obey orders. The three siege guns and other valuable stores that, for lack of transport animals, could not keep up with the retreating army, had to be destroyed. Souham pressed Wellington close, but refused to attack whenever he halted to offer battle. Salamanca and Valladolid were evacuated and the British fell back towards Ciudad Rodrigo. In accordance with orders from the quartermaster-general, Gordon [18], the commissaries emptied the magazines established along the Madrid road and moved their contents by the route furthest away from the enemy. As this was also the route furthest away from the army, rations were issued sparsely and on some days not at all. When fresh meat was found, there was rarely time to cook it before the army moved on. British troops, ostensibly searching for food, repeatedly broke into wine cellars and drank themselves insensible. This, plus the appalling weather of a Spanish November, led men who had been in both campaigns to say that the retreat from Burgos was harder than the **Retreat to Corunna (25 December 1808–11 January 1809)**.

At the passage of the Huelva (17 November 1812) the Light Division, acting as rearguard, only narrowly escaped from the pursuing French. The following day, William Stewart [39], who had just assumed command of the 1st Division after Paget [30] had been taken prisoner, held a Council of War with Clinton [8] commanding the 6th Division, and Dalhousie [34] commanding the 7th. They decided to disregard Wellington's orders to cross the Huelva by a ford and instead made for the only bridge, which he had allotted to their Spanish allies. This jammed the road and seriously delayed the retreat. Wellington found them the next day 'not knowing where to go or what to do', as he put it, and blamed Stewart for the fiasco. His starving army reached the magazines of Ciudad Rodrigo the next day.

Wellington blamed the sufferings of the troops on the failure of their officers to enforce discipline. During the retreat he had issued an order against the 'shameful and unmilitary practice of soldiers shooting pigs in the woods' and hanged two men caught doing so. Afterwards, he wrote to his generals that discipline had been worse than in 'any army with which I have ever served, or of which I have ever read', due to the 'habitual inattention of the officers of the regiments to their duty'. Some 3,000 men had been lost in the retreat and one third of the survivors were sick. The army went into winter quarters along the Portuguese border, but deaths from exposure, typhus, dysentery and malaria continued to run at 500 per week until the end of January 1813.

Wellington; Bisset [4]; Bock [5]; Clinton [8]; Cole [9]; Cotton [11]; Dalhousie [34]; Dickson [13]; Gordon [18]; Hill [21]; McGrigor [27]; Oswald [29]; Paget [30]; Robe [35]; W Stewart [39]

Vitoria (21 June 1813)

By the spring of 1813 Wellington's army, rested and reinforced to 52,000 British soldiers, 29,000 Portuguese, and 21,000 Spaniards under his direct command, with the capable Murray [28] re-appointed quartermaster-general, was again ready for operations. Facing him were some 5,000 French troops under King Joseph and his chief of staff, Marshal Jourdain, holding a 200-mile line between the Douro and the Tagus. General Bertrand Clausel, commanding the French Army of the North (reinforced with most of the infantry of the Army of Portugal), was engaged in counter-insurgency operations in Navarre. Another French corps was deployed around Bilbao, against the guerrillas of Biscaya.

Late in May 1813 Wellington sent most of his army northwards through the Tras-os-Montes, under Graham [19], while he advanced with Hill [21] and 30,000 men to take Salamanca on 25 May. Having successfully masked his intentions, he then rode north to join Graham at Miranda-do-Douro on 29 May. Joseph had already left Madrid in order to concentrate his forces at Valladolid where, by 2 June 1813, he had been joined by the French Army of the South, under General Gazan, and the remnant of the Army of Portugal under General Reille. The same day, appreciating that Wellington's main force had passed the Esla and was on the northern side of the Douro, he evacuated both Valladolid and Toro, where Hill rejoined Wellington on 4 June. With his river defence lines repeatedly outflanked as Wellington crossed upstream of them, Joseph retreated to Burgos, where the walls were still unrepaired after Wellington's siege of **Burgos (16 September–21 October 1812)** and the magazines had already been emptied. On 13 June the castle was blown up and the retreat continued along the road to Vitoria, while Wellington turned north to cross the upper reaches of the Ebro on 15 June and, after some fighting, crossed the Bayas on 20 June.

Vitoria (Vitoria-Gasteiz), at the north-western end of the valley of the Zadora, stands at the junction of the great highway from Burgos to Bayonne and a lesser road running eastwards to Pamplona. The French Army, 58,000 strong with 152 guns, took up a defensive position 3 miles west of Vitoria while its baggage-trains, carrying the ministers and officials of Joseph's government, with female dependants of all kinds, the Crown treasury and the plunder gained during six years of occupation, accompanied by some 20,000 refugees, struggled through the city's narrow streets. After a day concentrating his 72,000 men and ninety guns, Wellington attacked on 21 June 1813, before Clausel, still 20 miles away to the south-east, could come to Joseph's aid. On Wellington's right (south-western) flank, Hill, with the 2nd Division under William Stewart [39] and Spanish regulars under General Pablo Morillo, crossed the Zadora and the great highway and climbed the Puebla Ridge on which the French defences rested. This drew the French reserves from the centre, allowing Wellington to cross the Zadora with the 3rd Division under Picton [33] and 7th under Dalhousie [34], supported from their right flank by the Light Division under Alten [1] and 4th under Cole [9]. Graham [19] attacked on the north-eastern flank, with the 1st Division under Howard [25], the 5th under Oswald [29] and Spanish guerrillas under General Francisco Longa. Graham's corps was delayed by rough ground but, by late afternoon, Longa had reached Durana, 2 miles beyond Vitoria, and cut the road to Bayonne. Reille's much-reduced Army of Portugal fought a valiant rearguard action against Graham's regulars, but eventually the French fled in confusion towards Pamplona, leaving almost all their guns, vehicles, dependants and treasure to the victorious allies. Each side suffered about 5,000 killed or wounded, with an additional 2,000 French soldiers taken prisoner.

Wellington; Alten [1]; Barnard [2]; Bock [5]; Cole [9]; Colville [10]; Dalhousie [34]; Dickson [13]; Fletcher [17]; Graham [19]; Hay [20]; Hill [21]; Howard [25]; McGrigor [27]; Murray [28]; Oswald [29]; Picton [33]; W Stewart [39]

Pyrenees (25 July–1 August 1813)

After their defeat at Vitoria, the French withdrew to the Pyrenees, leaving strong garrisons at San Sebastian and Pamplona. Wellington took up a defensive line with an advanced corps under Hill [21] holding the passes of Roncesvalles and Maya. Marshal Soult, recalled from Germany to command the newly-formed French Army of Spain, planned to break through the passes, relieve Pamplona, capture the supplies of its Spanish besiegers and, by threatening his lines of communication, force Wellington to retreat. Soult attacked both passes at dawn on 25 July 1813, leading 35,000 men (two-thirds of his force) against Roncesvalles on Wellington's right flank and sending the remainder under General Jean Baptiste D'Erlon down the Maya, some 20 miles away to the north-west. At Roncesvalles, the 6,000 Allied troops held the pass until the late afternoon, when a mist descended, causing Cole [9], at the head of the 4th Division, to fear his flank would be turned by Soult's superior numbers. Prematurely (in Wellington's view), he fell back towards Picton [33] and the 3rd Division. Picton too feared for their flanks in the mountains and, to the chagrin of his men, joined the retreat and abandoned another 10 miles of ground. Cole halted on 27 July at the ridge of Sorauren, 6 miles north-east of Pamplona.

The lower approaches to the Maya Pass were held by the 2nd Division under William Stewart [39] who, hearing distant gunfire, decided there was no risk of an attack on his position, and rode back to see if his troops were needed elsewhere. In his absence, D'Erlon advanced down the Maya, taking the outnumbered defenders by surprise. Command was assumed by the recently-arrived Major General William Pringle, who hurried to the scene of the fighting line, ordering the rest of his men to follow as soon as they were formed, but with only two brigades against three divisions, he was steadily forced back. Stewart, on his return, joined the combat and was wounded while trying to re-deploy his troops, who had simply come into action wherever they reached the firing line. He ordered a retirement, in the course of which four Portuguese guns were lost, and was about to fall back further when reinforcements sent from the 7th Division under Dalhousie [34] reached him in the early evening. A counter-attack recovered the lost ground but Hill then arrived and ordered a retreat to straighten the line to Sorauren. D'Erlon, advancing the next day, found the pass unguarded and marched through with the intention of joining Soult's main force, while Hill moved towards Wellington.

Wellington, hastily returning from a conference with Graham [19] at San Sebastian, reached Sorauren just ahead of Soult on 27 July 1813. His army greeted him with cheering, a practice he normally discouraged but on this occasion allowed as a means of alerting the cautious Soult to his presence. Rather than pressing his numerical advantage of 32,000 to 16,000, Soult delayed for a day while he reconnoitred the ground and concentrated his forces. This gave Wellington time to summon the 6th Division, under Sir Dennis Pack, to join him, while the 2nd and 7th Divisions followed Pack at their best speed. The 6th Division reached Sorauren in the morning of 28 July, bringing Wellington's strength up to 24,000. Soult made a frontal attack shortly afterwards, his men moving bravely up the ridge against a concealed enemy. Exhausted by the climb and by lack of food, they twice reached the summit only to be met with disciplined volleys and bayonet charges while Wellington moved reserves to plug gaps in his line. On the approach of Dalhousie's 7th Division, Soult abandoned the attack, with some 3,000 casualties against the Allies' 2,600.

Having failed to reach Pamplona, Soult moved north-west to join D'Erlon and march on San Sebastian. Dawn on 30 July revealed his rear-guard, two divisions strong, still withdrawing from Sorauren, where Wellington immediately ordered a general advance and turned their retreat into a rout. Meanwhile Soult found D'Erlon facing Hill on a series of ridges near Marcalain. They drove Hill back to another ridge, which he held until Wellington's success at Sorauren forced Soult to abandon San Sebastian and retreat to France. At the Dona Maria Pass (31 July 1813), his rear-guard held off Stewart's 2nd and Dalhousie's 7th Divisions while the rest of the French army escaped over the mountains to St Esteban.

Wellington; Alten [1]; Cole [9]; Cotton [11]; Dalhousie [34]; Hill [21]; McGrigor [27]; Murray [28]; Pakenham [31]; Picton [33]; W Stewart [39]

San Sebastian (29 June–8 September 1813)

San Sebastian, on a peninsula of the Urumea estuary, came under blockade by the Spanish on 29 June 1813. Wellington viewed the defences on 12 July and ordered Graham [19] to take over operations, in command of two Portuguese brigades under Sir Dennis Pack, the 1st Division under Howard [25] and the 5th Division under Oswald [29]. Anticipating that Marshal Soult, commanding the newly-formed French Army of Spain, would attempt a relief, Wellington ordered the fortress to be stormed as soon as a practicable breach was made. The French commandant, General Louis Rey, with a garrison of 3,000 veterans and ninety-seven fortress guns, maintained a stout defence and a breach was not achieved until 22 July. Following a second breach, the assault was launched on 25 July 1813. Both breaches, created by siege guns firing across the estuary from the Choffre sand-hills, were on the city's eastern walls. The only ground in which saps could be dug lay on the southern side, so that to reach the breaches the stormers had to pass along the city's sea-girt eastern walls, between high and low water. Many were shot down before reaching the breaches and the survivors were beaten back. On the same day, Soult launched his offensive, not along the coast as Wellington had expected, but in the **Pyrenees (25 July–1 August 1813)**.

After Graham had been reinforced by heavy guns from the fleet and Burgos, a second attempt was made on 31 August 1813. New batteries re-opened the two breaches but Rey had built a strong inner wall behind them. The stormers, even after reaching the Great Breach, the southern-most of the two, were unable to make progress and after an hour's desperate fighting the British had lost several hundred men, with many more pinned down at the foot of a horn-work protecting the southern (landward) wall. The British then concentrated their artillery fire against the horn-work, shooting over the heads of the infantry and, after half an hour's bombardment, clearing a way forward. On the eastern side, a Portuguese brigade waded across the estuary under heavy fire and reached the northern-most, or Lesser, breach, but were stopped by the inner wall. Only when French magazines behind the Great Breach blew up did the defenders give way, allowing the Allies to take the horn-work and both breaches and enter the city. As at Ciudad Rodrigo and Badajoz, discipline immediately broke down and many crimes were committed during the next five days, ending only when the city was almost destroyed by a fire. Rey retreated to a castle beyond the northern walls, where he surrendered on 8 September 1813, having lost 1,900 casualties during the siege and another 1,200 taken prisoner with him. Allied casualties during the siege amounted to 3,700, over half of them during the final assault, in which their chief engineer, Fletcher [17], was killed.

To the local citizens, the siege was a disaster, with the sack and fire still remembered nearly two centuries later, when the Municipality refused permission for a British war memorial. To the British and French, who in this war generally respected each other far more than they did the Spaniards over whose country they fought, it was a combat in which both sides acquitted themselves with credit. Graham, when Rey asked for terms, gave him his own pen in tribute to a valiant defence, and told him to write them himself. Rey, with equal chivalry, stipulated only that the garrison should march out with the honours of war and the officers retain their swords.

Barnard [2]; Dickson [13]; Fletcher [17]; Graham [19]; Leith [26]; Oswald [29]

Passage of the Bidasoa (7 October 1813)

After being defeated at San Marcial (31 August–1 September 1813), the French under Marshal Soult fell back across the Bidasoa into France and established a 30-mile-long defence line. The western flank was held by 10,500 men deployed along the estuary of the Bidasoa, with 8,500 in reserve at the port of St Jean-de-Luz. The centre, with 15,300 men, was based on La Rhune (Mont Larrun), a twin-peak massif rising to 3,000 ft (900 m), from where the line extended to the Nivelle near Ainhoa. From there, 19,200 men under D'Erlon held the eastern flank as far as St Jean Pied-de-Port, securing the French side of the Maya and Roncesvalles passes.

Early in October 1813 Wellington quietly moved troops along the coast until he had 25,000 men at the mouth of the Bidasoa. At dawn on 7 October 1813 the 5th Division under Hay [20] waded across, surprising the defenders who were unaware that at low tide the estuary was only chest-deep. Hay then turned upstream from Hendaye to support the 1st Division under Howard [25], which forded the river at Behobie. Three Spanish divisions crossed higher up and within an hour the Allies were established on the French bank. Soult, who had been inspecting his line at Ainhoa, arrived too late to organise any counter-attack. On the eastern flank, Colville [10] advanced through the Maya Pass with the the the 6th Division and made a feint attack on D'Erlon's corps. In the centre, the Light Division captured La Bayonette redoubt on the French right flank, but made little progress up the Great Rhune. The advance of the 7th Division under Dalhousie [34] towards Sare, at the foot of the Great Rhune, caused the French to fear they would be surrounded. They withdrew from the mountainside on 8 October and held Sare against an assault by the 7th Division the next day. Each army suffered about 1,600 casualties in the three days of fighting, after which Soult fell back from the Bidasoa to the Nivelle.

Wellington; Colville [10]; Dalhousie [34]; Dickson [13]; Graham [19]; Hay [20]; Howard [25]

Passage of the Nivelle (10 November 1813)

After retreating from the Bidasoa, the French under Marshal Soult took up a line 20 miles long, with their western (right) flank at St Jean-de-Luz at the estuary of the Nivelle, their centre in a series of fortified hills between the Bidasoa and the Nivelle, and their eastern (left) flank behind the upper Nivelle in the mountains near Ainhoa. Wellington advanced on 10 November

1813. Hope [23], with the 1st Division under Howard [25] and the 5th under Hay [20], feinted along the coast, where Soult expected the main attack to fall. In the centre, the Light Division under Alten [1] stormed the Lesser Rhune, the smaller peak of the Rhune massif. On their right, Beresford [3], commanding the 3rd, 4th and 7th Divisions, took the redoubts protecting Sare and drove the French back to the Nivelle, where the loss of the bridge at Amotz effectively cut Soult's army in two. On the eastern flank, Hill [21], with the 2nd Division under William Stewart [39] and the 6th under Clinton [8], after fierce fighting through the French redoubts, crossed the river to join Beresford and Alten. Soult retreated to the Nive, having lost some 4,400 casualties against Wellington's 2,500.

Wellington; Alten [1]; Barnard [2]; Beresford [3]; Clinton [8]; Cole [9]; Colville [10]; Dickson [13]; Elphinstone [15]; Hill [21]; Hon J Hope [23]; Howard [25]; Murray [28]; Pakenham [31]; W Stewart [39]; Walker [41]

Passage of the Nive (10–13 December 1813)

After their defeat on the Nivelle, the French under Marshal Soult concentrated their forces in an entrenched camp at Bayonne, at the confluence of the Nive and Adour. Wellington, confined between these rivers and the Pyrenees, decided to gain space by crossing the Nive to reach open country. On 9 December 1813 Hope [23] advanced towards the Adour on the coastal side of Bayonne with three divisions (the 1st under Howard [25], 5th under Hay [20] and Light under Alten [1]) and three independent brigades. At the same time, Beresford [3] and Hill [21] crossed the Nive upstream of the city with five British divisions (the 2nd under William Stewart [39], 3rd under Colville [10], 4th under Cole [9], 6th under Clinton [8] and 7th under Walker [41]), one Portuguese division and two Spanish divisions, forcing the locally outnumbered French to withdraw to their entrenchments. While Wellington's army was divided by the Nive, Soult used the bridges at Bayonne to concentrate his entire force in a counter-attack against Hope on 10 December. When this failed, he attacked again on 11 and 12 December, on both occasions driving Hope back, but then retiring to Bayonne as Wellington brought the 3rd, 6th and 7th Divisions back across the Nive to meet the threat. During the night of 12–13 December, swollen by heavy rains, the Nive swept away the British pontoon bridge at Villefranque and left Hill isolated on the northern side. Soult then attacked near St Pierre d'Irube with six divisions. Hill's centre held for four hours, 'like a thin red line of old bricks' as one veteran recalled, though both flanks were lost and it seemed that victory was at last within the French grasp. Hill committed his last reserves just as Wellington arrived with the 6th Division, having crossed the river by the remaining pontoon bridge at Ustaritz. Beresford sent the 3rd, 4th and 7th Divisions across the repaired bridge at Villefranque to join them and the French retreated towards Bayonne. The fighting around St Pierre cost 2,000 Allied and 3,000 French casualties along a 3-mile front. Wellington said afterwards that he had never seen the dead lie so thick.

Wellington; Alten [1]; Beresford [3]; Clinton [8]; Cole [9]; Colville [10]; Dickson [13]; Elphinstone [15]; Hay [20]; Hill [21]; Hon J Hope [23]; Howard [25]; Murray [28]; Pakenham [31]; W Stewart [39]; Walker [41]

Orthez (27 February 1814)

After the French defeats on the Nive, Marshal Soult left a strong garrison to hold Bayonne (with its motto *nunquam polluta*, 'never defiled') and deployed the rest of his army behind the Adour. Unable to provision his men from the sandy heaths stretching north to Bordeaux, he depended on supplies from the more fertile east. When Wellington began to march eastwards with 45,000 men on 12 February 1814, Soult was obliged to retreat to Orthez, where he stood on the Gave de Pau with 36,000 men. On 26 February 1814 Beresford [3] crossed the river several miles downstream of Orthez with the 4th Division under Cole [9], the 7th under Walker [41] and a cavalry brigade. The 3rd Division under Picton [33], the 6th under Clinton [8] and the Light under Alten [1], with another cavalry brigade, joined him during the night. Leaving Hill [21] on the south bank with a Portuguese division and the 2nd Division under William Stewart [39], Wellington joined Beresford early on 27 February and attacked Soult's position on the high ground west of Orthez. At first the Allies made little headway and the 4th Division was driven back down the hillside. The 7th Division came to its support and after six hours of fighting the 3rd Division carried the heights while Hill crossed the river and threatened Soult's retreat. Soult then abandoned Orthez and retreated north-eastwards, having lost 3,985 casualties against Wellington's 2,174.

Wellington; Alten [1]; Barnard [2]; Beresford [3]; Clinton [8]; Cole [9]; Cotton [11]; Hill [21]; Pakenham [31]; Picton [33]; W Stewart [39]; Walker [41]

Toulouse (10 April 1814)

After the French defeat at Orthez, Marshal Soult retreated 140 miles eastwards to Toulouse on the upper Garonne. There, with 42,000 men re-equipped from the main arsenal of southern France and protected by water obstacles and strong field works, he awaited the approach of Wellington's 49,000-strong army. The Garonne, swollen by spring floods, made Toulouse's western walls impregnable. After two attempts, a pontoon bridge was built 15 miles downstream of the city on 4 April 1814 and Beresford [3] led two divisions (the 4th under Cole [9] and the 6th under Clinton [8]) across to the east bank. The pontoons then gave way under the force of the current, leaving Beresford's 18,000 men isolated. Soult made no move against them, telling his generals 'You do not know what stuff two British divisions are made of. They would not be conquered as long as there is a man left to stand.'

While the French continued to fortify Calvinet Ridge, dominating Toulouse's eastern defences, Wellington's engineers repaired the bridge so that by 9 April most of his army had crossed and was deployed between the Garonne and the Hers, flowing a few miles to its east. Hill [21] remained on the west bank with the 2nd Division under William Stewart [39] and a Portuguese division. Wellington attacked on 10 April 1814, beginning with a diversionary assault by Hill against St Cyprien, Toulouse's suburb on the western side of the Garonne. Across the river, Picton [33] and the 3rd Division feinted against the western end of the Languedoc Canal, which protected the city's northern side. On Picton's left flank, Alten [1] and the Light Division moved against the canal where it turned southwards. The main attack was launched against the Calvinet Ridge.

Wellington's plan was for Beresford to move along the Hers before turning west to climb the southern end of the Calvinet Ridge, while two Spanish divisions simultaneously attacked its northern end, 2 miles away. Beresford was delayed by boggy ground, but the Spaniards heard his guns firing and, assuming he had begun the attack, advanced gallantly up the ridge. After a brief success, they were driven back in disarray, causing Wellington to remark that he had never seen 10,000 men running a race before. He moved the Light Division to fill the gap in his line, while Beresford's men continued to struggle on through the Hers marshes. The two hours that they took to reach their allotted position allowed Soult to move his reserves, concealed behind the skyline, to meet them. A pre-emptive attack on the 6th Division at the foot of the ridge failed but as the 4th Division clambered upwards, it seemed that it would be defeated by the same tactics so often used by

Wellington. 'There they are, General Taupin,' shouted Soult to his divisional commander, 'I give them to you.' The British, though surprised, replied with musketry volleys that killed Taupin and many of his men and forced the rest back. Despite repeated counter-attacks, Beresford's divisions fought their way northwards through Soult's redoubts until the whole ridge was in British hands. Meanwhile, at the Languedoc Canal, Picton decided to reprise his achievement at **Badajoz (17 March–6 April 1812)** by converting his feints into real attacks, intended to cover the Spaniards while they rallied, and to prevent Soult from reinforcing the ridge. Launched against well-prepared defences, they proved a costly failure, contributing over 400 casualties to the Allied total of 4,568 against the French 3,236. After losing the ridge, Soult evacuated Toulouse on 11 April.

Wellington; Alten [1]; Barnard [2]; Beresford [3]; Clinton [8]; Cole [9]; Cotton [11]; Dickson [13]; Hill [21]; McGrigor [27]; Pakenham [31]; Picton [33]; W Stewart [39]

Waterloo (18 June 1815)

After Napoleon's return to power in March 1815, the Great Powers declared him an outlaw and mobilised against him. Flanders, in the newly-formed United Kingdom of the Netherlands, became the base of a multi-national army of British, Germans and Dutch-Belgians under Wellington while a Prussian army, under Field Marshal Count von Blucher, concentrated at Namur. In a pre-emptive strike, Napoleon suddenly advanced from Charleroi on 15 June, intending to defeat Blucher and Wellington in turn and capture Brussels. On 16 June he gained a victory over Blucher at Ligny while Marshal Ney fought a drawn battle with Wellington at Quatre Bras, 6 miles to the west. As Blucher retreated northwards to Wavre, Wellington, to keep in touch with him, fell back towards Waterloo. Despite the misgivings of the Prussian Chief of Staff, Count von Gneisenau, who feared that the British would, as so often, retreat to their ships, Blucher promised Wellington that he would move westwards to join him.

Wellington halted accordingly on 17 June, in a position he had selected several weeks earlier as well suited to holding the road to Brussels. Confident that his left (eastern) flank would be secured by the approaching Prussians, he placed Hill [21] 10 miles away on his western flank, with a corps of British, Hanoverian and Dutch-Belgian troops, in case Napoleon moved by that route to seize Brussels and cut communications with Ostend.

Wellington's main force was deployed on a plateau south of Mont St Jean, mostly concealed behind a series of low ridges. The right of his line, vulnerable to an outflanking movement from the plain below, was allotted to the 1st British (Guards) Division, with the 2nd British Division under Clinton [8] behind it as a mobile reserve and Brunswickers and Dutch-Belgians stationed further behind them. In front of the line, the château of Hougoumont was garrisoned by light companies from the Foot Guards, supported by 700 Hanoverians and Nassauers in the surrounding woods. In the centre, Alten [1] with the 3rd British Division held the west side of the road to Brussels. Below them, riflemen of the King's German Legion occupied the farm buildings of La Haye Sainte, supported by sharpshooters from the 95th Rifles in a nearby sand quarry. The east side of the road was held by Picton [33] with five brigades (two British, two Hanoverian, and one Dutch-Belgian). The strongly-built manor house and farm of La Haye and Papelotte protected their front and two British light cavalry brigades on their left flank held the eastern end of the line. All told, Wellington could deploy 68,000 men and 156 guns against Napoleon's 72,000 men and 246 guns.

Napoleon waited for the ground (soaked by heavy rains the previous night) to dry. This improved conditions for the French artillery but gave precious time to the Prussians as they struggled along the muddy roads from Wavre, urged on by Blucher with 'I have promised Lord Wellington; you would not have me break my word.' Napoleon began the battle with a heavy artillery bombardment followed by a frontal attack on Wellington's centre and a diversionary flank attack on Hougoumont. The latter held out throughout the day, eventually absorbing almost an entire French corps. The bombardment lost much of its effect due to the muddy state of the ground, though in Picton's division the Dutch-Belgian brigade under Count Bylandt, standing in front of, rather than behind, a ridge, suffered badly. At 1.30 p.m. D'Erlon advanced with his First Corps and routed Bylandt's brigade, but elsewhere was driven back, though Picton himself was killed. A charge by British heavy cavalry turned D'Erlon's retreat into a rout, only for one brigade to press the pursuit too recklessly and be routed by French lancers in its turn. Ney, commanding in Napoleon's temporary absence, mistakenly decided that Wellington was about to retreat and launched a cavalry attack. This reached the ridge, only to be met by British infantry formed in squares to receive them. The attack failed, but was renewed many times, with the British squares bombarded by French artillery in the intervals. The Prussians began to appear in force on the French right, where Napoleon had formed a new flank with his Fifth Corps. Napoleon returned to the field at about 4.30 p.m. and, condemning Ney for using cavalry against infantry in position, contrary to all standard tactical procedures, ordered an infantry division forward to cover the horsemen who had at last been recalled.

At 6 p.m. Ney made a determined attack on Wellington's left centre, where La Haye Sainte, out of ammunition, was taken, and a King's German Legion brigade, advancing in line on the orders of the young Prince of Orange, was destroyed by French cavalry. Ney begged Napoleon for reserves to make a final breakthrough, but almost all had gone to their right flank, where the Prussians were arriving in force. Only at 7.30, when there was no hope of stopping the Prussians, did Napoleon himself lead forward eleven battalions of the Imperial Guard to a point between La Haye Sainte and Hougoumont. From there Ney took them on to reach the ridge at a point where Wellington awaited them with the British 1st Division which, after a prolonged struggle, drove the attackers back down the slope. The sight of the previously invincible Imperial Guard in retreat, and the arrival of the Prussians (whom Napoleon had assured his men were Grouchy's Third Corps coming to their aid) turned the French army into a dissolving mass, with only a few units still continuing the fight. On the ridge, Wellington, silhouetted against the setting sun, waved his cocked hat as the signal for a general advance. At about 9 p.m. Blucher met him at Napoleon's former command post, the inn of La Belle Alliance, embracing him and saying 'Mein lieber Kamerad' and 'Quelle affaire.' Wellington's casualties had amounted to 15,000, almost half of them British. Napoleon left 30,000 men on the field. Blucher, whose cavalry kept up the pursuit throughout the night, suffered some 9,000 casualties out of his 50,000-strong army.

Wellington; Alten [1]; Barnard [2]; Clinton [8]; Colville [10]; Dickson [13]; Hill [21]; Picton [33]

ARMY SENIORITY LIST (excluding ordnance, commissariat and medical officers)

	Major	Lt Col	Col	Maj Gen	Lt Gen	Gen	Remarks
HOPE, Hon J [23]	25 Apr 92	26 Apr 93	3 May 96	29 Apr 02	25 Apr 08	12 Aug 19	loc lt gen 21 Feb 10
GRAHAM [19]	—	10 Feb 94	26 Jan 97	25 Sep 03	25 Jul 10	19 Jul 21	loc lt gen 12 Apr 09
SHERBROOKE [36]	30 Sep 93	24 May 94	1 Jan 98	1 Jan 05	4 Jun 11	27 May 25	loc lt gen 12 Apr 09
PAYNE [32]	1 Feb 94	1 Mar 94	1 Jan 98	1 Jan 05	4 Jun 11	27 May 25	loc lt gen 12 Apr 09
PAGET [30]	14 Nov 93	30 Apr 94	1 Jan 98	1 Jan 05	4 Jun 11	27 May 25	loc lt gen 12 Apr 09
SPENCER [38]	6 Mar 91	2 May 94	1 Jan 98	1 Jan 05	4 Jun 11	27 May 25	loc lt gen 5 May 10
COTTON [11]	28 Apr 94	9 May 94	1 Jan 00	30 Oct 05	1 Jan 12	27 May 25	loc lt gen 31 Aug 09
HILL [21]	10 Feb 94	13 May 94	1 Jan 00	30 Oct 05	1 Jan 12	27 May 25	loc lt gen 31 Aug 09
BERESFORD [3]	1 Mar 94	1 Aug 94	1 Jan 00	25 Apr 08	1 Jan 12	27 May 25	loc lt gen 16 Feb 09
DALHOUSIE [34]	27 Jun 92	22 Aug 94	1 Jan 00	25 Apr 08	4 Jun 13	22 Jul 30	loc lt gen 3 Sep 12
LEITH [26]	1 Mar 94	25 Oct 94	1 Jan 01	25 Apr 08	4 Jun 13	—	loc lt gen 6 Sep 11
PICTON [33]	22 Jun 95	19 Nov 94	1 Jan 01	25 Apr 08	4 Jun 13	—	loc lt gen 6 Sep 11
COLE [9]	31 Oct 93	26 Nov 94	1 Jan 01	25 Apr 08	4 Jun 13	22 Jul 30	loc lt gen 6 Sep 11
ERSKINE [16]	1 Mar 93	14 Dec 94	1 Jan 01	25 Apr 08	—	—	
STEWART, W [39]	1 Mar 94	14 Jan 94	2 Apr 01	25 Apr 08	4 Jun 13	—	
HOUSTON [24]	30 May 94	18 Mar 95	29 Apr 02	25 Oct 09	4 Jun 14	10 Jan 37	
SLADE [37]	1 Mar 94	29 Apr 95	29 Apr 02	25 Oct 09	4 Jun 14	10 Jan 37	loc lt gen 3 Sep 12
CLINTON [8]	22 Apr 94	30 Sep 95	25 Sep 02	25 Jul 10	4 Jun 14	—	loc lt gen 8 Apr 13
DUNLOP [14]	1 Mar 94	12 Oct 95	25 Sep 03	25 Jul 10	4 Jun 14	—	

CAMPBELL [7]	1 Sep 95	4 Dec 95	25 Sep 03	25 Jul 10	4 Jun 14	–	loc lt gen 9 Mar 12
STEWART, C [40]	4 Aug 96	1 Jan 97	25 Sep 03	25 Jul 10	4 Jun 14	10 Jan 37	
BOCK [5]	–	–	1 Apr 04	25 Jul 10	–	–	
ALTEN [1]	–	–	22 Dec 04	25 Jul 10	–	–	
HOPE, J [22]	25 Mar 95	20 Feb 96	1 Jan 05	25 Jul 10	12 Aug 19	10 Jan 37	
COLVILLE [10]	1 Sep 95	26 Aug 96	1 Jan 05	25 Jul 10	12 Aug 19	10 Jan 37	
HOWARD [25]	–	30 Dec 97	1 Jan 05	25 Jul 10	12 Aug 19	10 Jan 37	
OSWALD [29]	1 Sep 95	30 Mar 97	30 Oct 05	4 Jun 11	12 Aug 19	10 Jan 37	
CRAUFURD [12]	1 Nov 87	30 Dec 97	30 Oct 05	–	–	–	loc maj gen 4 June 11
HAY [20]	1 Sep 94	1 Jan 98	25 Apr 08	4 Jun 11	–	–	
BURNE [6]	1 Mar 94	1 Jan 98	25 Apr 08	4 Jun 11	19 Jul 21	–	
WALKER [41]	27 Aug 96	6 Sep 98	25 Sep 08	4 Jun 11	19 Jul 21	28 Jun 38	
MURRAY [28]	–	5 Aug 99	9 Mar 09	1 Jan 12	27 May 25	23 Nov 41	loc lt gen 19 Dec 14
PAKENHAM [31]	6 Dec 94	17 Oct 99	25 Oct 09	4 Jun 12	–	–	loc maj gen 26 Oct 11
GORDON [18]	9 Nov 97	1 May 01	25 Jul 10	4 Jun 13	27 May 25	23 Nov 41	
BARNARD [2]	6 Jan 08	28 Jan 08	4 June 13	12 Aug 19	10 Oct 37	11 Nov 51	

Bibliography

Aspinall-Oglander, Cecil, *Freshly Remembered. The Story of Thomas Graham, Lord Lynedoch*, Hogarth Press, London, 1956.

Atkinson, C.T., *The Royal Hampshire Regiment*, Robert Macklehose & Co. Ltd., Glasgow, 1950.

Bailey, Sidney D., *Ceylon*, Hutchinson's University Library, London, 1952.

Bannatyne, Neil, *The History of the Thirtieth Regiment now the First Battalion, East Lancashire Regiment*, Littlebury Bros., Liverpool, 1923.

Beamish, N. Ludlow, *History of the King's German Legion* (2 vols.), London, 1832–37, repub. Naval and Military Press, Dallington, 1997.

Bell, Douglas, *Wellington's Officers*, Collins, London, 1938.

Brett-James, Antony, *General Graham, Lord Lynedoch*, Macmillan, London, 1959

—— *Wellington at War 1794–1815. A selection of his war-time letters*, Macmillan, London, 1961.

Bryant, Arthur, *The Years of Endurance 1793–1802*, Collins, London, 1941.

—— *The Years of Victory 1802–1812*, Collins, London, 1944.

—— *The Age of Elegance 1812–1822*, Collins, London, 1950.

—— *The Great Duke or the Invincible General*, Collins, London, 1971.

Burke, Bernard, *Genealogical and Heraldic Dictionary of the Peerage and Baronetage*, Harrison & Son, London, 1887.

Burns, Alan, *History of the British West Indies*, George Allen and Unwin, London, 1954.

Butler, Lewis, *Wellington's Operations in the Peninsula*, 2 vols., T. Fisher Unwin, London, 1904.

Cannon, Richard, *Historical Records of the 1st Foot, The Royal Scots*, Parker, Furnivall & Parker, London, 1847.

—— *Historical Records of the 15th Yorkshire East Riding Regiment of Foot*, Parker, Furnivall & Parker, London, 1848.

—— *Historical Records of the 36th or Herefordshire Regiment of Foot*, Parker, Furnivall & Parker, London, 1847.

—— *Historical Records of the 56th or West Essex Regiment of Foot*, Parker, Furnivall and Parker, London, 1844.

Cantlie, N., *A History of the Army Medical Department*, 2 vols., Churchill Livingstone, Edinburgh, 1974.

Carmichael, Gertrude, *The History of the West Indian Islands of Trinidad and Tobago, 1498–1900*, Alvin Redman, London, 1961.

Chandler, David, ed., *Dictionary of Battles. The World's Key Battles from 405 BC to today*, Ebury Press, London, 1987.

—— *The Dictionary of the Napoleonic Wars*, Macmillan, London, 1979.

Cole, John William, *Memoirs of British Generals distinguished during the Peninsular War*, 2 vols., Richard Bentley, London, 1835.

Cole, Maud Lowry, and Gwynn, Stephen, *Memoirs of Sir Lowry Cole*, Macmillan, London, 1934.

Conelly, T.W.J., ed. Edwards, R.F., *Roll of Officers of the Corps of Royal Engineers, 1660–1898*, R.E. Institute, Chatham, 1898.

Corrigan, Gordon, *Wellington. A Military Life*, Hambledon and London, London, 2001.

Craufurd, Alexander H., *General Craufurd and his Light Division*, Griffith, Farrow, Okeden & Welsh, London [c.1870].

Davis, John, *The History of the Second, Queen's Royal Regiment*, Richard Bentley, London, 1894.

De Silva, C.R., *Sri Lanka. A History*, Vikra Publishing, New Delhi, 1987, 1994.

Delavoye, A., *Life of Thomas Graham, Lord Lynedoch*, Richardson & Co., London, 1880.

Duncan, Francis, *History of the Royal Regiment of Artillery*, 2 vols., John Murray, London, 1874.

Esdale, Charles, *The Peninsular War*, Allen Lane, London, 2002.

Everett, Henry, *The History of the Somerset Light Infantry (Prince Albert's) 1685–1914*, Methuen & Co. Ltd., London, 1934.

Ferrar, M.L., *A History of the Services of the 19th Regiment, now Alexandra, Princess of Wales's Own (Yorkshire Regiment)*, Eden Fisher and Co. Ltd, London, 1911.

Fletcher, C.R.L., *Historical Portraits 1700–1850*, 2 vols., Clarendon Press, Oxford, 1919.

Fortescue, Hon. Sir J. W., *A History of the British Army*, 15 vols., 1899–1930.

Frederick, J.B.M., *Lineage Book of the British Land Forces, 1660–1978*, 2 vols., Microform Academic Publishers, East Ardsley, 1984.

Fyler, Arthur Evelyn, *The History of the 50th or the Queen's Own Regiment*, Chapman & Hall Ltd., London, 1895.

Gale, R., *The Worcestershire Regiment (The 29th and 36th Regiments of Foot)*, Leo Cooper, London, 1970.

Glover, Michael, *Wellington's Peninsular Victories*, Batsford, London, 1962.

Glover, Richard, *Peninsular Preparations: The Reform of the British Army 1795–1809*, Cambridge University Press, 1963.

Gordon, Lawrence L., *British Orders and Awards*, pub. privately, Stafford, 1959.

Graham, Henry, *History of the Sixteenth, the Queen's, Light Dragoons (Lancers) 1759–1912*, pub. privately, Devizes, 1912.

Gretton, G. le M., Moxsey, A.R., et al, *The Royal Inniskilling Fusiliers 1688–1914*, Constable, London, 1928.

Griffith, Paddy, *A History of the Peninsular War. Vol. IX. Modern Studies of the War in Spain and Portugal, 1808–1814*, Greenhill Books, London, 1999.

—— (ed.), *Wellington as Commander. The Iron Duke's Generalship*. Antony Bird Publications, London, 1983.

Gurwood, John, *The Dispatches of Field Marshal the Duke of Wellington 1799–1818*, John Murray, London, 1824.

Hamilton, F.W., *The Origins and History of the First or Grenadier Guards*, John Murray, London, 1874.

Havard, R., *Wellington's Welsh General. Life of Sir Thomas Picton*, Aurum Press, London, 1996.

Haythornthwaite, Philip J., *The Armies of Wellington*, Arms and Armour Press, London, 1994.

—— *The Peninsular War: the complete companion to the Iberian Campaigns, 1807–14*, Brassey's Almanac, London, 2004.

Heathcote, T.A., *The British Field Marshals 1736–1997. A Biographical Dictionary*, Leo Cooper, Pen & Sword, Barnsley, 1999.

Hibbert, Christopher, *Wellington. A personal History*, HarperCollins, London, 1997.

Holmes, Richard, *Wellington: The Iron Duke*, HarperCollins, London 2002.

Hunt, Keith S., *Sir Lowry Cole: A Study in Colonial Administration*, Durban, South Africa, 1974.

Hylton, Earl of, *The Paget Brothers*, John Murray, London, 1918.

Ingham, David, *Sudden Death, Sudden Glory, The 59th Regiment 1793–1830*, Jade Publishing, Oldham, 1996.

Jacques, Tony, *Dictionary of Battles and Sieges*, 3 vols., Greenwood Press, Westport and London, 2007.

James, Lawrence, *The Iron Duke. A Military Biography of Wellington*, Weidenfeld and Nicolson, London, 1992.

Johnstone, S.H.F., *The History of the Cameronians (Scottish Rifles), 26th and 90th*, Gale and Polden, Aldershot, 1957.

Jourdain, H.F.N., and Fraser, Edward, *The Connaught Rangers*, RUSI, London, 1924.

Kane, John, and Askwith, W.H., *List of Officers of the Royal Regiment of Artillery*, 4th edn., R. A. Institution, Woolwich, 1900.

Kingsford, Charles Lethbridge, *The Story of the Royal Warwickshire Regiment*, Country Life, London, 1921.

—— *The Story of the Duke of Cambridge's Own (Middlesex Regiment)*, Country Life, London, 1916.

Lee, Albert, *History of the Third Foot (Duke of Wellington's) West Riding Regiment*, The Empire Press, Norwich, 1922.

Liddell, R.S., *The Memoirs of the Tenth Royal Hussars*, Longmans, Green & Co., London, 1891.

Longford, Earl of, ed., *The Pakenham Letters* [1800–14], privately printed, 1914.

McGrigor, James, *Sir James McGrigor. The Scalpel and the Sword. The autobiography of the Father of Army Medicine*, Scottish Cultural Press, Dalkeith, 2000.

MacKinnon, Col., *Origin and Services of the Coldstream Guards*, vol. I, Richard Bentley, London, 1833.

Mostert, Noel, *Frontiers. The Epic of South Africa's Creation and the Tragedy of the Xhosa People*, Jonathan Cape, London, 1992.

Moxsy, A.R., (ed.), *The Royal Inniskilling Fusiliers, Dec 1688 – July 1914*, Constable & Co., London, 1928.

Myatt, Frederick, *British Sieges of the Peninsular War*, Spellmount, Tunbridge Wells, 1987.

—— *Peninsular Generals: Sir Thomas Picton, 1758–1815*, David and Charles, Newton Abbot, 1980.

Napier, W.F.P., *History of the War in the Peninsula and the South of France, 1807–1814*, 6 vols., David and Charles, Newton Abbot, 1980, Thomas and William Boone, London, 1840.

—— *English Battles and Sieges in the Peninsula*, John Murray, London, 1906.

Oman, Charles, *A History of the Peninsula War*, 7 vols., Clarendon, Oxford, 1930.

—— *Wellington's Army, 1809–1814*, Edward Arnold, London, 1913.

Paget, Harriet Mary (ed.), *Letters and Memorials of General the Honourable Sir Edward Paget, GCB*, privately published, 1898.

Pearse, Hugh W., *History of the 31st and 70th Foot, the 1st and 2nd Bns., the East Surrey Regiment, Vol. I*, Spottiswoode, Ballantyne & Co., London, 1916.

Peterkin, A., and Johnstone, W., *Commissioned Officers in the Medical Services of the British Army, 1660–1960*, Wellcome Medical Library, London, 1968.

Petrie, Charles, *Wellington. A Re-assessment*, James Barrie, London, 1956.

Petrie, F. Loraine, *The Royal Berkshire Regiment (49th and 66th Foot)*, 2 vols., The Barracks, Reading, 1925.

Pomeroy, Ralph Legge, *The Story of a Regiment of Horse, being the regimental history from 1688 to 1922 of the 5th Princess Charlotte of Wales's Dragoon Guards*, William Blackwood & Sons, Edinburgh and London 1924.

Porter, Whitworth, *History of the Corps of Royal Engineers, Vol. I*, Longmans, Green & Co., London, 1889.

Purdon, H.G., *Memoirs of the Services of the 64th Regiment (Second Staffordshire) 1758–1881*, W.H. Allen & Co., London, [1882].

Reid, Stuart, *Wellington's Army in the Peninsula*, Osprey, Oxford, 2004.

—— *Wellington's Officers. A Biographical Dictionary*, Partizan Press, Leigh-on-Sea, 2008.

Robertson, Ian C., *Wellington at War in the Peninsula, 1808–1814, an overview and guide*, Leo Cooper, Pen & Sword, Barnsley, 2000.

Robinson, H.B., *Memoirs of Lieutenant-General Sir Thomas Picton*, 2 vols., Richard Bentley, London, 1835.

Royle, Trevor, *The Gordon Highlanders. A concise history*, Mainstream Publishing, Edinburgh, 2007.

Sandes, E.W.C., *The Military Engineer in India, Vol. I*, R.E. Institute, Chatham, 1933.

Schaumann, A.L.F., (trans. and ed. Ludovici, A.M.,) *On the Road with Wellington*, William Heinemann, London, 1924.

Seymour, E., *The Life of Lord Hill, commander of the forces*, John Murray, London, 1845.

Sutherland, Douglas, *Tried and Valiant. The History of the Border Regiment, the 34th and 55th Regiments of Foot*, Leo Cooper, London, 1972.

Teffeteiler, Gordon L., *The Surpriser: the life of Rowland, Lord Hill*, Associated University Press, London, 1983.

Toussant, Auguste, (trans. Ward, W.C.F.), *History of Mauritius*, Macmillan Education, London, 1977.

Trimen, Richard, *An Historical Memoir of the 35th Royal Sussex Regiment of Foot*, Southampton Times, Southampton, 1873.

Uffindel, Andrew, *Wellington's Armies. Britain's Campaigns in the Peninsula and at Waterloo*, Sidgwick & Jackson, London, 2003.

—— *Waterloo Commanders: Napoleon, Wellington and Blucher*, Pen & Sword Military, Barnsley, 2007.

Walker, H.M., *A History of the Northumberland Fusiliers, 1674–1902*, John Murray, London, 1919.

Ward, S.G.P., *Wellington*, B.T. Batsford, London, 1963.

Weller, Jac, *Wellington in the Peninsula 1808–1814*, Greenhill Books, London, 1992.

Wheeler, W., *Historical Records of the Seventh or Royal Regiment of Fusiliers*, pub. privately, Leeds, 1875.

Whitehorne, A.C., *History of the Welch Regiment*, Western Mail and Echo, Cardiff, 1932.

Whitton, F.E., *The History of the Prince of Wales's Leinster Regiment*, Gale and Polden, Aldershot, 1924.

Wilson, W.J., *History of the Madras Army*, 3 vols., Government Press, Madras, 1882.

Wylly, H.C., *XVth (The King's) Hussars 1759 to 1913*, Caxton House Publishing, London, 1914.

—— *The Loyal North Lancashire Regiment, vol. I, 1741– 1914*, RUSI, London, 1933.

Index